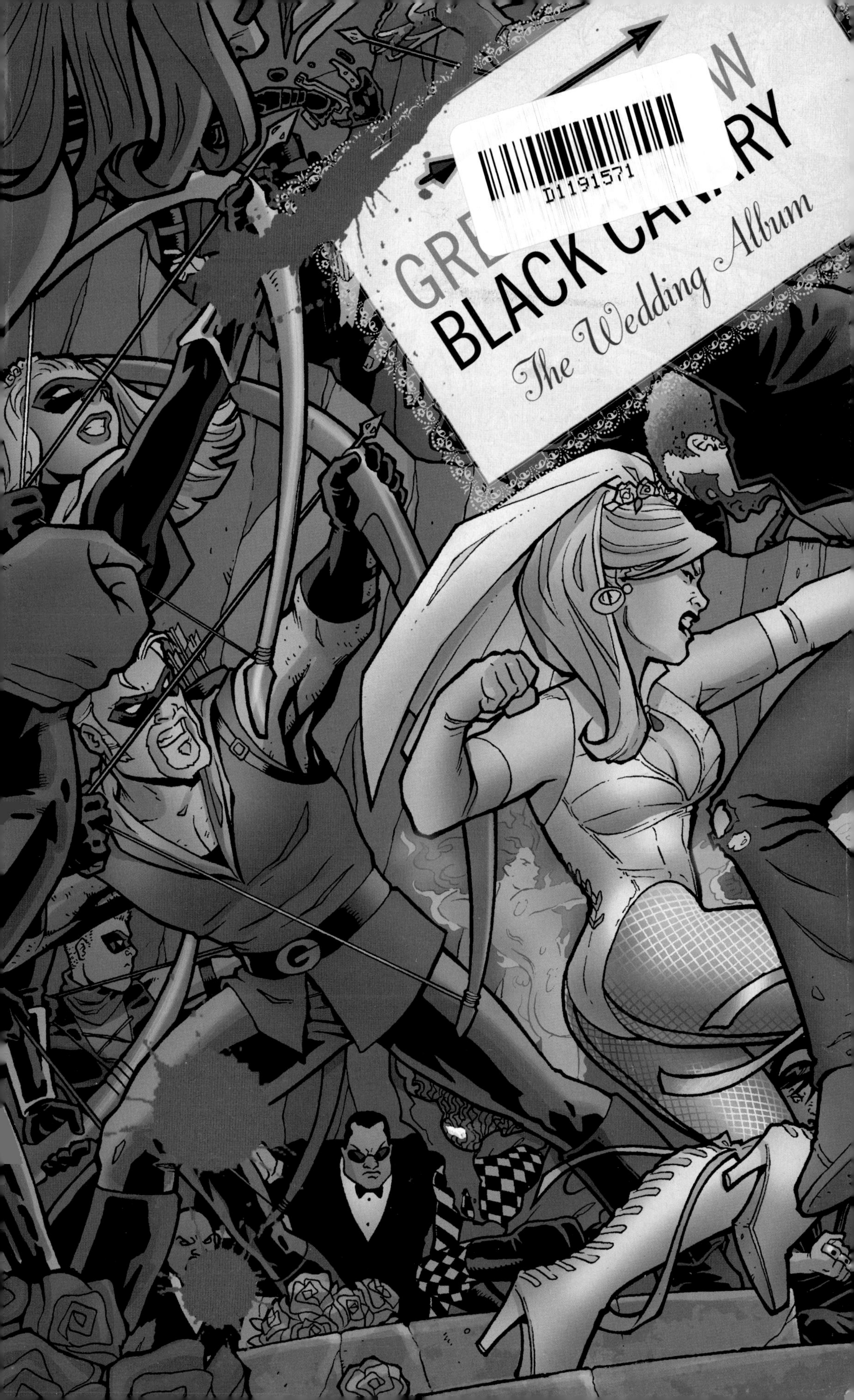
GRE W
BLACK CAN RY
The Wedding Album

DAN DIDIO Senior VP-Executive Editor / **MIKE CARLIN** Editor-original series / **ELISABETH GEHRLEIN** Assistant Editor-original series
BOB JOY Editor-collected edition / **ROBBIN BROSTERMAN** Senior Art Director / **PAUL LEVITZ** President & Publisher
GEORG BREWER VP-Design & DC Direct Creative / **RICHARD BRUNING** Senior VP-Creative Director
PATRICK CALDON Executive VP-Finance & Operations / **CHRIS CARAMALIS** VP-Finance / **JOHN CUNNINGHAM** VP-Marketing
TERRI CUNNINGHAM VP-Managing Editor / **ALISON GILL** VP-Manufacturing / **DAVID HYDE** VP-Publicity
HANK KANALZ VP-General Manager, WildStorm / **JIM LEE** Editorial Director-WildStorm / **PAULA LOWITT** Senior VP-Business & Legal Affairs
MARYELLEN McLAUGHLIN VP-Advertising & Custom Publishing / **JOHN NEE** Senior VP-Business Development
GREGORY NOVECK Senior VP-Creative Affairs / **SUE POHJA** VP-Book Trade Sales / **STEVE ROTTERDAM** Senior VP-Sales & Marketing
CHERYL RUBIN Senior VP-Brand Management / **JEFF TROJAN** VP-Business Development, DC Direct / **BOB WAYNE** VP-Sales

Cover art by Cliff Chiang. Publication design by Amelia Grohman.

GREEN ARROW/BLACK CANARY: THE WEDDING ALBUM
Published by DC Comics. Cover and compilation Copyright © 2008 DC Comics. All Rights Reserved.

Originally published in single magazine form in GREEN ARROW AND BLACK CANARY WEDDING SPECIAL 1,
GREEN ARROW AND BLACK CANARY 1-5 Copyright © 2007, 2008 DC Comics. All Rights Reserved.
All characters, their distinctive likenesses and related elements featured in this publication are trademarks of DC Comics.
The stories, characters and incidents featured in this publication are entirely fictional.
DC Comics does not read or accept unsolicited submissions of ideas, stories or artwork.

DC Comics, 1700 Broadway, New York, NY 10019 / A Warner Bros. Entertainment Company
Printed in USA. First Printing. HC ISBN-13: 978-1-4012-1841-6 SC ISBN-13: 978-1-4012-2219-2

GREEN ARROW
BLACK CANARY
The Wedding Album

Judd Winick
writer

Amanda Conner
Cliff Chiang
André Coelho
artists

Paul Mounts
Trish Mulvihill
David Baron
colorists

Ken Lopez
Pat Brosseau
letterers

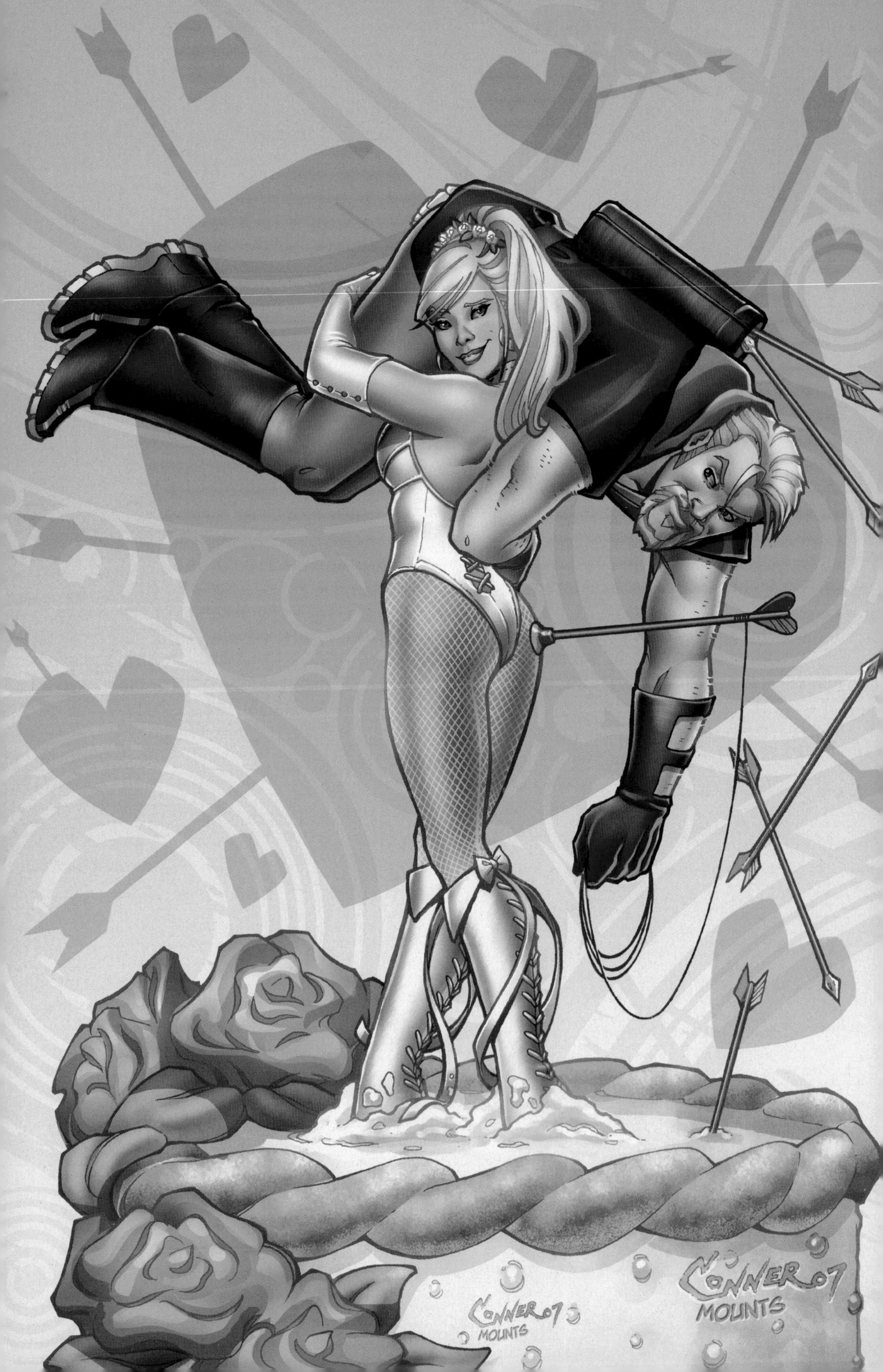
CONNER 07
MOUNTS
CONNER 07
MOUNTS

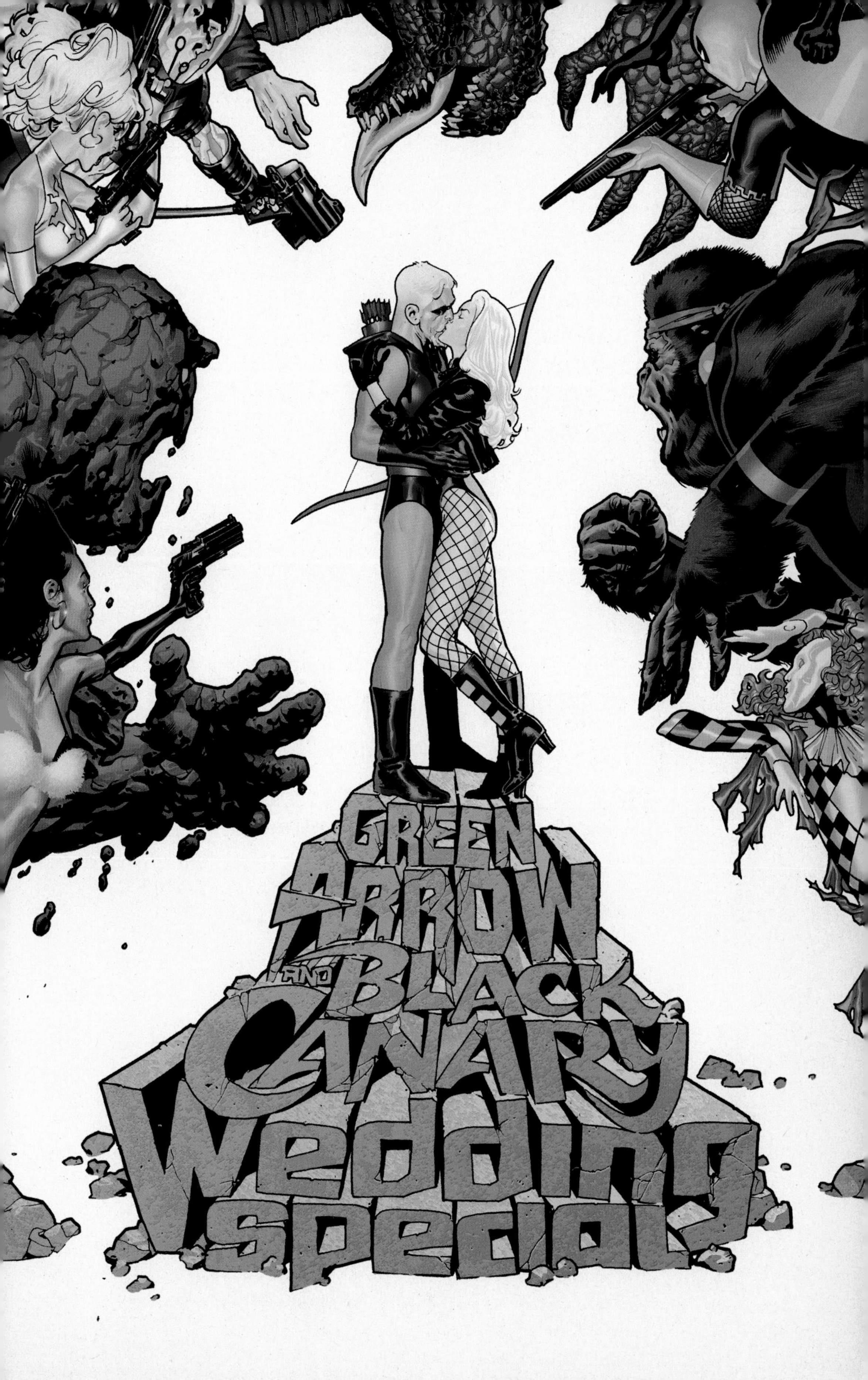
GREEN ARROW AND BLACK CANARY Wedding Special

GREEN ARROW AND BLACK CANARY WEDDING SPECIAL *Ryan Sook*

AND THEY SAID IT WOULDN'T LAST
THE WEDDING OF GREEN ARROW
AND BLACK CANARY

Story: **Judd Winick**   *Art:* **Amanda Conner**   *Color:* **Paul Mounts**

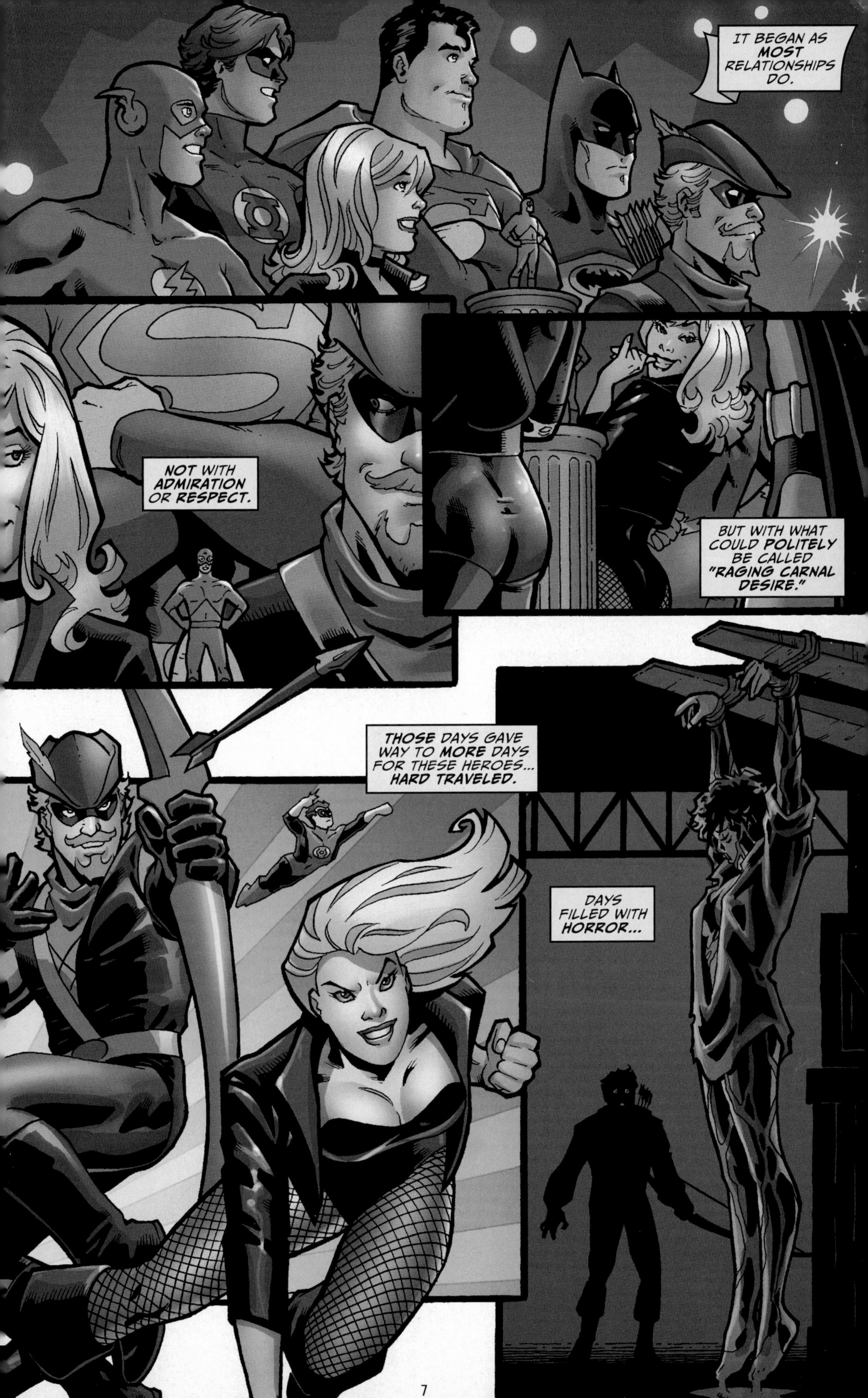
IT BEGAN AS MOST RELATIONSHIPS DO.
NOT WITH ADMIRATION OR RESPECT.
BUT WITH WHAT COULD POLITELY BE CALLED "RAGING CARNAL DESIRE."
THOSE DAYS GAVE WAY TO MORE DAYS FOR THESE HEROES... HARD TRAVELED.
DAYS FILLED WITH HORROR...

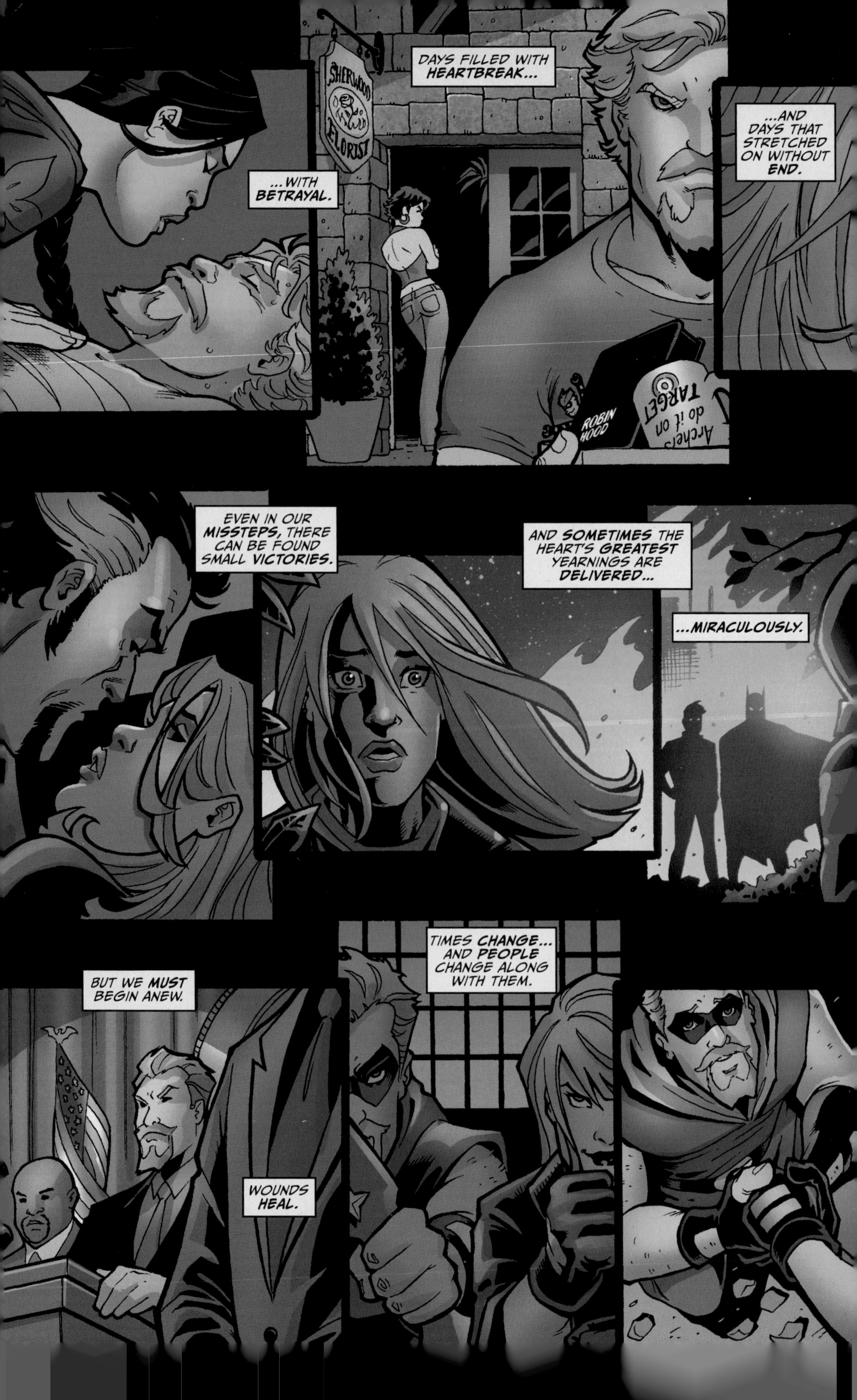

DAYS FILLED WITH HEARTBREAK...
...WITH BETRAYAL.
SHERWOOD FLORIST
ROBIN HOOD
Archers do it on TARGET
...AND DAYS THAT STRETCHED ON WITHOUT END.
EVEN IN OUR MISSTEPS, THERE CAN BE FOUND SMALL VICTORIES.
AND SOMETIMES THE HEART'S GREATEST YEARNINGS ARE DELIVERED...
...MIRACULOUSLY.
BUT WE MUST BEGIN ANEW.
WOUNDS HEAL.
TIMES CHANGE... AND PEOPLE CHANGE ALONG WITH THEM.

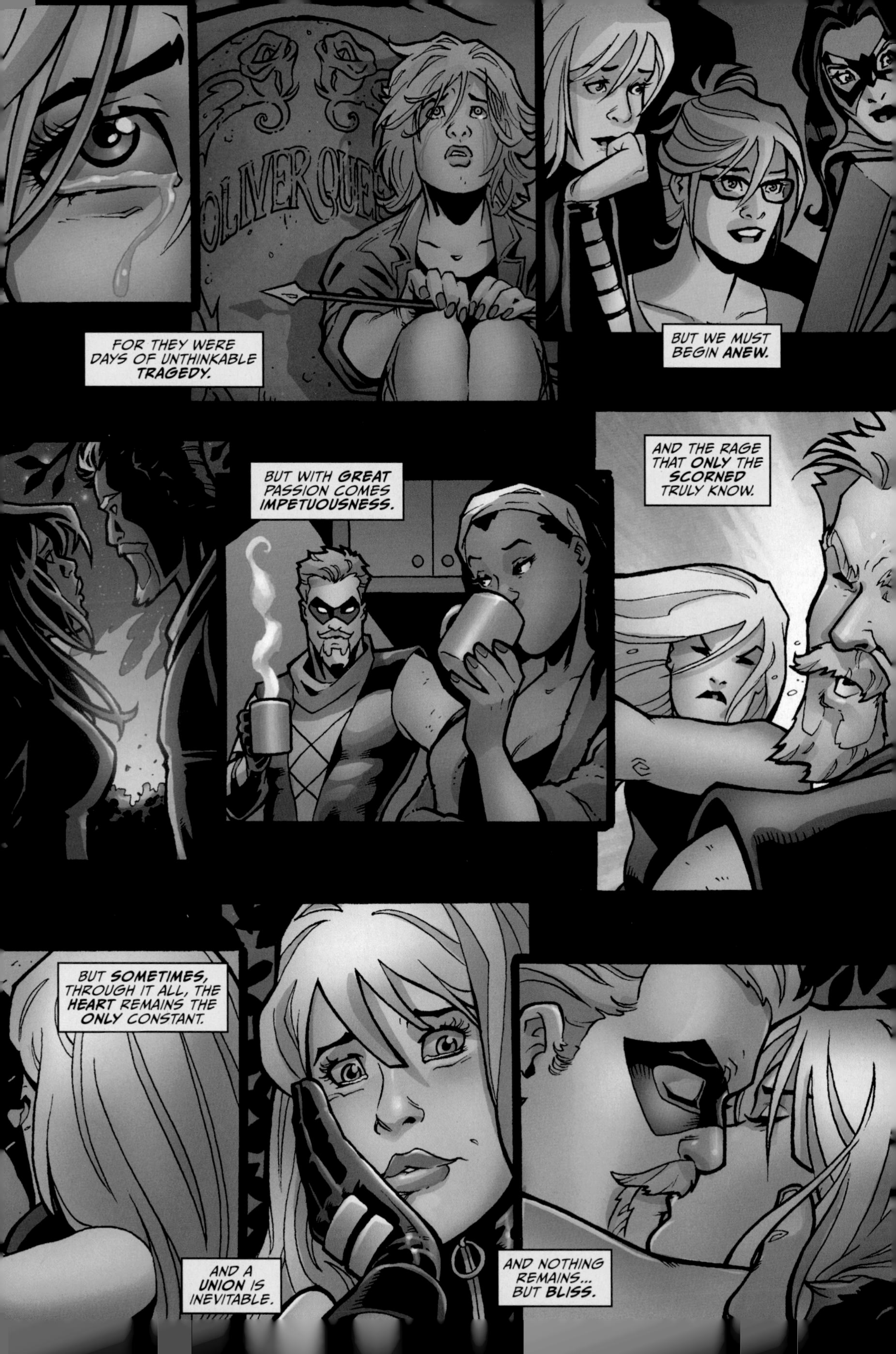
OLIVER QUE
FOR THEY WERE DAYS OF UNTHINKABLE TRAGEDY.
BUT WE MUST BEGIN ANEW.
BUT WITH GREAT PASSION COMES IMPETUOUSNESS.
AND THE RAGE THAT ONLY THE SCORNED TRULY KNOW.
BUT SOMETIMES, THROUGH IT ALL, THE HEART REMAINS THE ONLY CONSTANT.
AND A UNION IS INEVITABLE.
AND NOTHING REMAINS... BUT BLISS.

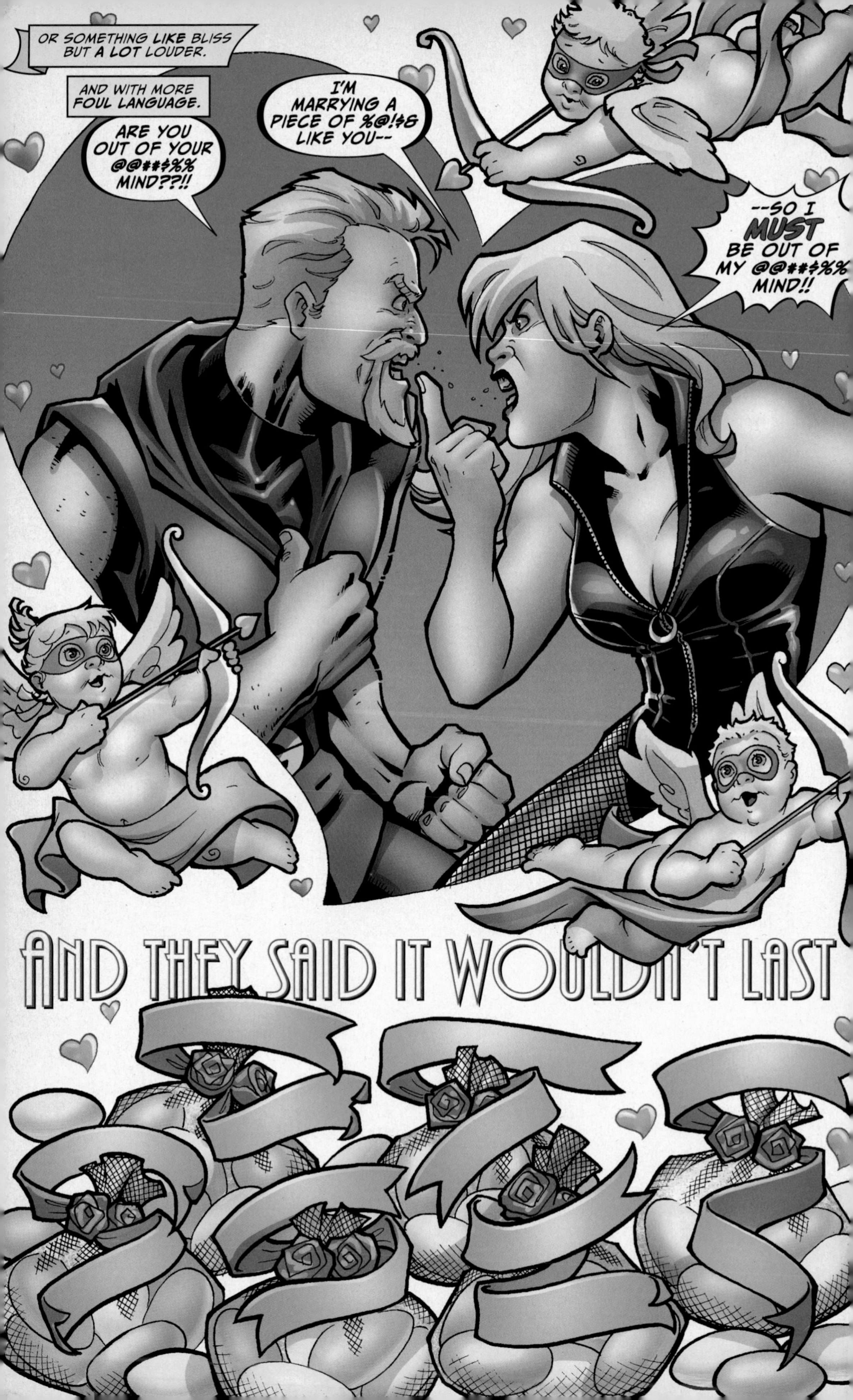
OR SOMETHING LIKE BLISS BUT A LOT LOUDER.
AND WITH MORE FOUL LANGUAGE.
ARE YOU OUT OF YOUR @@##$%% MIND??!!
I'M MARRYING A PIECE OF %@!$& LIKE YOU--
--SO I MUST BE OUT OF MY @@##$%% MIND!!
AND THEY SAID IT WOULDN'T LAST

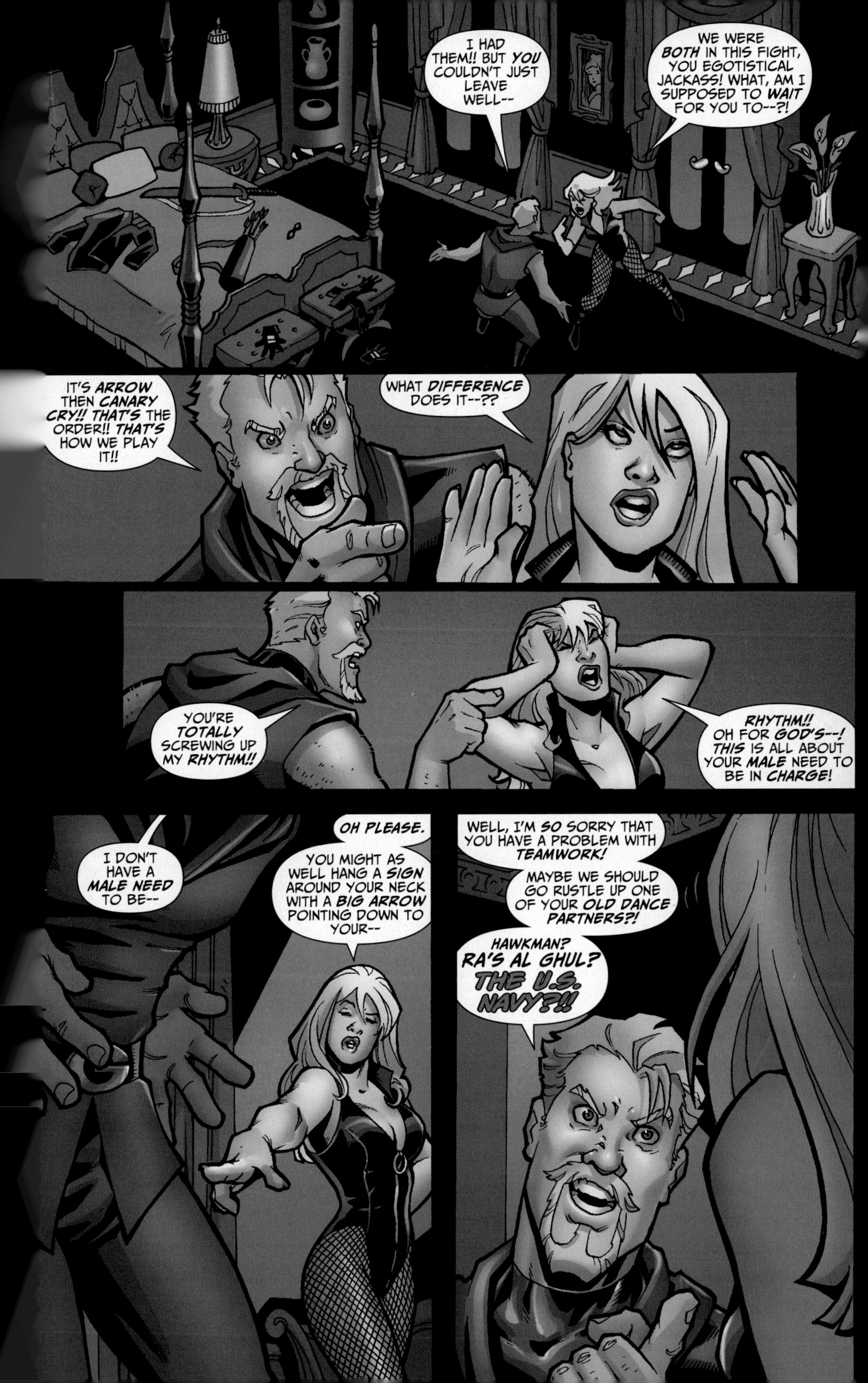
I HAD THEM!! BUT YOU COULDN'T JUST LEAVE WELL--
WE WERE BOTH IN THIS FIGHT, YOU EGOTISTICAL JACKASS! WHAT, AM I SUPPOSED TO WAIT FOR YOU TO--?!
IT'S ARROW THEN CANARY CRY!! THAT'S THE ORDER!! THAT'S HOW WE PLAY IT!!
WHAT DIFFERENCE DOES IT--??
YOU'RE TOTALLY SCREWING UP MY RHYTHM!!
RHYTHM!! OH FOR GOD'S--! THIS IS ALL ABOUT YOUR MALE NEED TO BE IN CHARGE!
I DON'T HAVE A MALE NEED TO BE--
OH PLEASE.
YOU MIGHT AS WELL HANG A SIGN AROUND YOUR NECK WITH A BIG ARROW POINTING DOWN TO YOUR--
WELL, I'M SO SORRY THAT YOU HAVE A PROBLEM WITH TEAMWORK!
MAYBE WE SHOULD GO RUSTLE UP ONE OF YOUR OLD DANCE PARTNERS?!
HAWKMAN? RA'S AL GHUL? THE U.S. NAVY?!!

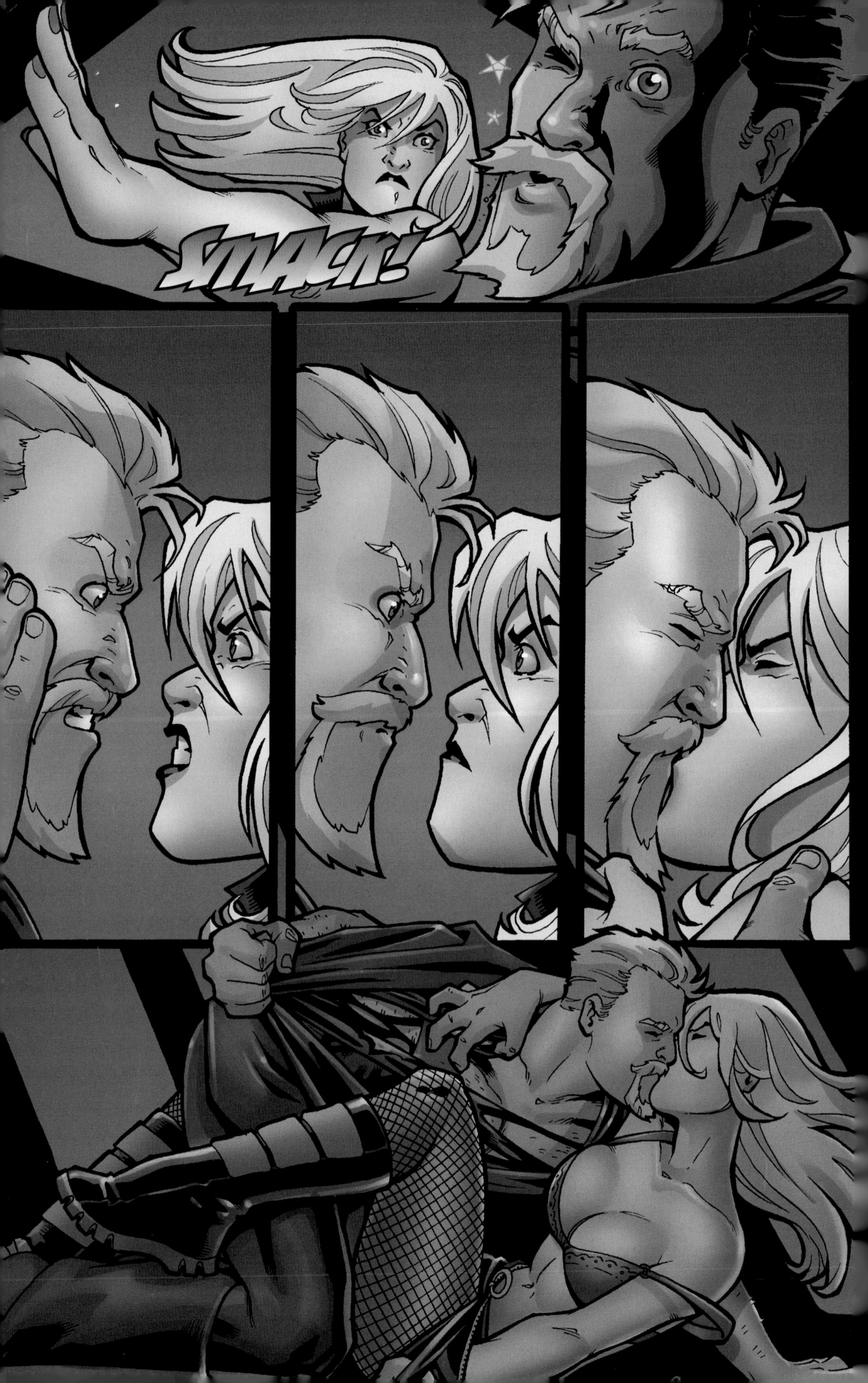
SMACK!

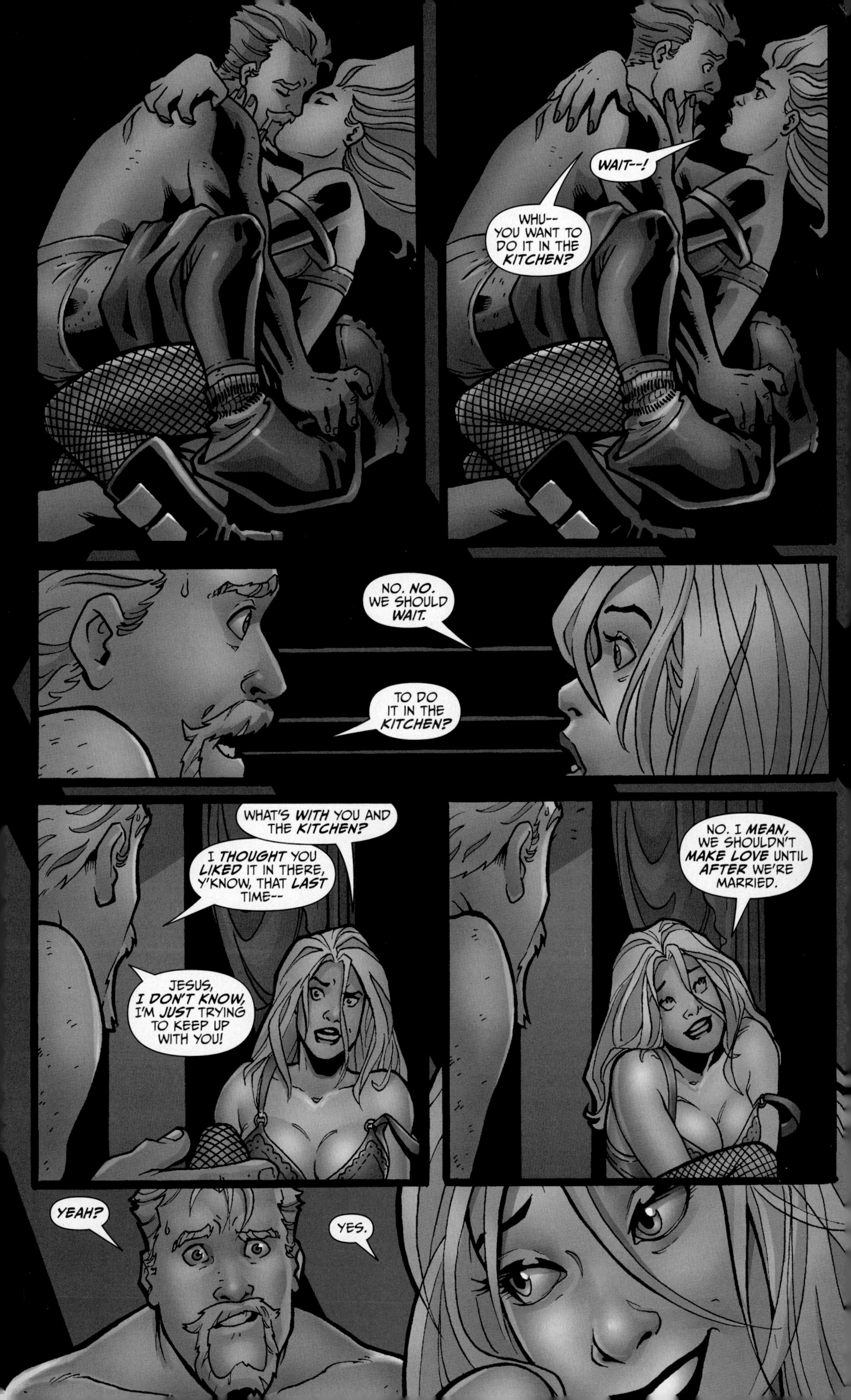
WAIT--!
WHU-- YOU WANT TO DO IT IN THE KITCHEN?
NO. NO. WE SHOULD WAIT.
TO DO IT IN THE KITCHEN?
WHAT'S WITH YOU AND THE KITCHEN?
I THOUGHT YOU LIKED IT IN THERE, Y'KNOW, THAT LAST TIME--
JESUS, I DON'T KNOW, I'M JUST TRYING TO KEEP UP WITH YOU!
NO. I MEAN, WE SHOULDN'T MAKE LOVE UNTIL AFTER WE'RE MARRIED.
YEAH?
YES.

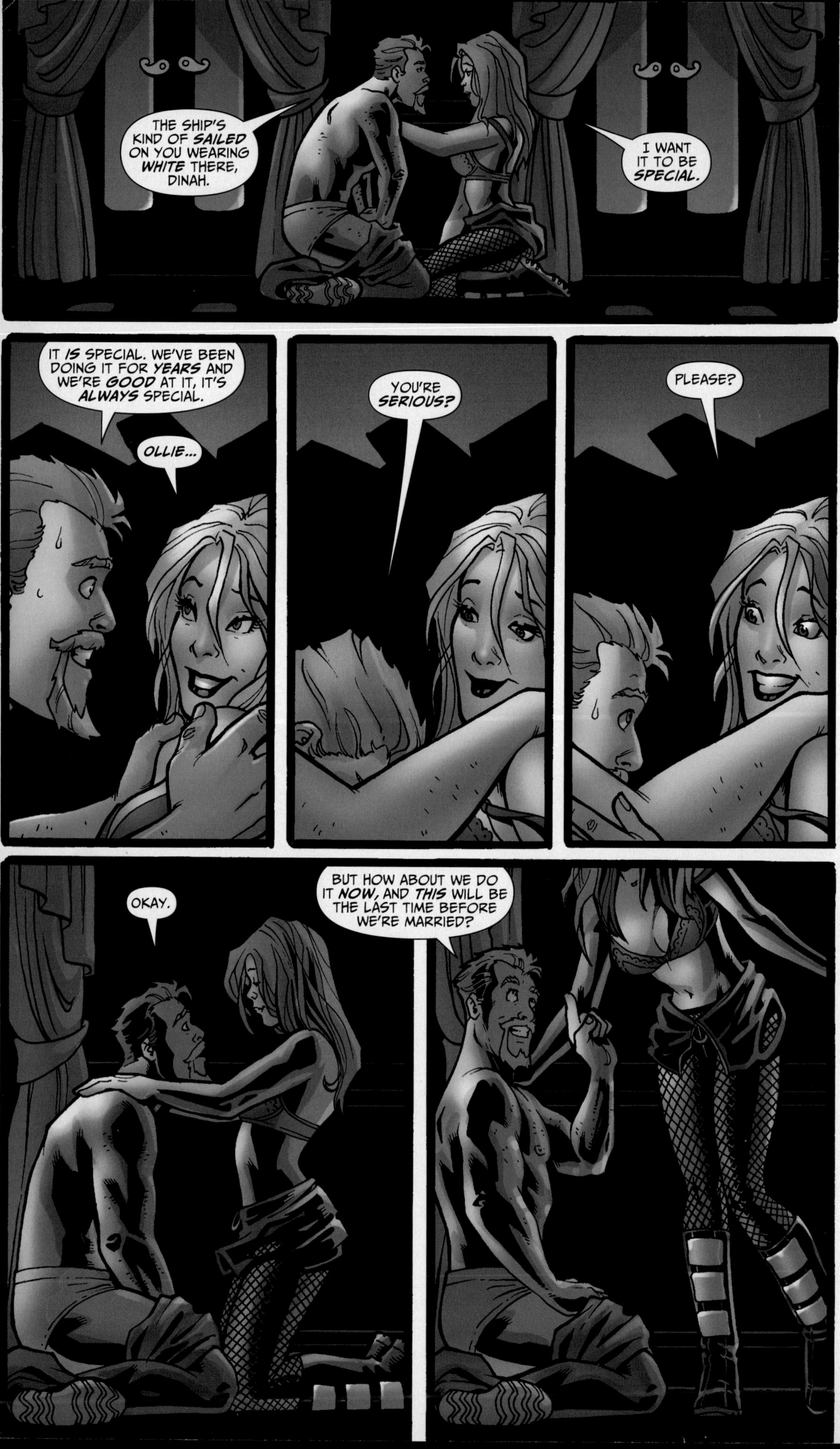
THE SHIP'S KIND OF SAILED ON YOU WEARING WHITE THERE, DINAH.
I WANT IT TO BE SPECIAL.
IT IS SPECIAL. WE'VE BEEN DOING IT FOR YEARS AND WE'RE GOOD AT IT, IT'S ALWAYS SPECIAL.
OLLIE...
YOU'RE SERIOUS?
PLEASE?
OKAY.
BUT HOW ABOUT WE DO IT NOW, AND THIS WILL BE THE LAST TIME BEFORE WE'RE MARRIED?

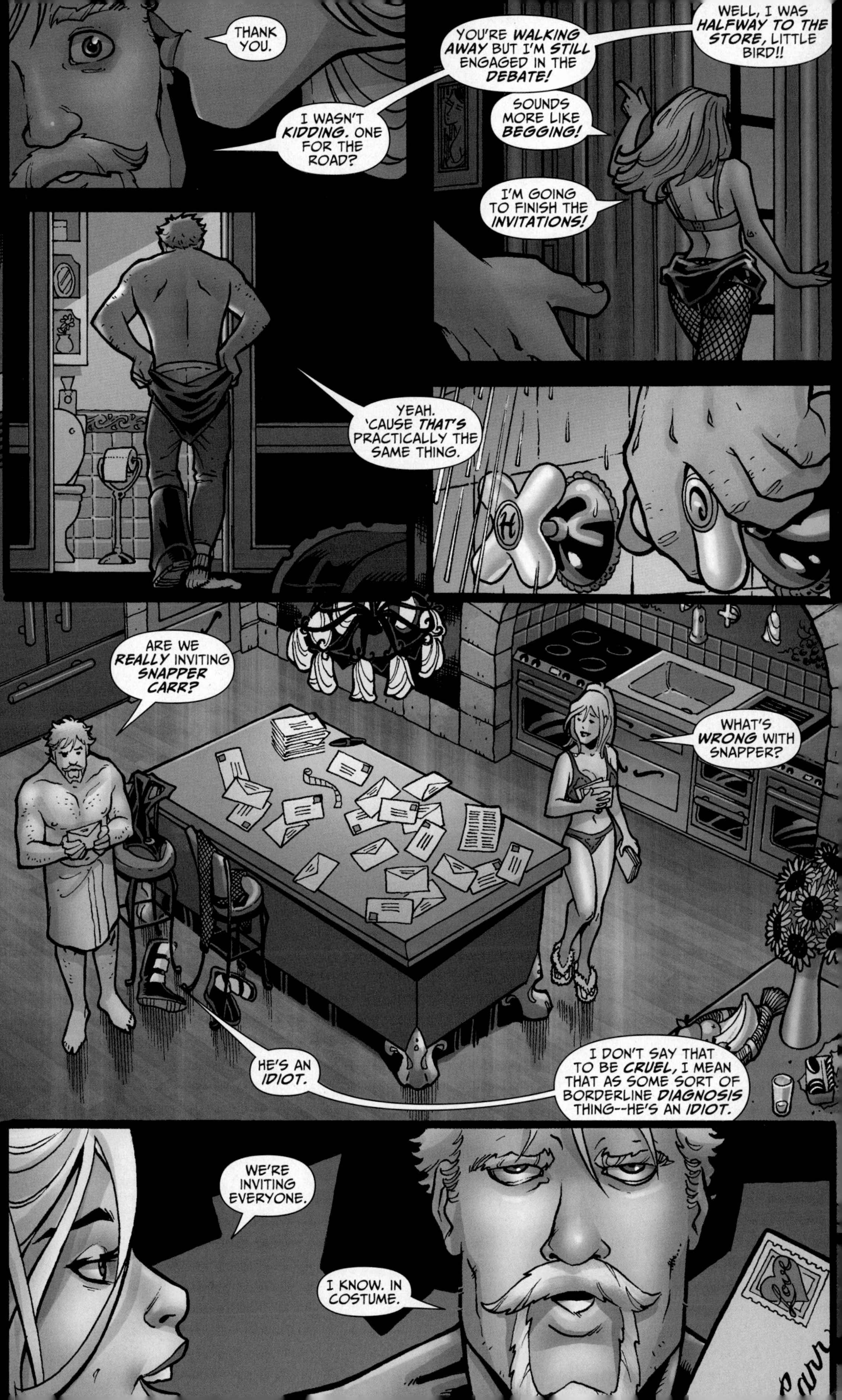

THANK YOU.
YOU'RE WALKING AWAY BUT I'M STILL ENGAGED IN THE DEBATE!
WELL, I WAS HALFWAY TO THE STORE, LITTLE BIRD!!
I WASN'T KIDDING. ONE FOR THE ROAD?
SOUNDS MORE LIKE BEGGING!
I'M GOING TO FINISH THE INVITATIONS!
YEAH. 'CAUSE THAT'S PRACTICALLY THE SAME THING.
ARE WE REALLY INVITING SNAPPER CARR?
WHAT'S WRONG WITH SNAPPER?
HE'S AN IDIOT.
I DON'T SAY THAT TO BE CRUEL, I MEAN THAT AS SOME SORT OF BORDERLINE DIAGNOSIS THING--HE'S AN IDIOT.
WE'RE INVITING EVERYONE.
I KNOW. IN COSTUME.

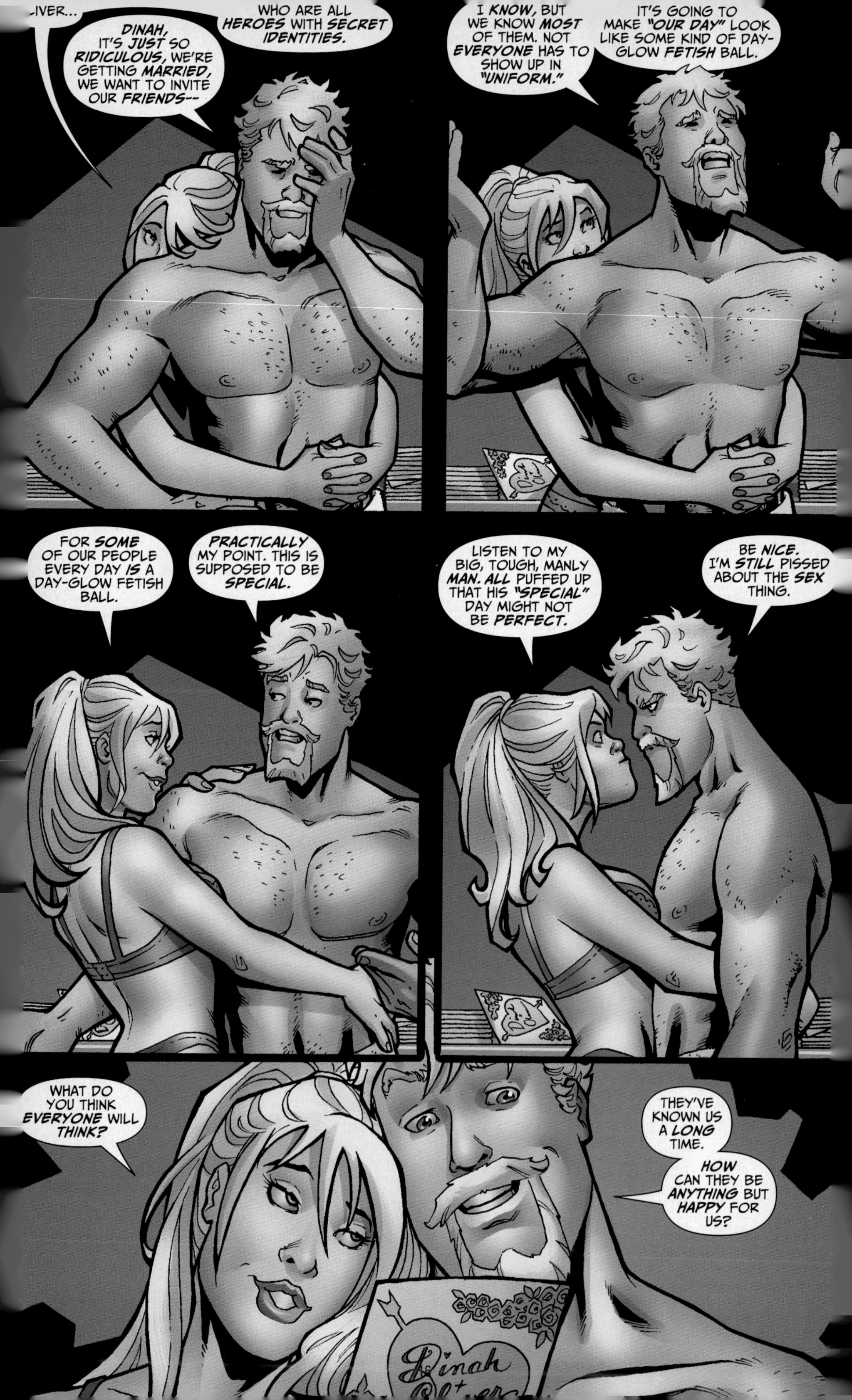

LIVER...
DINAH, IT'S JUST SO RIDICULOUS, WE'RE GETTING MARRIED, WE WANT TO INVITE OUR FRIENDS--
WHO ARE ALL HEROES WITH SECRET IDENTITIES.
I KNOW, BUT WE KNOW MOST OF THEM. NOT EVERYONE HAS TO SHOW UP IN "UNIFORM."
IT'S GOING TO MAKE "OUR DAY" LOOK LIKE SOME KIND OF DAY-GLOW FETISH BALL.
FOR SOME OF OUR PEOPLE EVERY DAY IS A DAY-GLOW FETISH BALL.
PRACTICALLY MY POINT. THIS IS SUPPOSED TO BE SPECIAL.
LISTEN TO MY BIG, TOUGH, MANLY MAN. ALL PUFFED UP THAT HIS "SPECIAL" DAY MIGHT NOT BE PERFECT.
BE NICE. I'M STILL PISSED ABOUT THE SEX THING.
WHAT DO YOU THINK EVERYONE WILL THINK?
THEY'VE KNOWN US A LONG TIME.
HOW CAN THEY BE ANYTHING BUT HAPPY FOR US?
Dinah

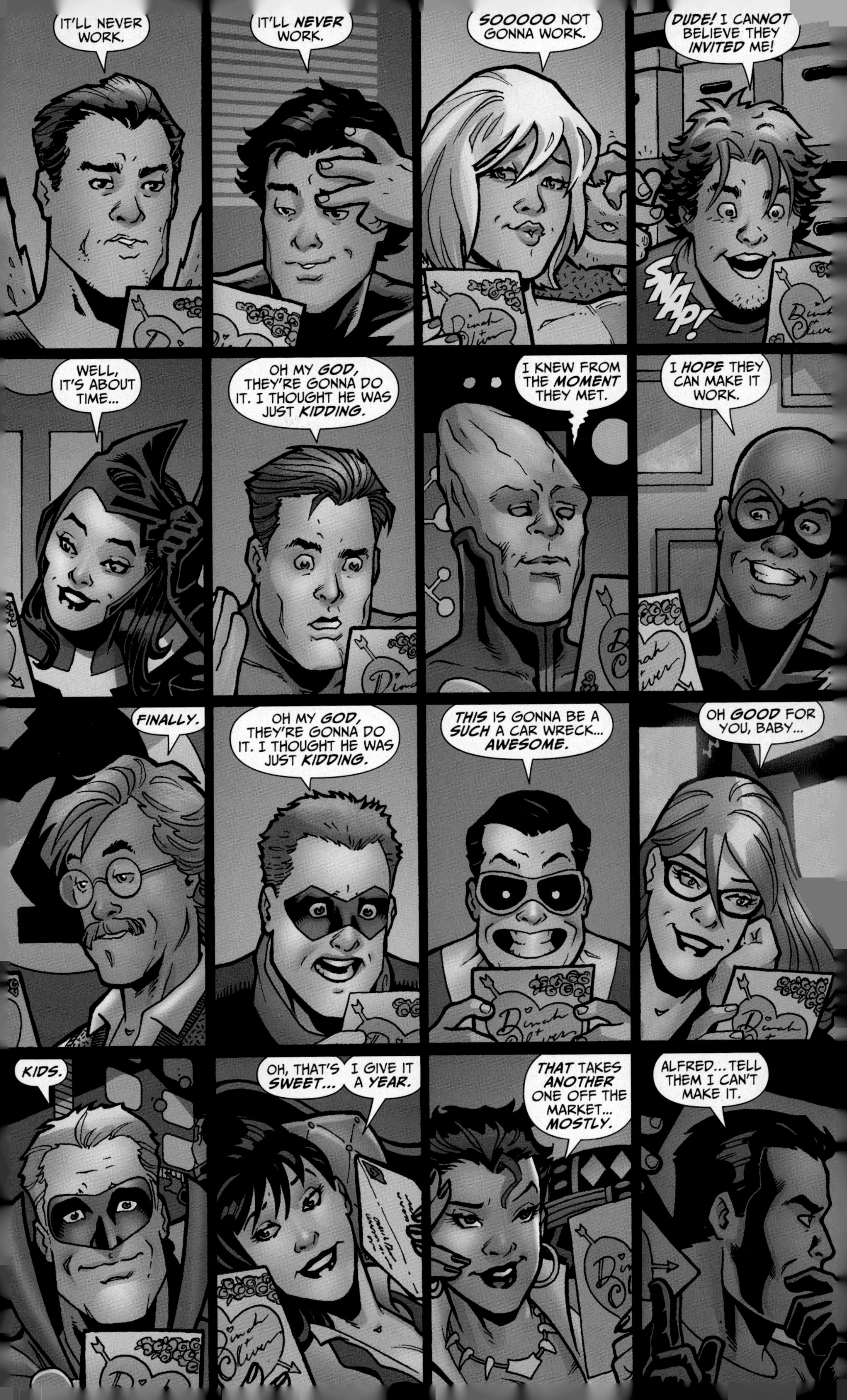
IT'LL NEVER WORK.
IT'LL NEVER WORK.
SOOOOO NOT GONNA WORK.
DUDE! I CANNOT BELIEVE THEY INVITED ME!
SNAP!
WELL, IT'S ABOUT TIME...
OH MY GOD, THEY'RE GONNA DO IT. I THOUGHT HE WAS JUST KIDDING.
I KNEW FROM THE MOMENT THEY MET.
I HOPE THEY CAN MAKE IT WORK.
FINALLY.
OH MY GOD, THEY'RE GONNA DO IT. I THOUGHT HE WAS JUST KIDDING.
THIS IS GONNA BE A SUCH A CAR WRECK... AWESOME.
OH GOOD FOR YOU, BABY...
KIDS.
OH, THAT'S SWEET...
I GIVE IT A YEAR.
THAT TAKES ANOTHER ONE OFF THE MARKET... MOSTLY.
ALFRED... TELL THEM I CAN'T MAKE IT.

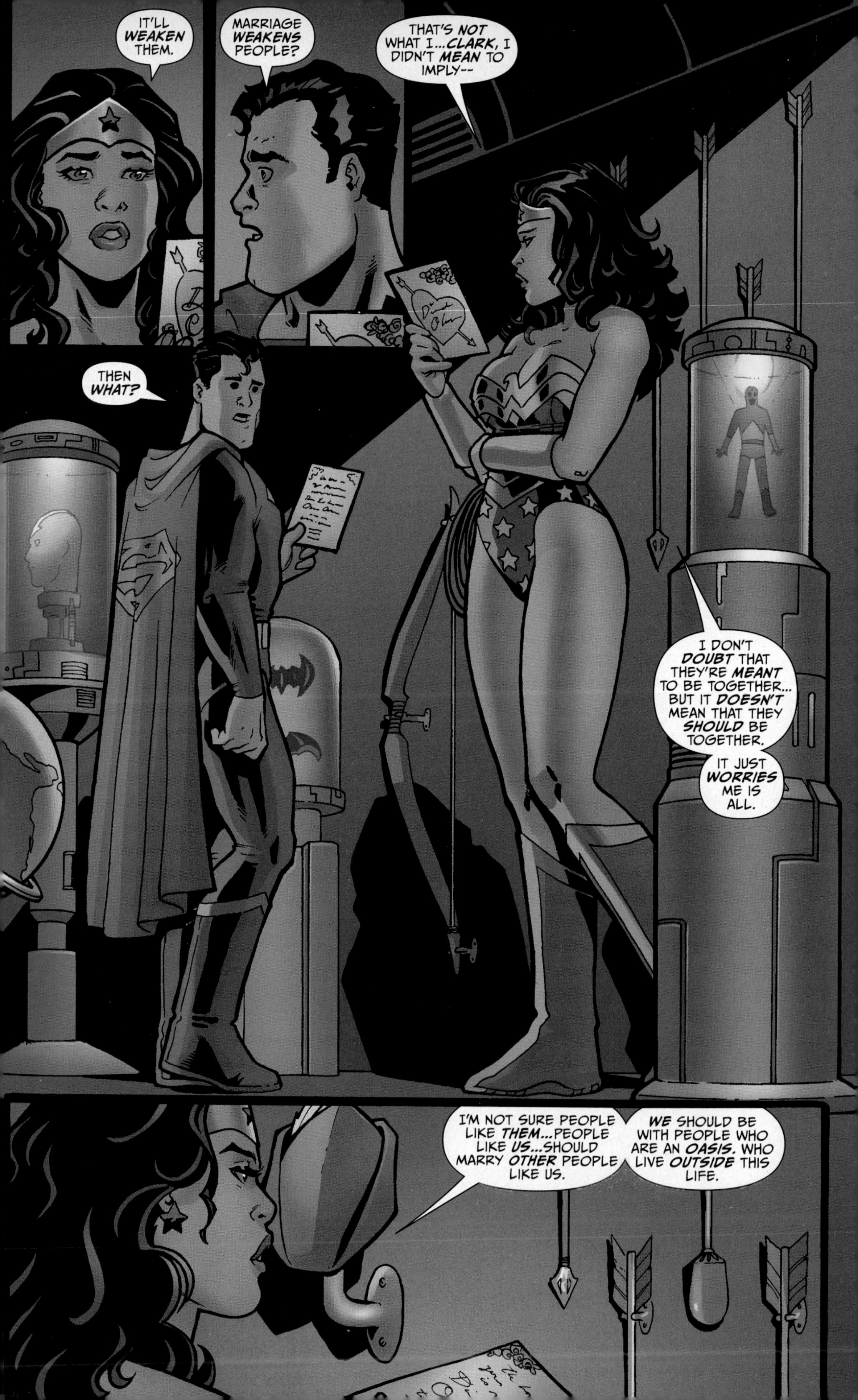
IT'LL WEAKEN THEM.
MARRIAGE WEAKENS PEOPLE?
THAT'S NOT WHAT I...CLARK, I DIDN'T MEAN TO IMPLY--
THEN WHAT?
I DON'T DOUBT THAT THEY'RE MEANT TO BE TOGETHER... BUT IT DOESN'T MEAN THAT THEY SHOULD BE TOGETHER.
IT JUST WORRIES ME IS ALL.
I'M NOT SURE PEOPLE LIKE THEM...PEOPLE LIKE US...SHOULD MARRY OTHER PEOPLE LIKE US.
WE SHOULD BE WITH PEOPLE WHO ARE AN OASIS. WHO LIVE OUTSIDE THIS LIFE.

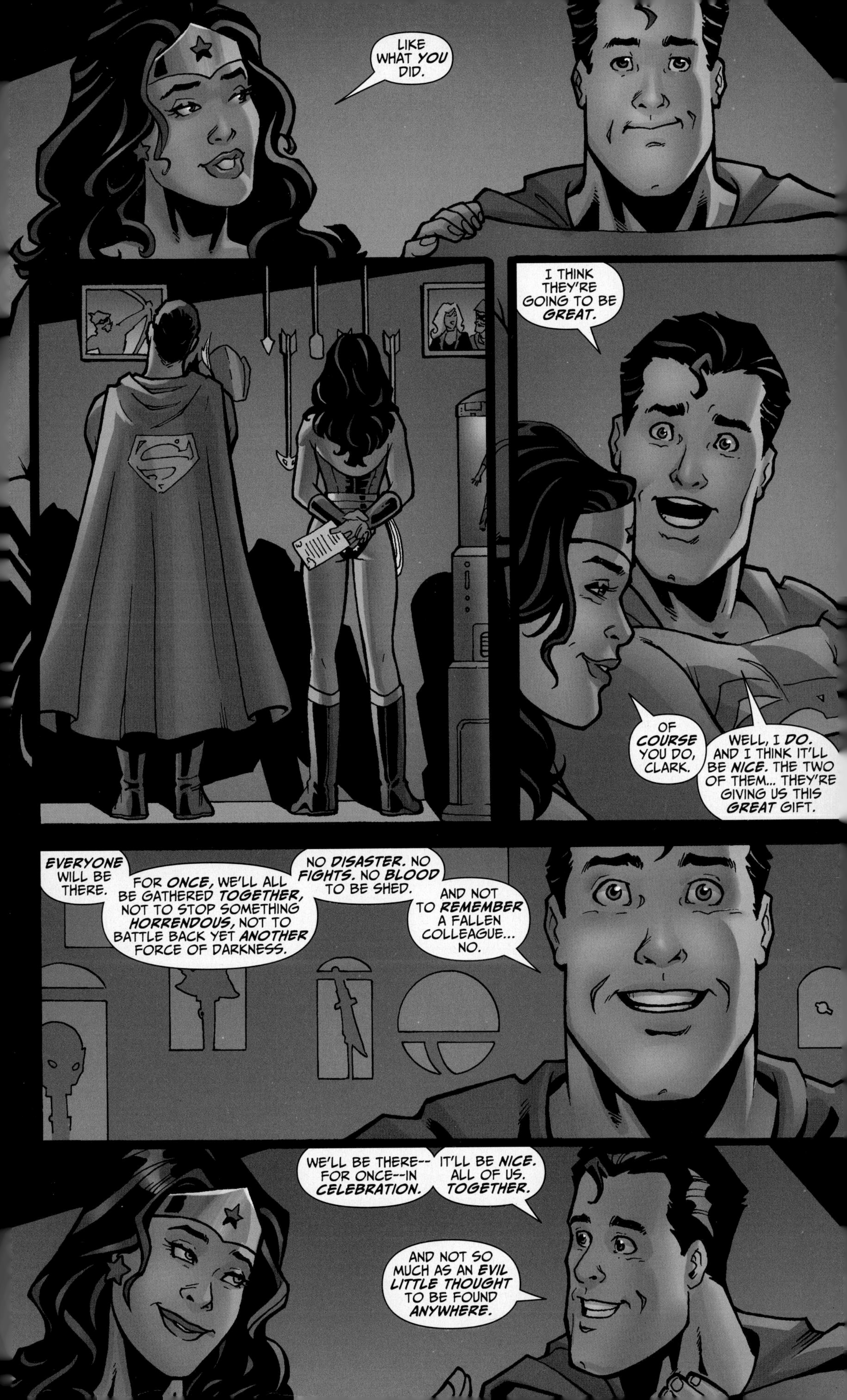

LIKE WHAT *YOU* DID.
I THINK THEY'RE GOING TO BE *GREAT.*
OF *COURSE* YOU DO, CLARK.
WELL, I *DO.* AND I THINK IT'LL BE *NICE.* THE TWO OF THEM... THEY'RE GIVING US THIS *GREAT* GIFT.
EVERYONE WILL BE THERE.
FOR *ONCE,* WE'LL ALL BE GATHERED *TOGETHER,* NOT TO STOP SOMETHING *HORRENDOUS,* NOT TO BATTLE BACK YET *ANOTHER* FORCE OF DARKNESS.
NO *DISASTER.* NO *FIGHTS.* NO *BLOOD* TO BE SHED.
AND NOT TO *REMEMBER* A FALLEN COLLEAGUE... NO.
WE'LL BE THERE-- FOR ONCE--IN *CELEBRATION.*
IT'LL BE *NICE.* ALL OF US. *TOGETHER.*
AND NOT SO MUCH AS AN *EVIL LITTLE THOUGHT* TO BE FOUND *ANYWHERE.*

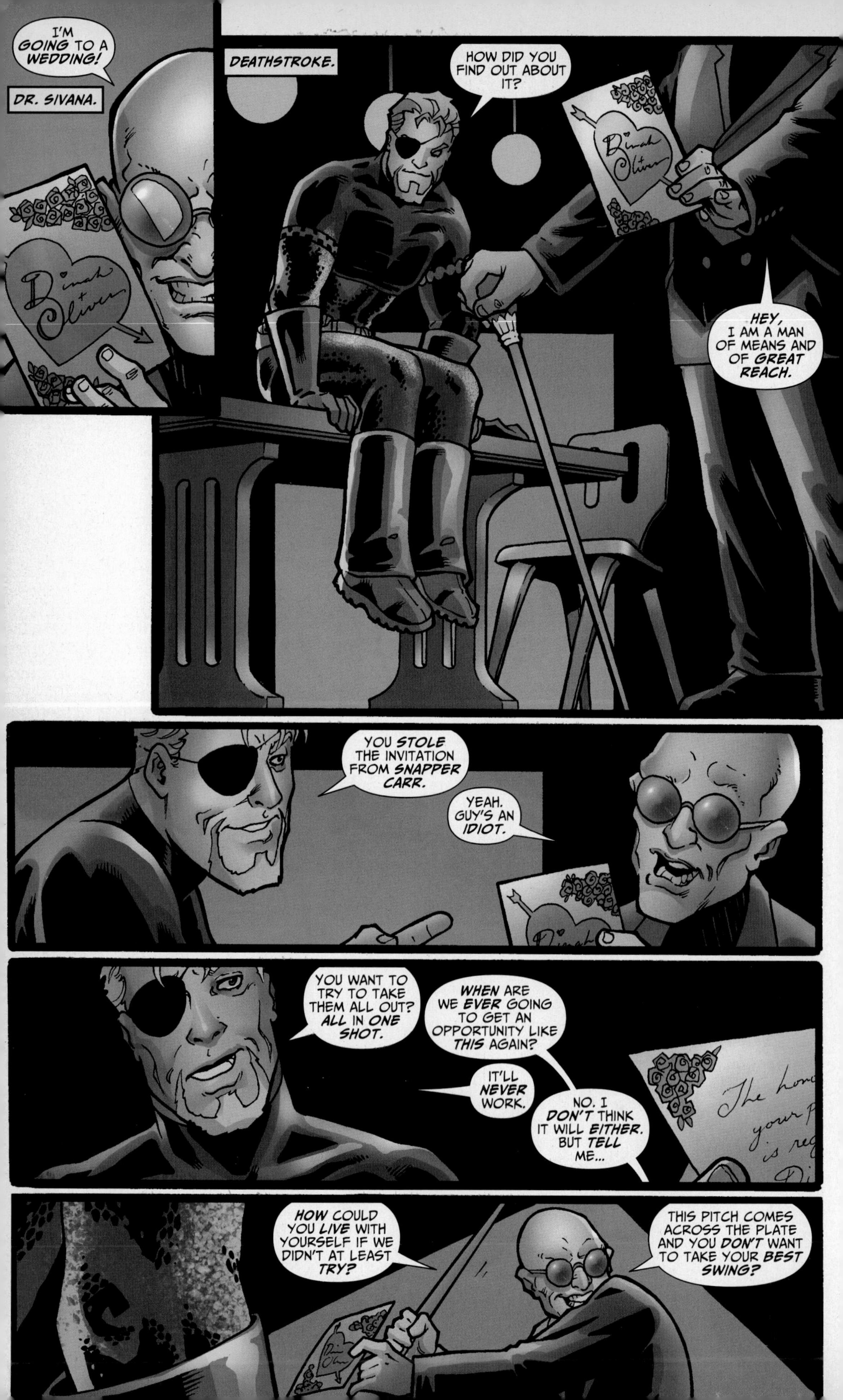
I'M GOING TO A WEDDING!
DR. SIVANA.
DEATHSTROKE.
HOW DID YOU FIND OUT ABOUT IT?
HEY, I AM A MAN OF MEANS AND OF GREAT REACH.
YOU STOLE THE INVITATION FROM SNAPPER CARR.
YEAH. GUY'S AN IDIOT.
YOU WANT TO TRY TO TAKE THEM ALL OUT? ALL IN ONE SHOT.
WHEN ARE WE EVER GOING TO GET AN OPPORTUNITY LIKE THIS AGAIN?
IT'LL NEVER WORK.
NO. I DON'T THINK IT WILL EITHER. BUT TELL ME...
HOW COULD YOU LIVE WITH YOURSELF IF WE DIDN'T AT LEAST TRY?
THIS PITCH COMES ACROSS THE PLATE AND YOU DON'T WANT TO TAKE YOUR BEST SWING?

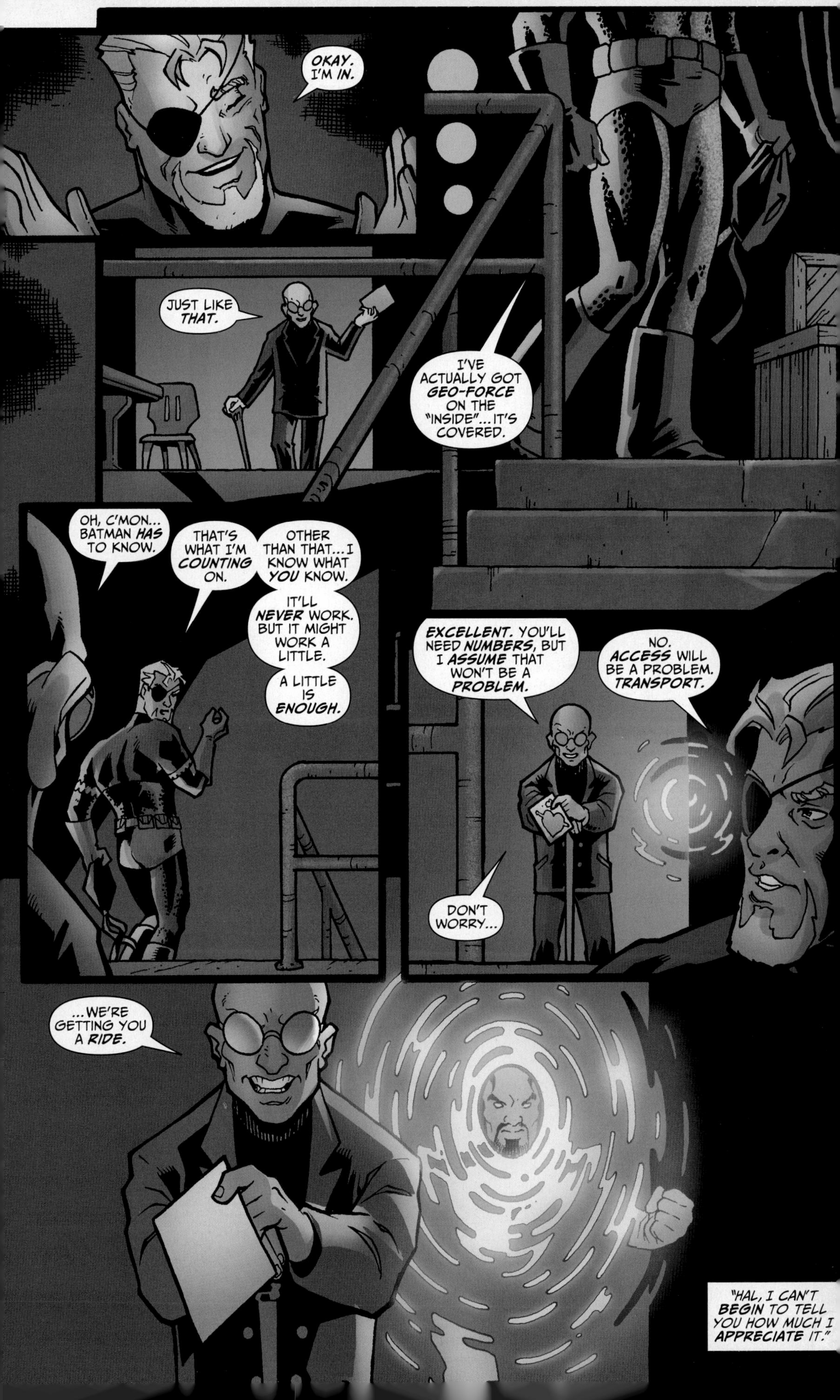

OKAY. I'M IN.
JUST LIKE THAT.
I'VE ACTUALLY GOT GEO-FORCE ON THE "INSIDE"... IT'S COVERED.
OH, C'MON... BATMAN HAS TO KNOW.
THAT'S WHAT I'M COUNTING ON.
OTHER THAN THAT... I KNOW WHAT YOU KNOW.
IT'LL NEVER WORK. BUT IT MIGHT WORK A LITTLE.
A LITTLE IS ENOUGH.
EXCELLENT. YOU'LL NEED NUMBERS, BUT I ASSUME THAT WON'T BE A PROBLEM.
NO. ACCESS WILL BE A PROBLEM. TRANSPORT.
DON'T WORRY...
...WE'RE GETTING YOU A RIDE.
"HAL, I CAN'T BEGIN TO TELL YOU HOW MUCH I APPRECIATE IT."

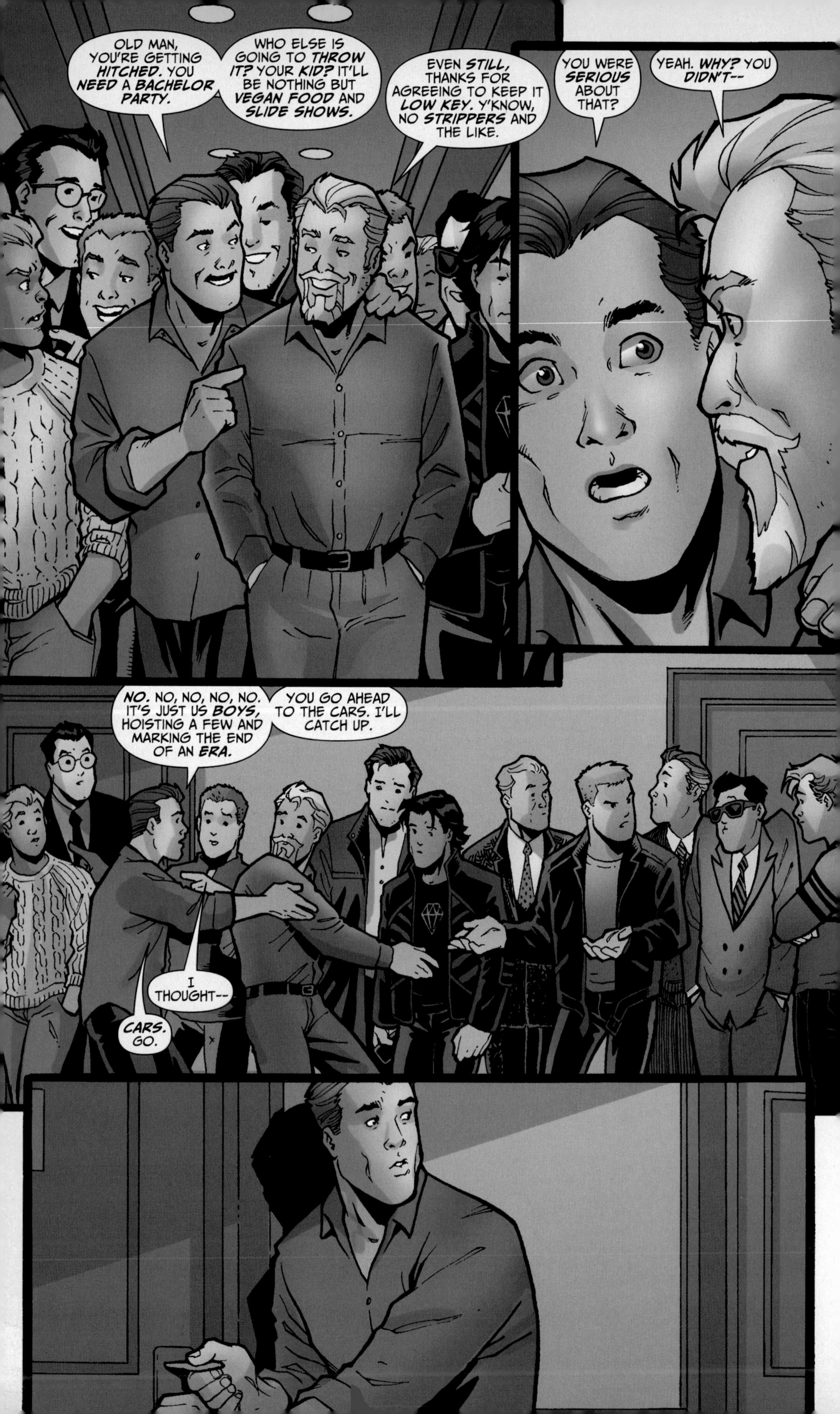
OLD MAN, YOU'RE GETTING *HITCHED*. YOU *NEED* A *BACHELOR PARTY*.
WHO ELSE IS GOING TO *THROW IT*? YOUR *KID*? IT'LL BE NOTHING BUT *VEGAN FOOD* AND *SLIDE SHOWS*.
EVEN *STILL*, THANKS FOR AGREEING TO KEEP IT *LOW KEY*. Y'KNOW, NO *STRIPPERS* AND THE LIKE.
YOU WERE *SERIOUS* ABOUT THAT?
YEAH. *WHY?* YOU *DIDN'T*--
NO. NO, NO, NO, NO. IT'S JUST US *BOYS*, HOISTING A FEW AND MARKING THE END OF AN *ERA*.
YOU GO AHEAD TO THE CARS. I'LL CATCH UP.
I THOUGHT--
CARS. GO.

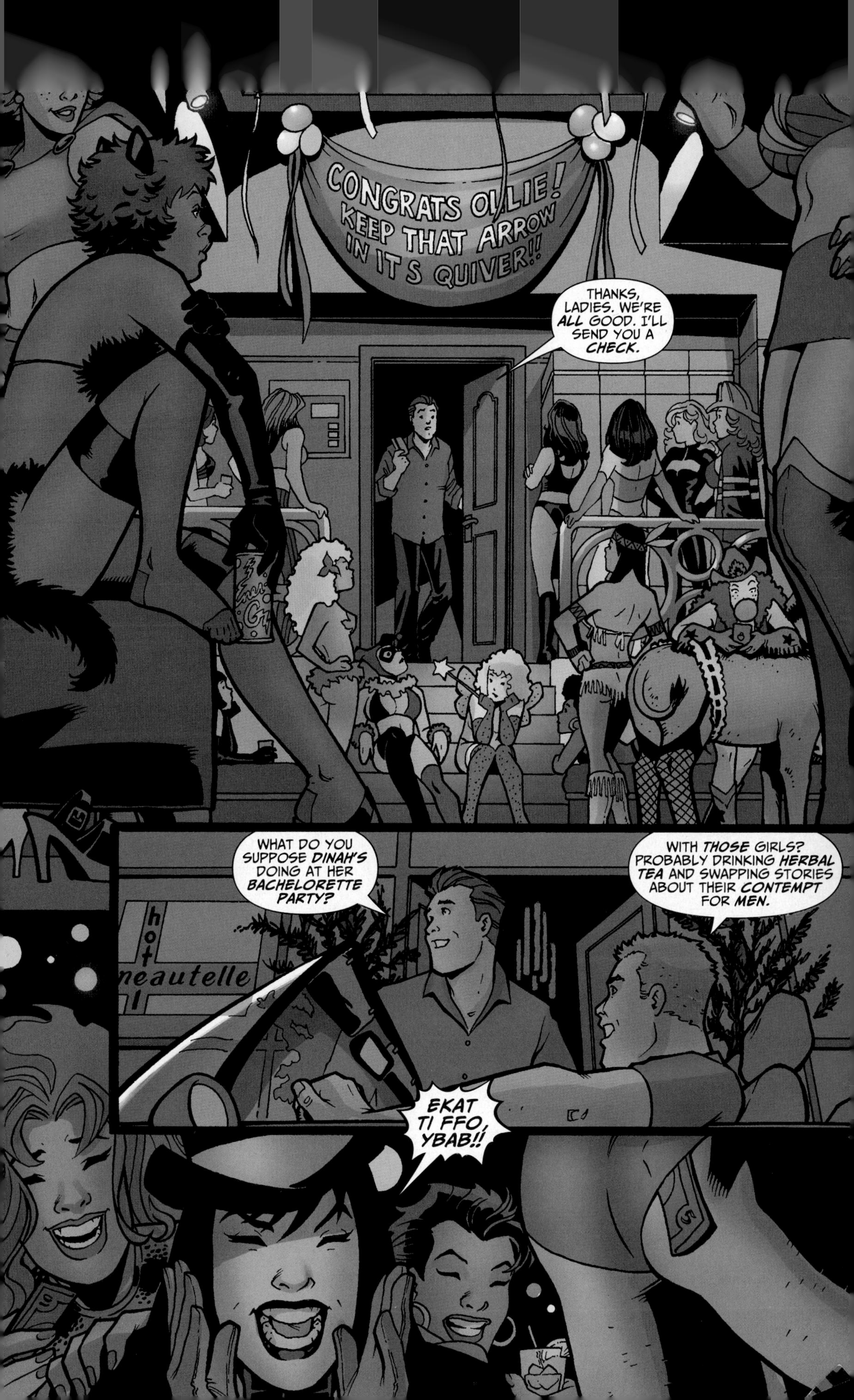
CONGRATS OLLIE! KEEP THAT ARROW IN IT'S QUIVER!!
THANKS, LADIES. WE'RE ALL GOOD. I'LL SEND YOU A CHECK.
WHAT DO YOU SUPPOSE DINAH'S DOING AT HER BACHELORETTE PARTY?
WITH THOSE GIRLS? PROBABLY DRINKING HERBAL TEA AND SWAPPING STORIES ABOUT THEIR CONTEMPT FOR MEN.
hot
neautelle
EKAT TI FFO, YBAB!!

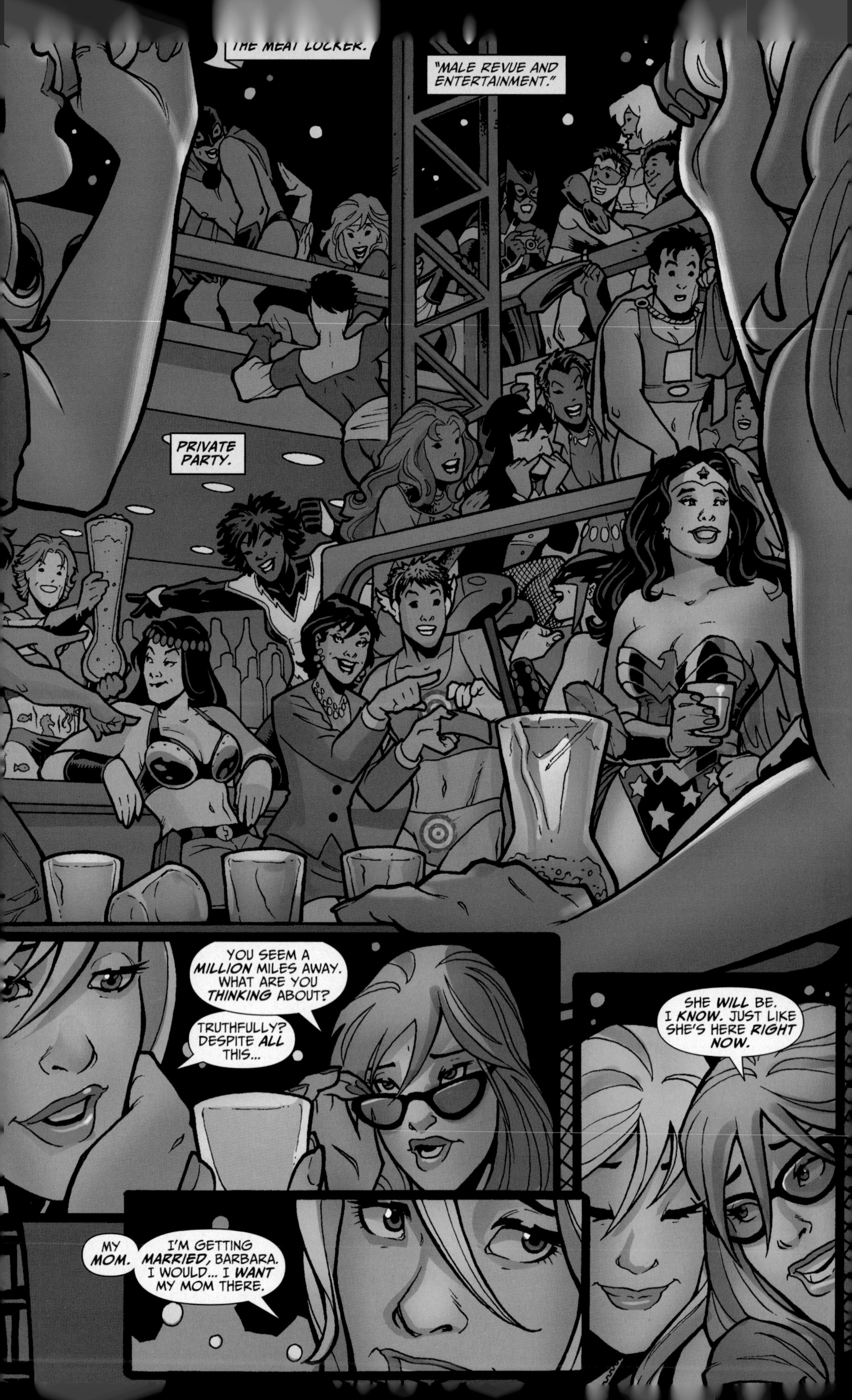
THE MEAT LOCKER.
"MALE REVUE AND ENTERTAINMENT."
PRIVATE PARTY.
YOU SEEM A MILLION MILES AWAY. WHAT ARE YOU THINKING ABOUT?
TRUTHFULLY? DESPITE ALL THIS...
MY MOM.
I'M GETTING MARRIED, BARBARA. I WOULD... I WANT MY MOM THERE.
SHE WILL BE. I KNOW. JUST LIKE SHE'S HERE RIGHT NOW.

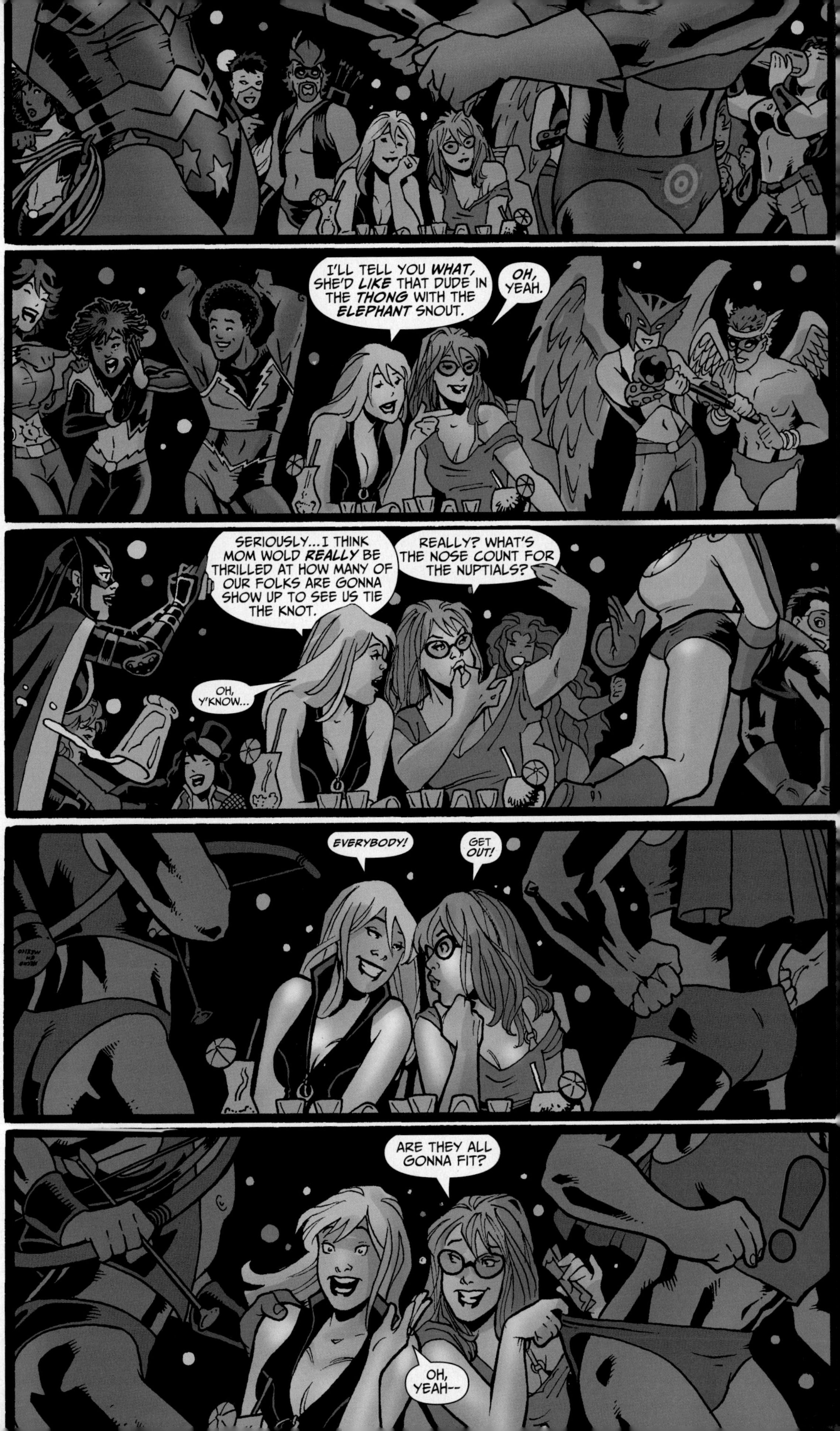
I'LL TELL YOU WHAT, SHE'D LIKE THAT DUDE IN THE THONG WITH THE ELEPHANT SNOUT.
OH, YEAH.
SERIOUSLY...I THINK MOM WOLD REALLY BE THRILLED AT HOW MANY OF OUR FOLKS ARE GONNA SHOW UP TO SEE US TIE THE KNOT.
REALLY? WHAT'S THE NOSE COUNT FOR THE NUPTIALS?
OH, Y'KNOW...
EVERYBODY!
GET OUT!
ARE THEY ALL GONNA FIT?
OH, YEAH--

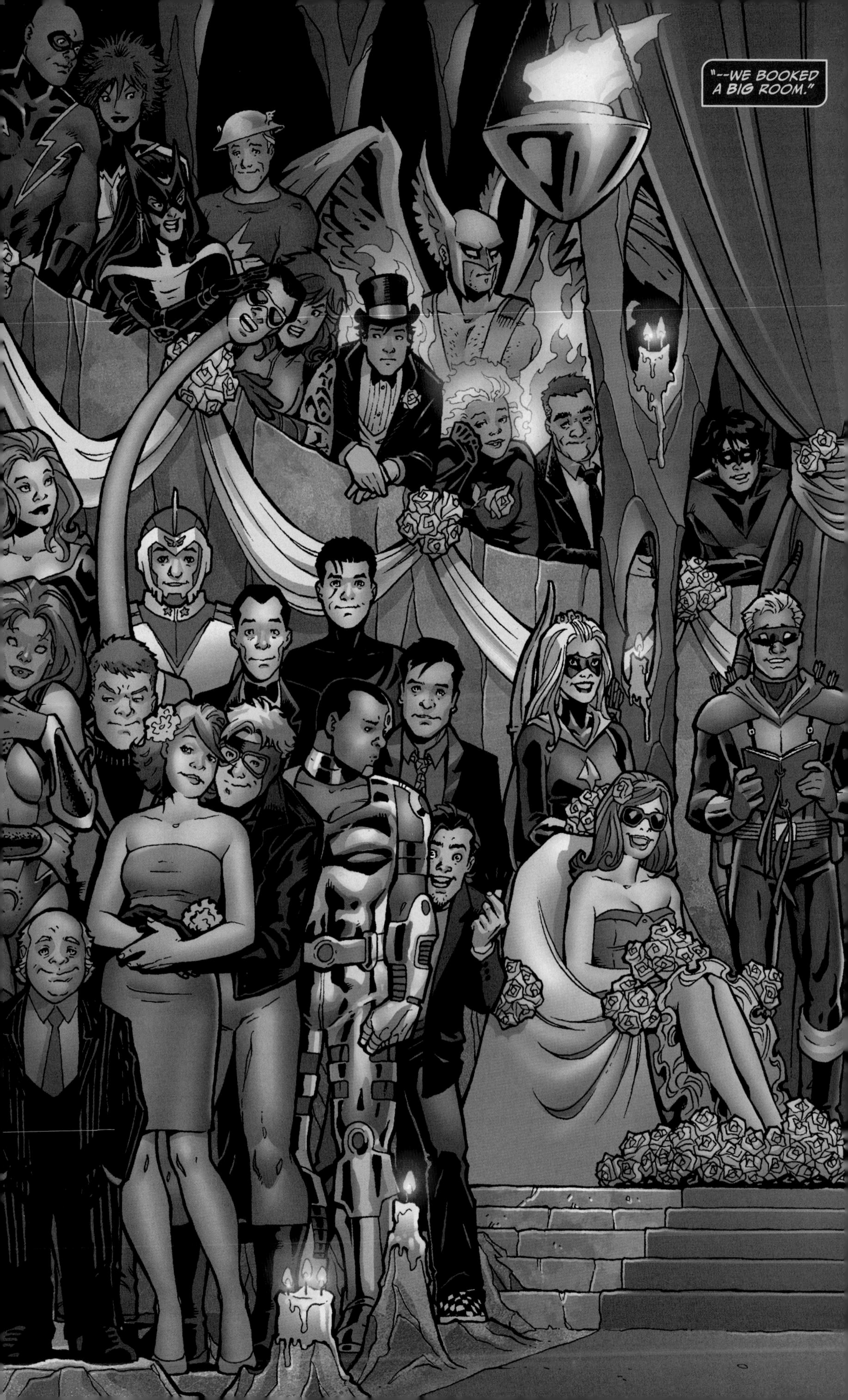
"--WE BOOKED
A BIG ROOM."

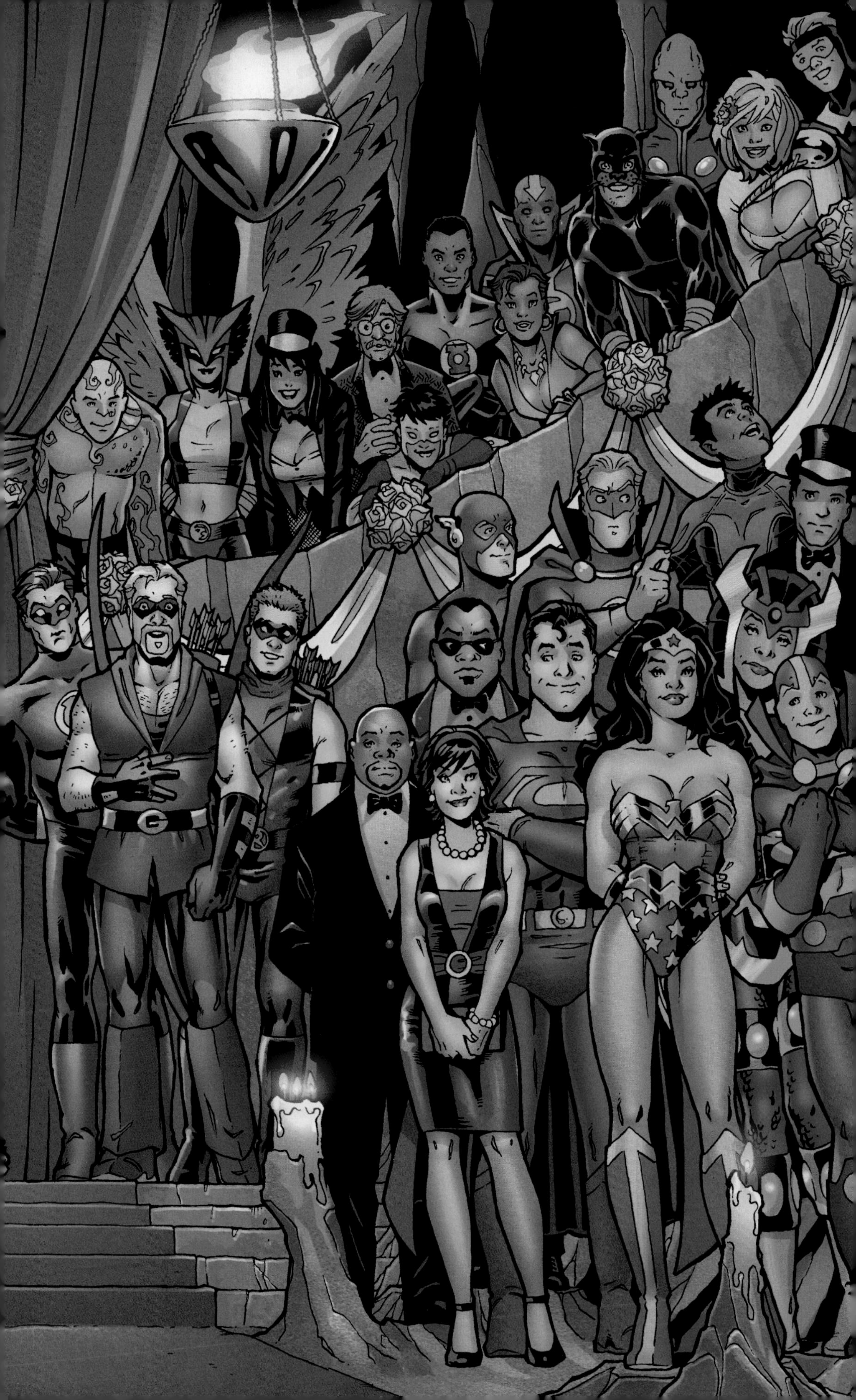

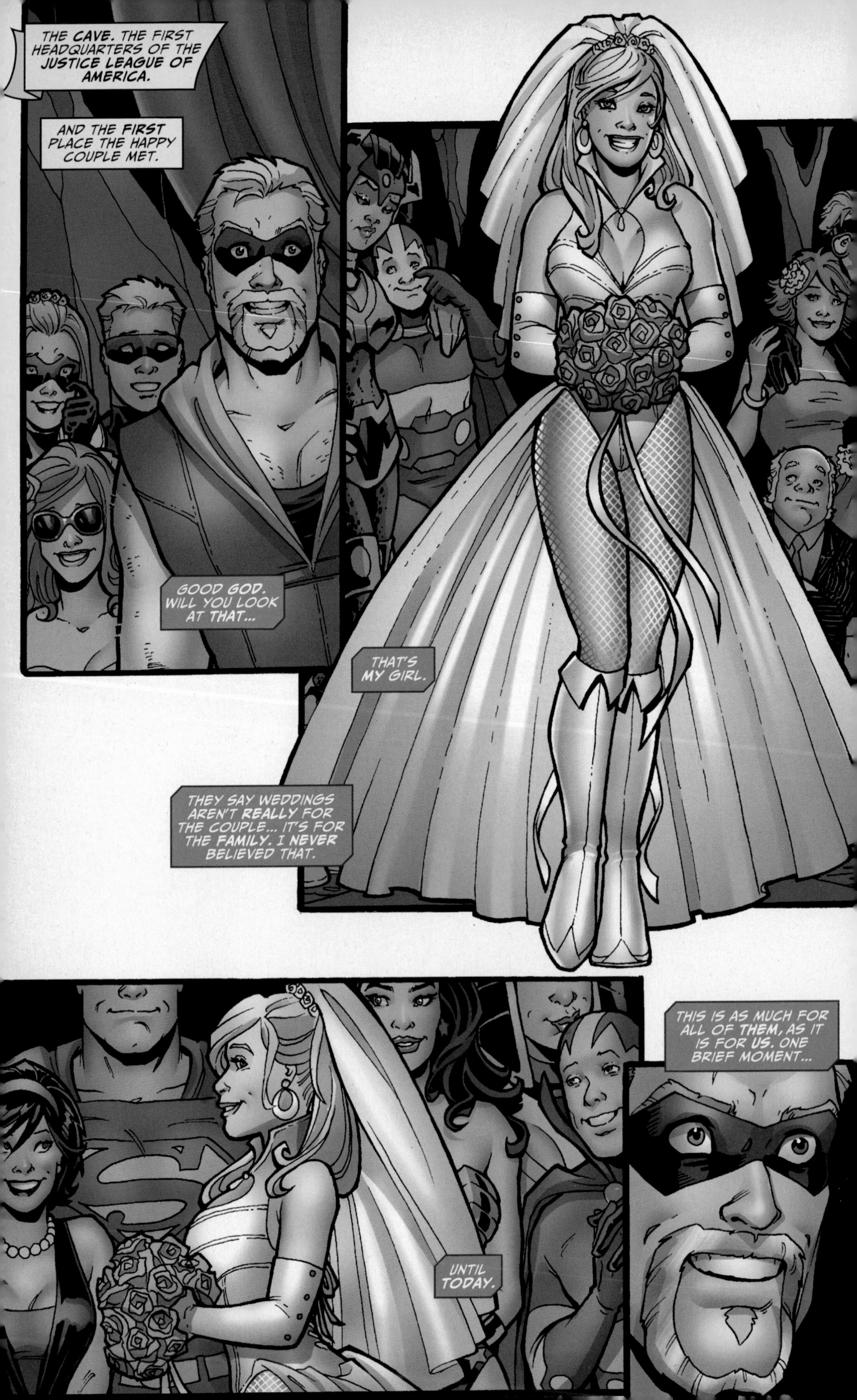
THE CAVE. THE FIRST HEADQUARTERS OF THE JUSTICE LEAGUE OF AMERICA.
AND THE FIRST PLACE THE HAPPY COUPLE MET.
GOOD GOD. WILL YOU LOOK AT THAT...
THAT'S MY GIRL.
THEY SAY WEDDINGS AREN'T REALLY FOR THE COUPLE... IT'S FOR THE FAMILY. I NEVER BELIEVED THAT.
UNTIL TODAY.
THIS IS AS MUCH FOR ALL OF THEM, AS IT IS FOR US. ONE BRIEF MOMENT...

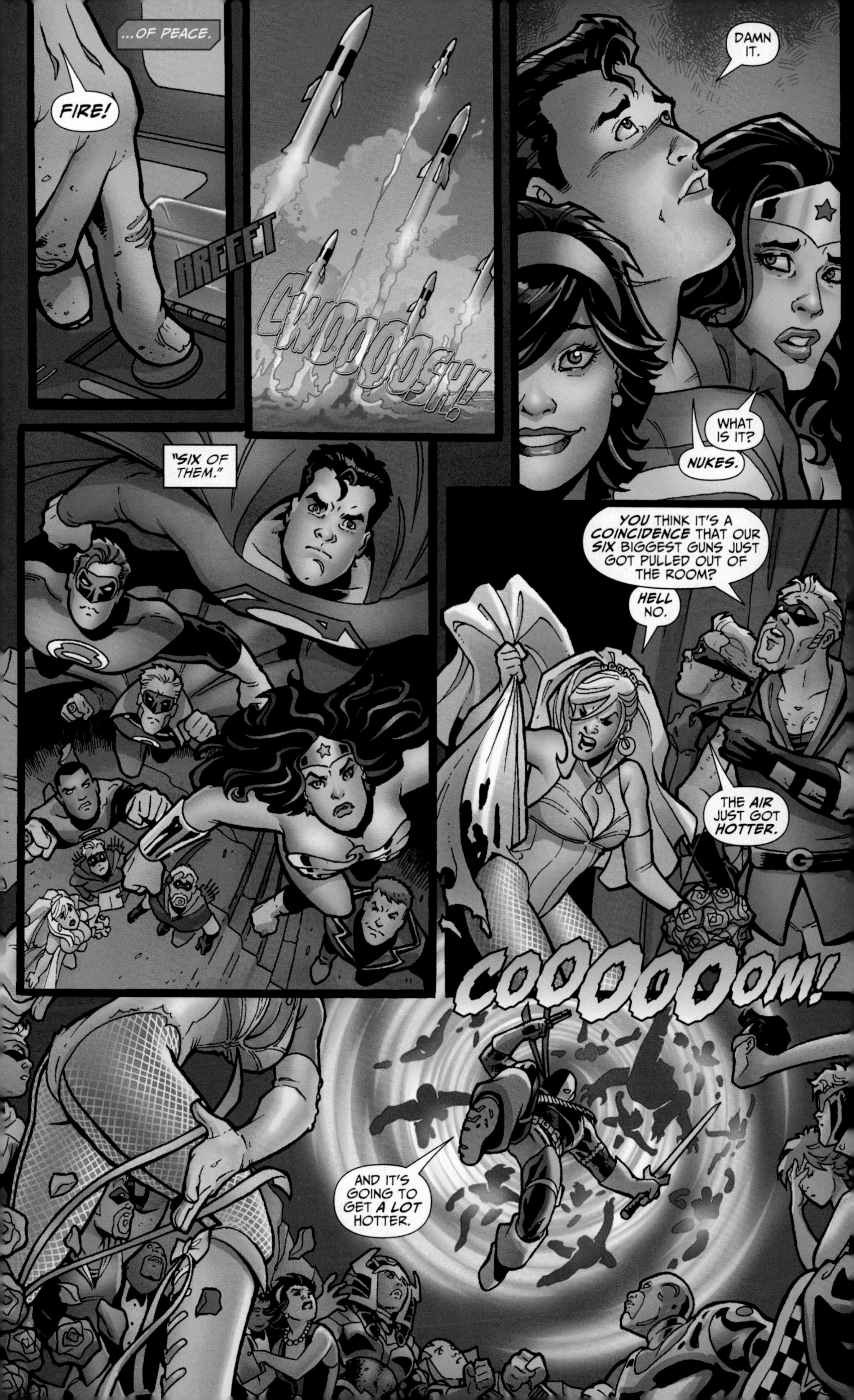
...OF PEACE.
FIRE!
BREEET
CWOOOOSH!
DAMN IT.
WHAT IS IT?
NUKES.
"SIX OF THEM."
YOU THINK IT'S A COINCIDENCE THAT OUR SIX BIGGEST GUNS JUST GOT PULLED OUT OF THE ROOM?
HELL NO.
THE AIR JUST GOT HOTTER.
COOOOOOM!
AND IT'S GOING TO GET A LOT HOTTER.

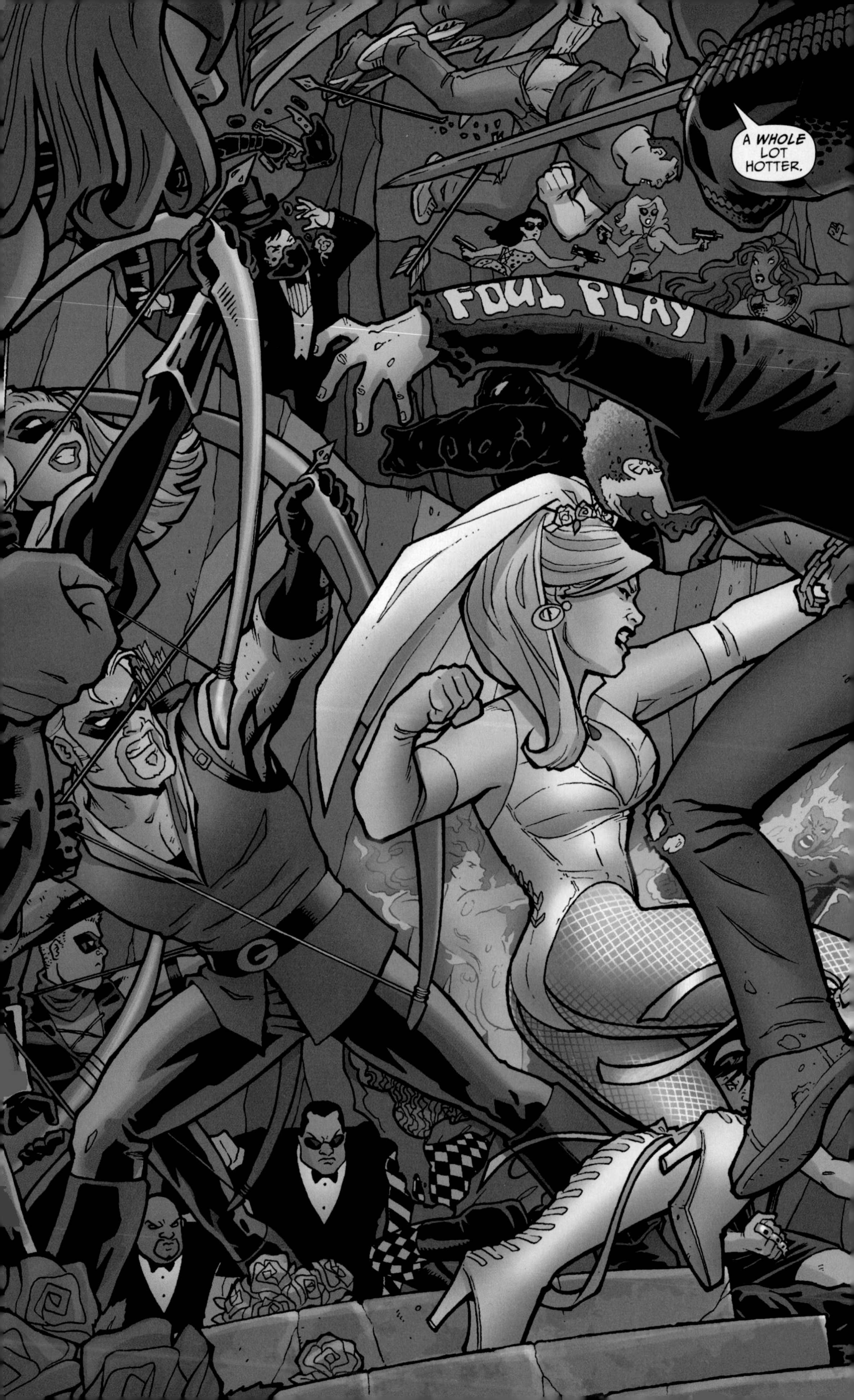
A WHOLE LOT HOTTER.
FOUL PLAY

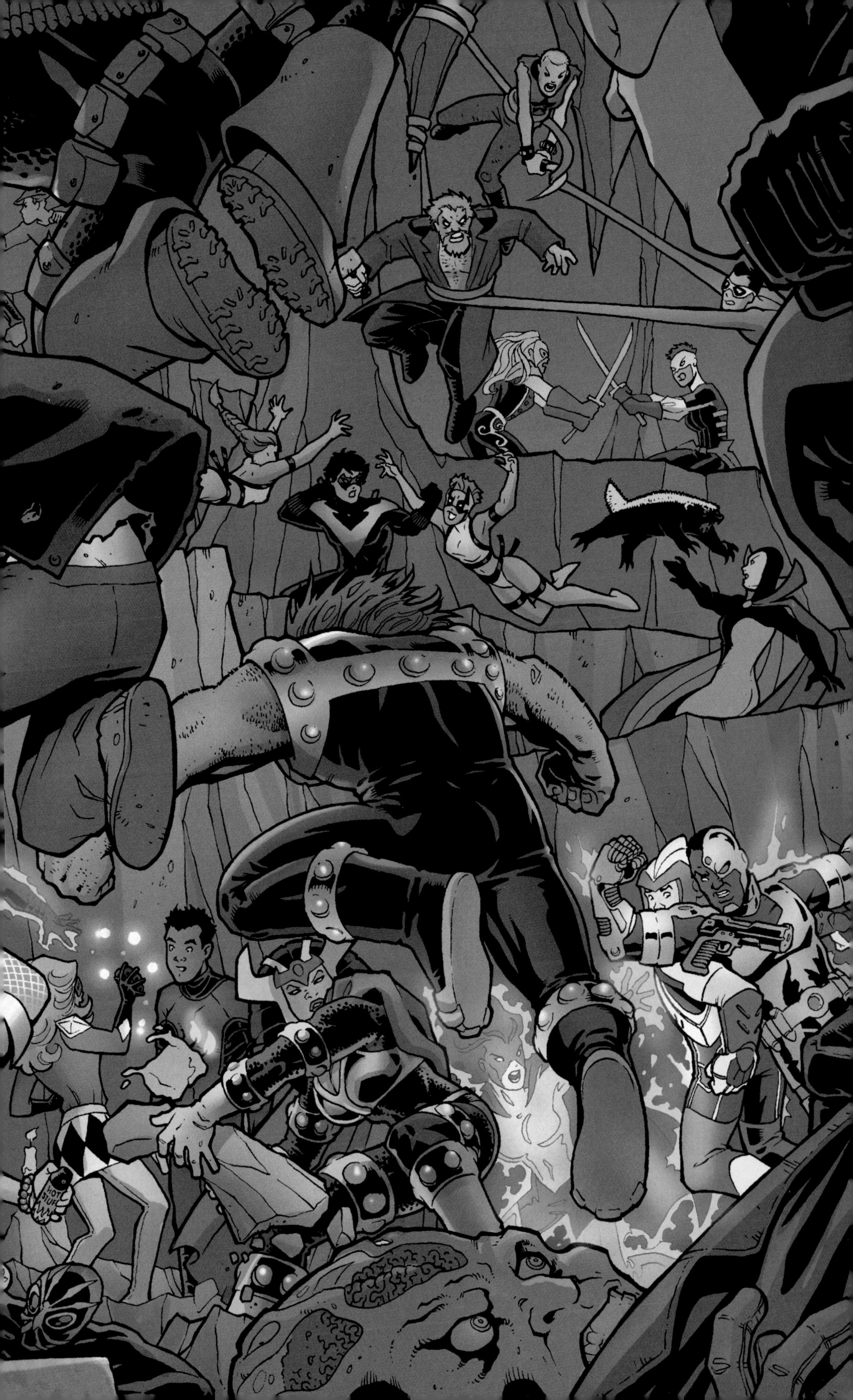
HOT
STUF

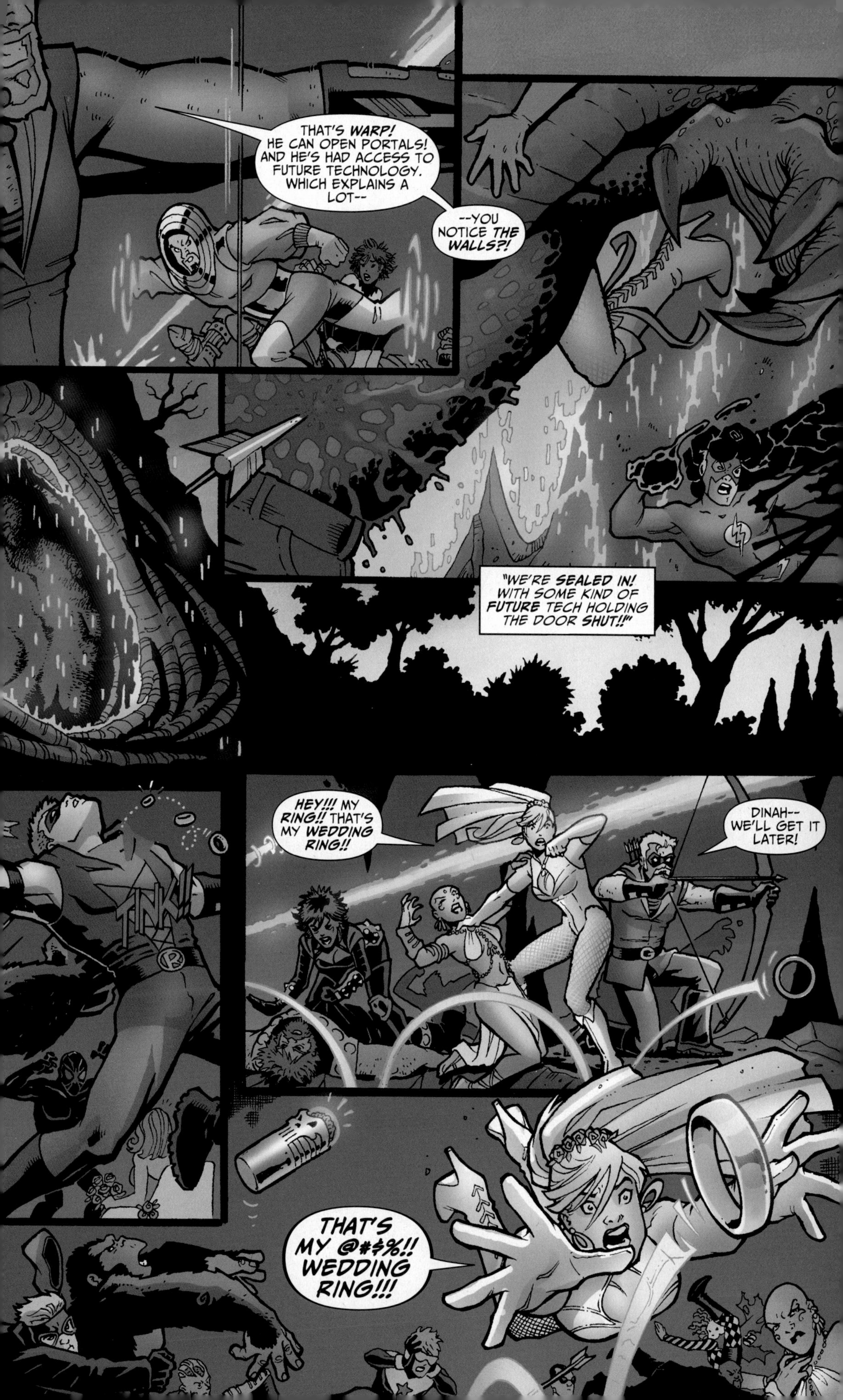
THAT'S WARP! HE CAN OPEN PORTALS! AND HE'S HAD ACCESS TO FUTURE TECHNOLOGY. WHICH EXPLAINS A LOT--
--YOU NOTICE THE WALLS?!
"WE'RE SEALED IN! WITH SOME KIND OF FUTURE TECH HOLDING THE DOOR SHUT!!"
TINK!!
HEY!!! MY RING!! THAT'S MY WEDDING RING!!
DINAH-- WE'LL GET IT LATER!
THAT'S MY @#$%!! WEDDING RING!!!

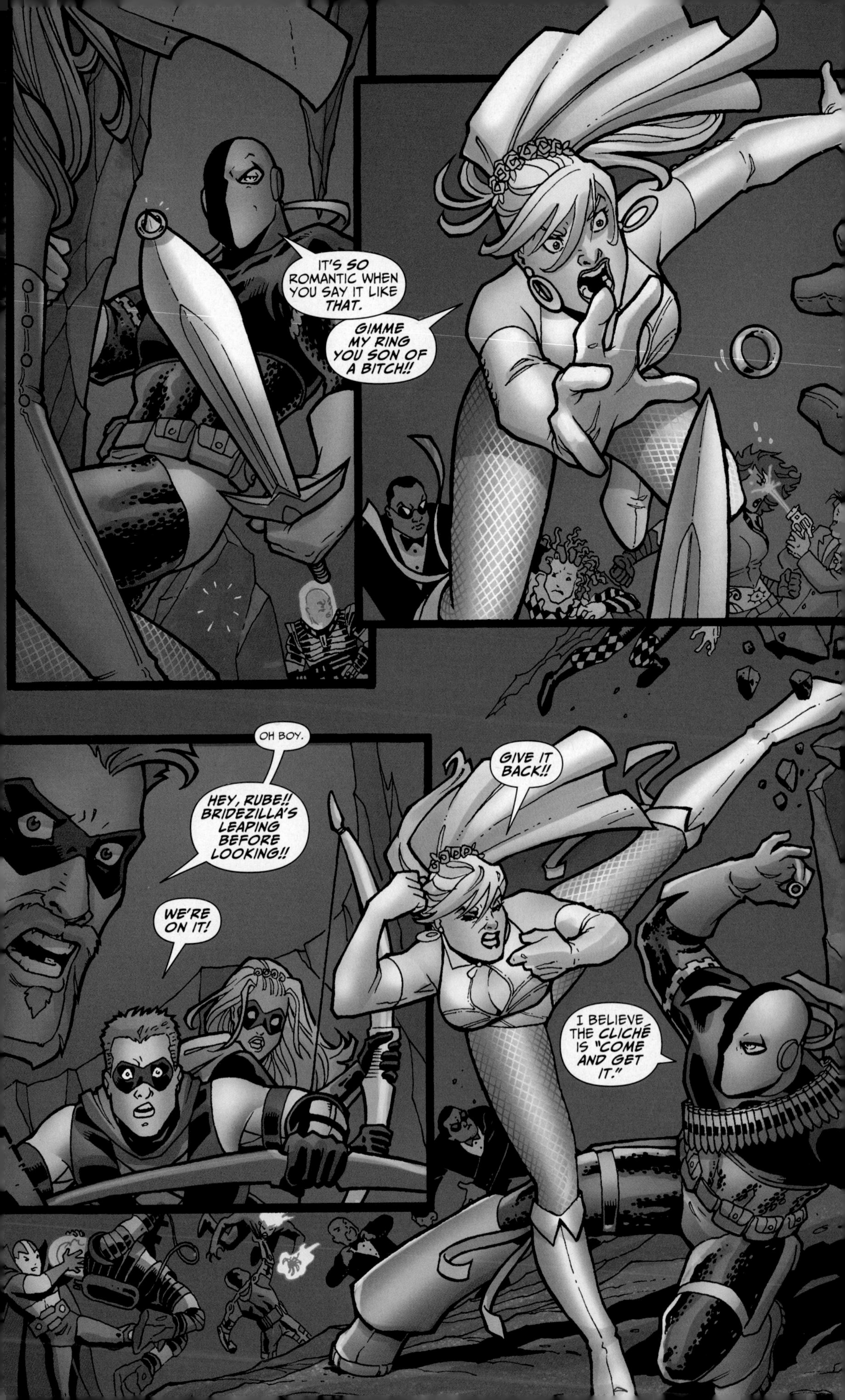
IT'S SO ROMANTIC WHEN YOU SAY IT LIKE THAT.
GIMME MY RING YOU SON OF A BITCH!!
OH BOY.
HEY, RUBE!! BRIDEZILLA'S LEAPING BEFORE LOOKING!!
WE'RE ON IT!
GIVE IT BACK!!
I BELIEVE THE CLICHÉ IS "COME AND GET IT."

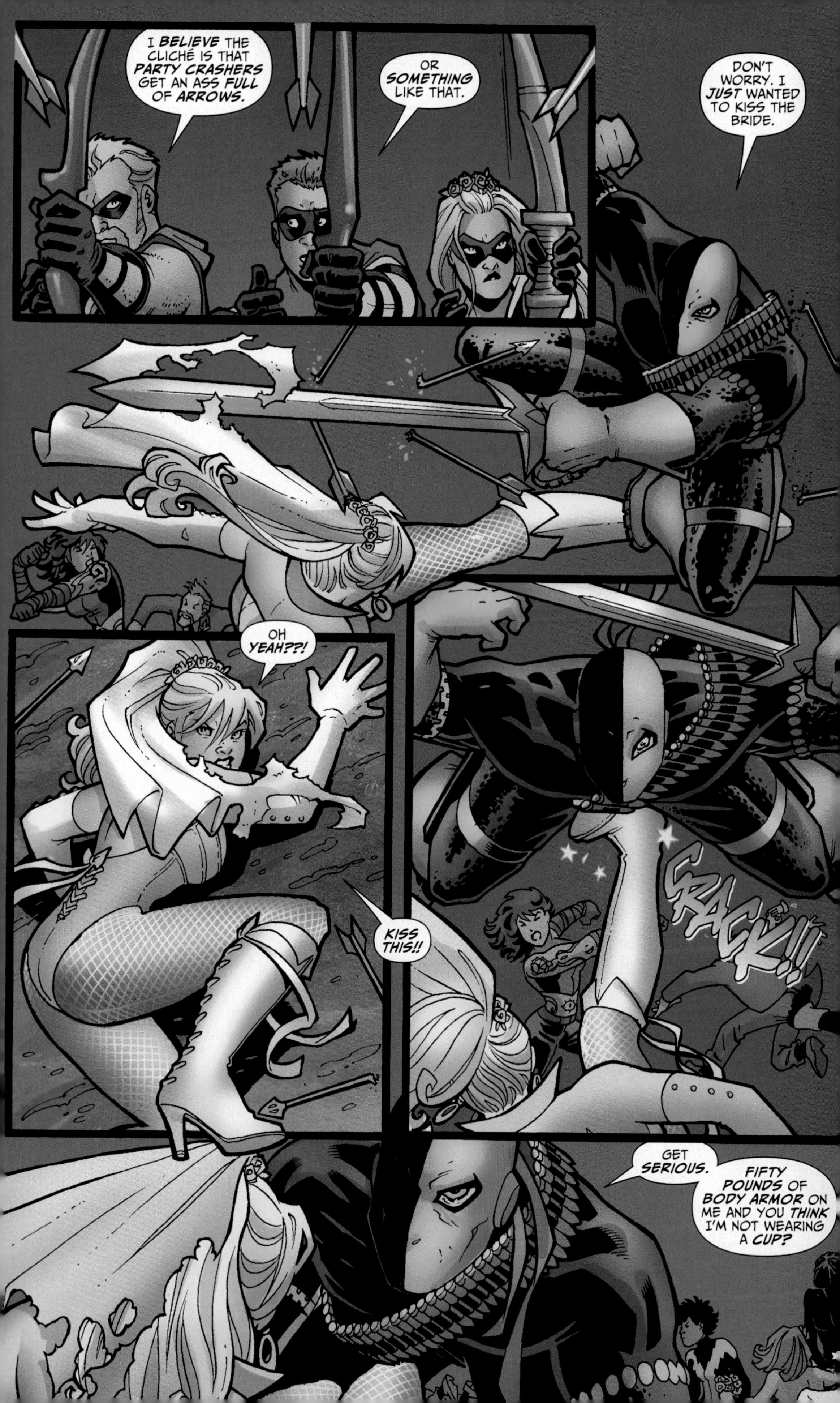

I BELIEVE THE CLICHÉ IS THAT PARTY CRASHERS GET AN ASS FULL OF ARROWS.
OR SOMETHING LIKE THAT.
DON'T WORRY. I JUST WANTED TO KISS THE BRIDE.
OH YEAH??!
KISS THIS!!
CRACK!!
GET SERIOUS.
FIFTY POUNDS OF BODY ARMOR ON ME AND YOU THINK I'M NOT WEARING A CUP?

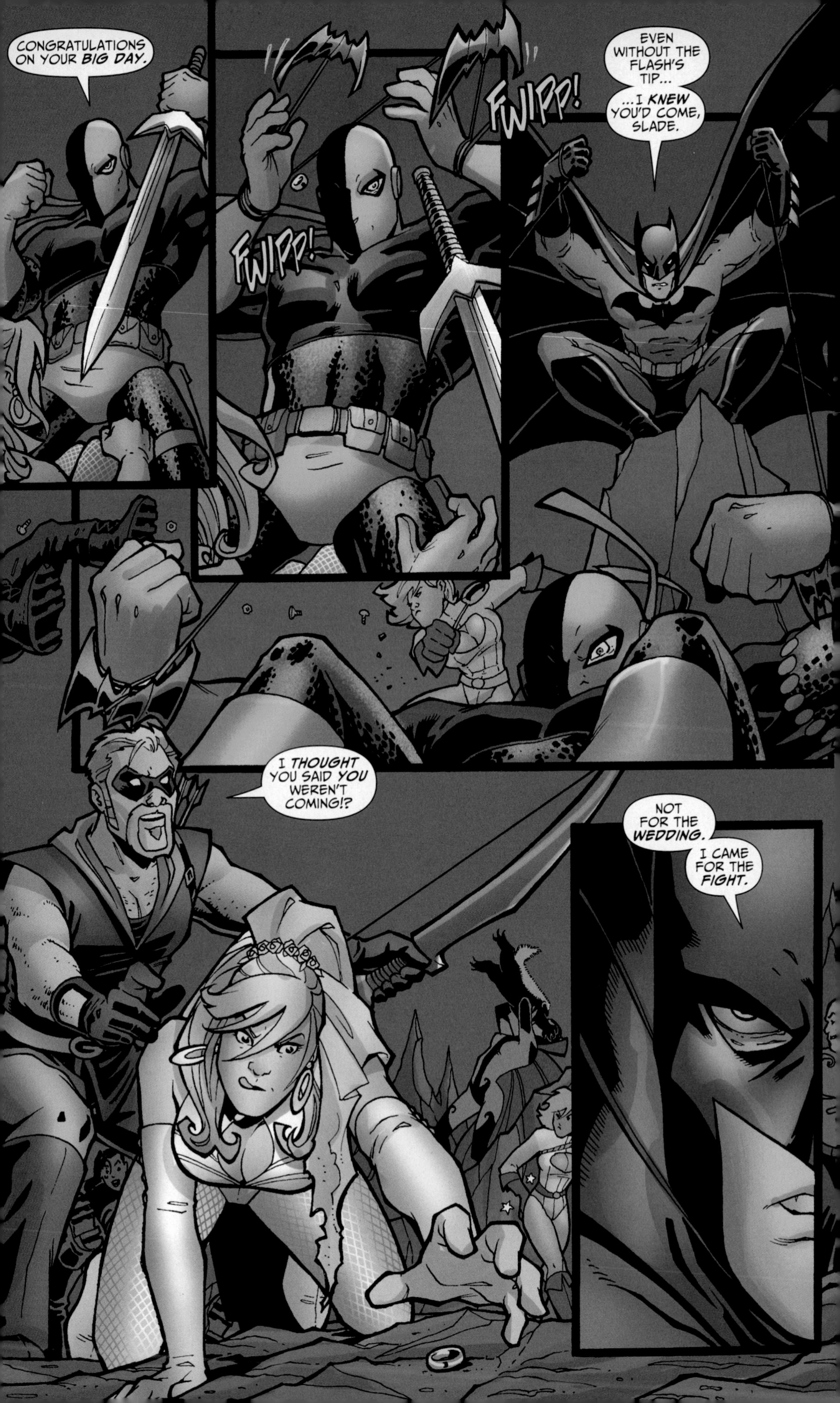
CONGRATULATIONS ON YOUR BIG DAY.
FWIPP!
FWIPP!
EVEN WITHOUT THE FLASH'S TIP...
...I KNEW YOU'D COME, SLADE.
I THOUGHT YOU SAID YOU WEREN'T COMING!?
NOT FOR THE WEDDING.
I CAME FOR THE FIGHT.

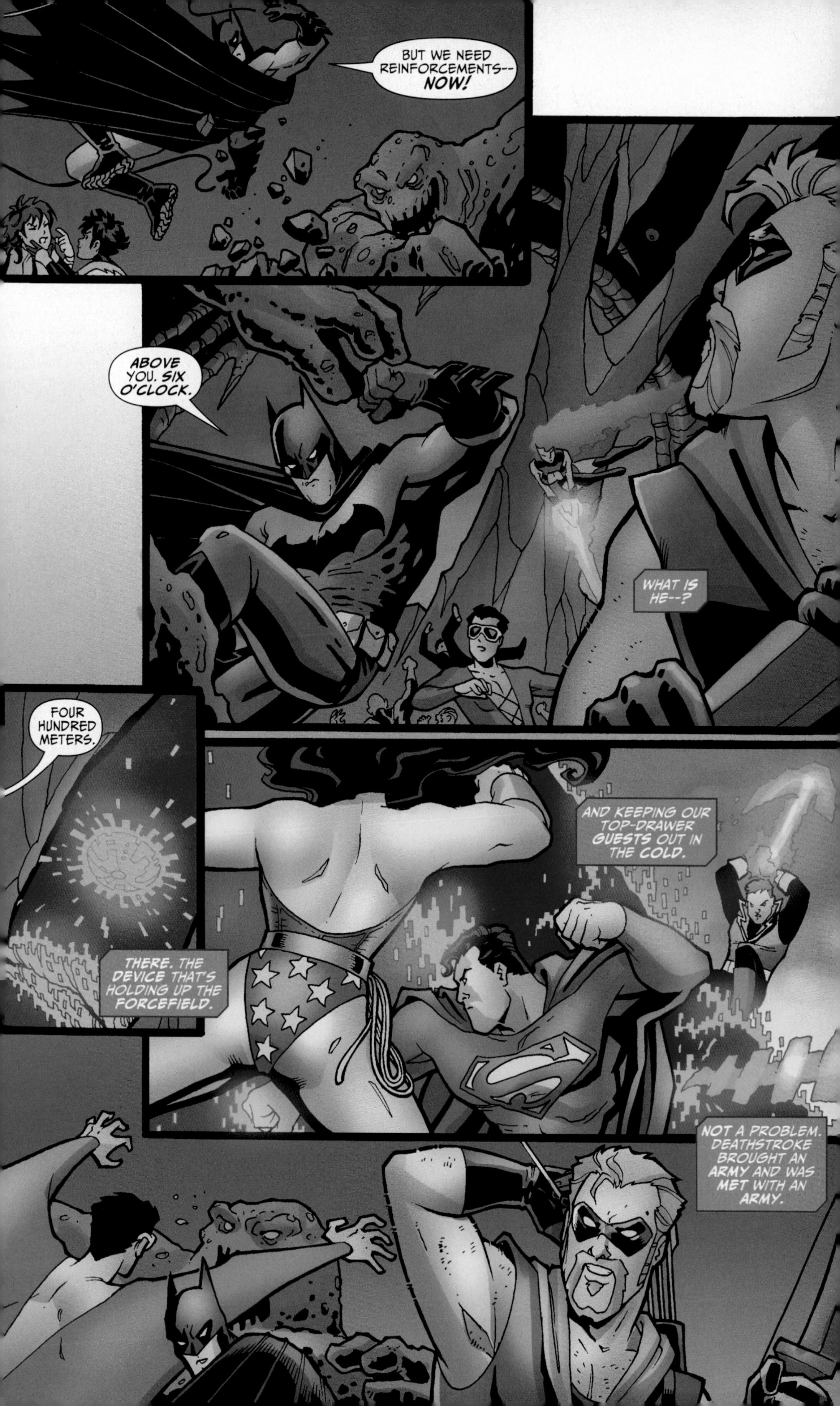
BUT WE NEED REINFORCEMENTS-- NOW!
ABOVE YOU. SIX O'CLOCK.
WHAT IS HE--?
FOUR HUNDRED METERS.
THERE. THE DEVICE THAT'S HOLDING UP THE FORCEFIELD.
AND KEEPING OUR TOP-DRAWER GUESTS OUT IN THE COLD.
NOT A PROBLEM. DEATHSTROKE BROUGHT AN ARMY AND WAS MET WITH AN ARMY.

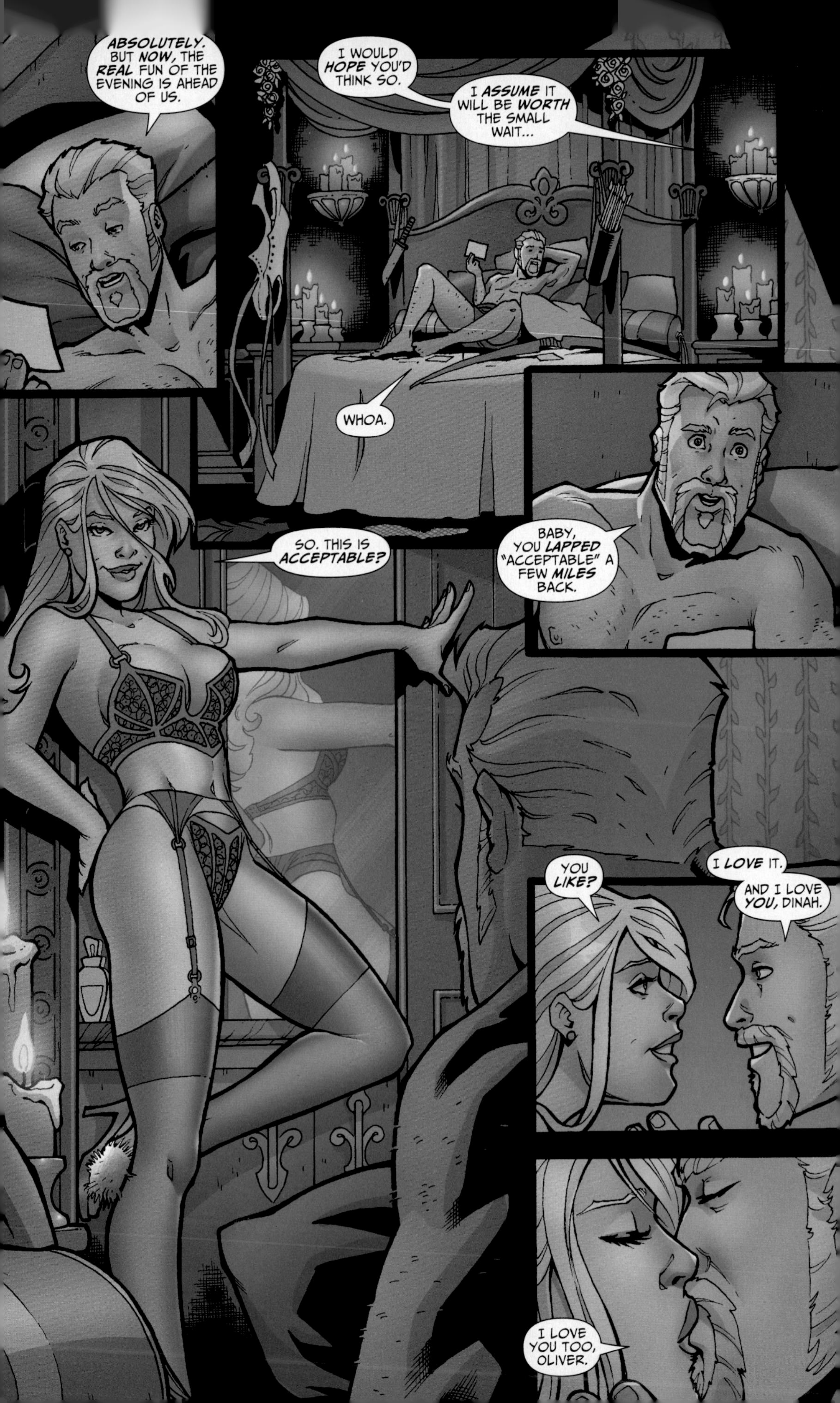

ABSOLUTELY. BUT NOW, THE REAL FUN OF THE EVENING IS AHEAD OF US.
I WOULD HOPE YOU'D THINK SO.
I ASSUME IT WILL BE WORTH THE SMALL WAIT...
WHOA.
SO. THIS IS ACCEPTABLE?
BABY, YOU LAPPED "ACCEPTABLE" A FEW MILES BACK.
YOU LIKE?
I LOVE IT.
AND I LOVE YOU, DINAH.
I LOVE YOU TOO, OLIVER.

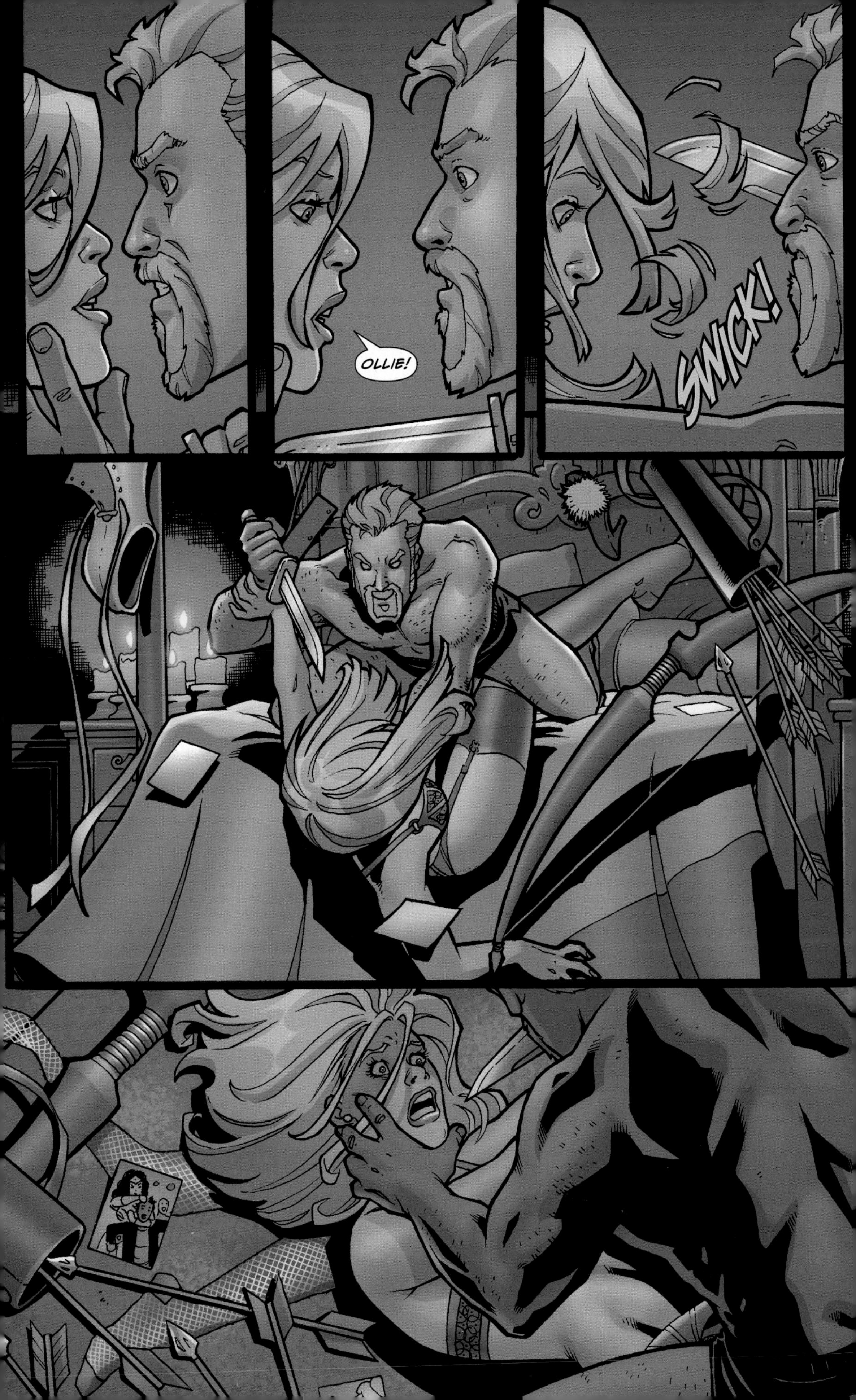
OLLIE!
SWICK!

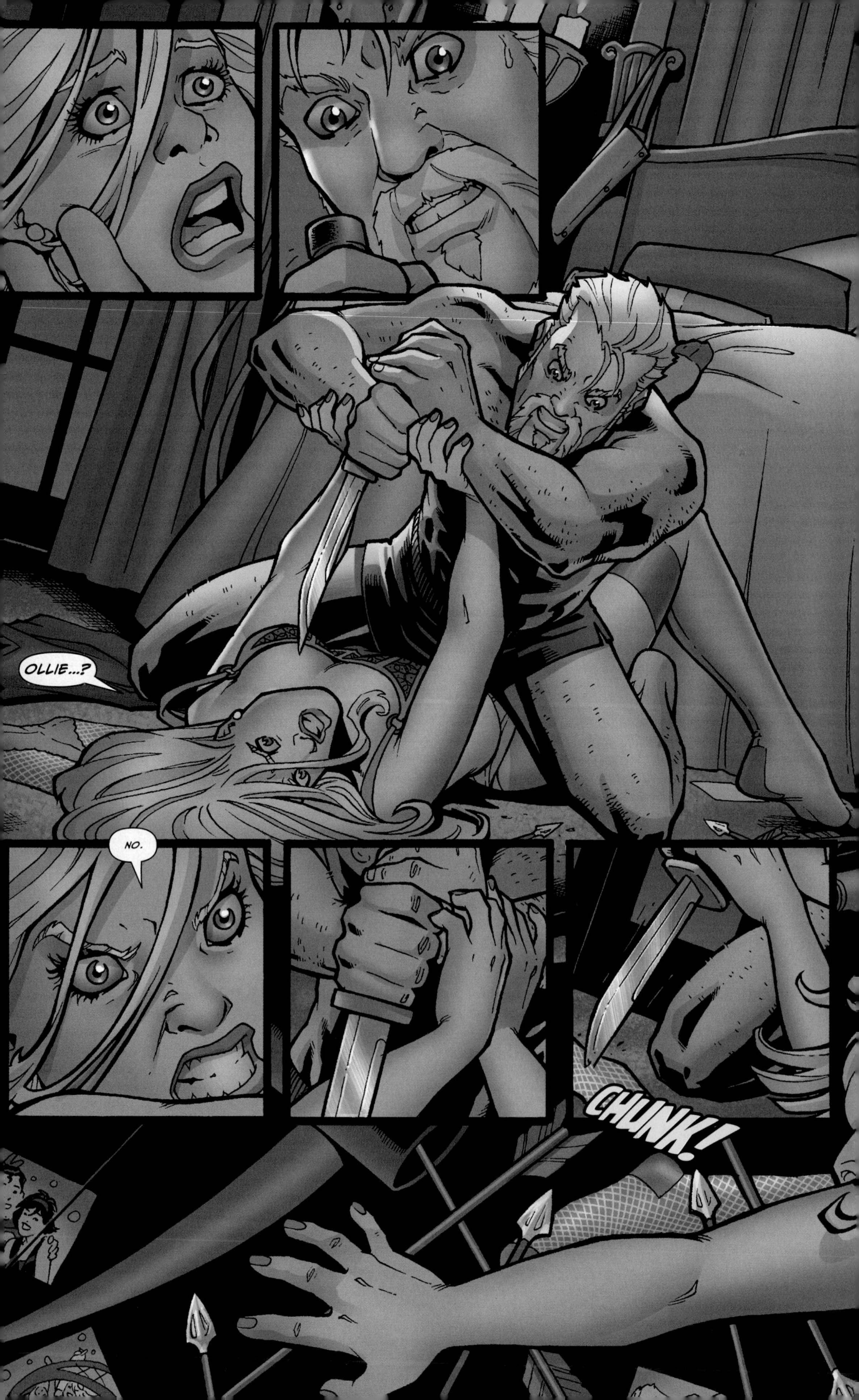
OLLIE...?
NO.
CHUNK!

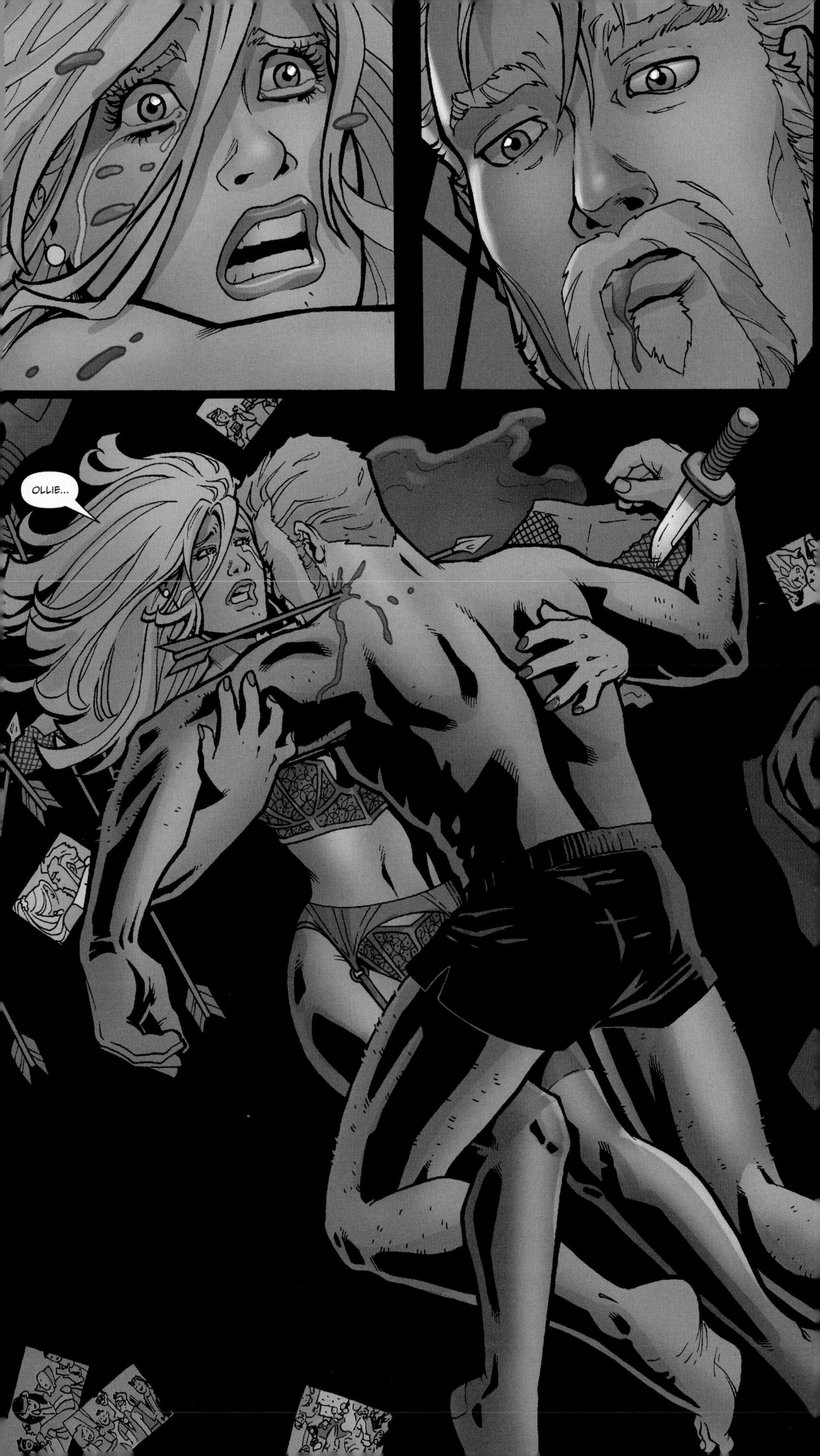
OLLIE...

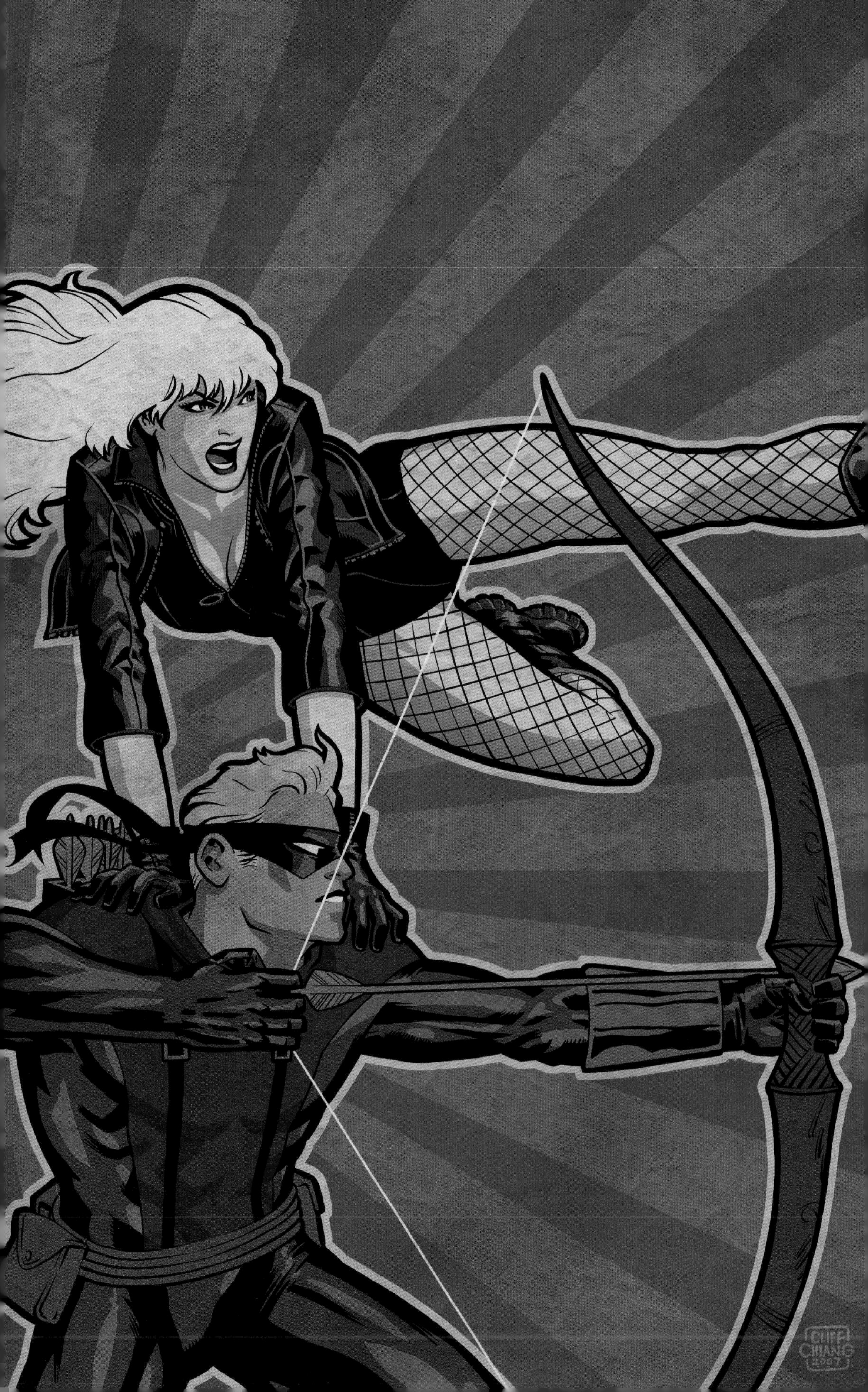
CLIFF
CHIANG
2007

GREEN ARROW AND BLACK CANARY #1

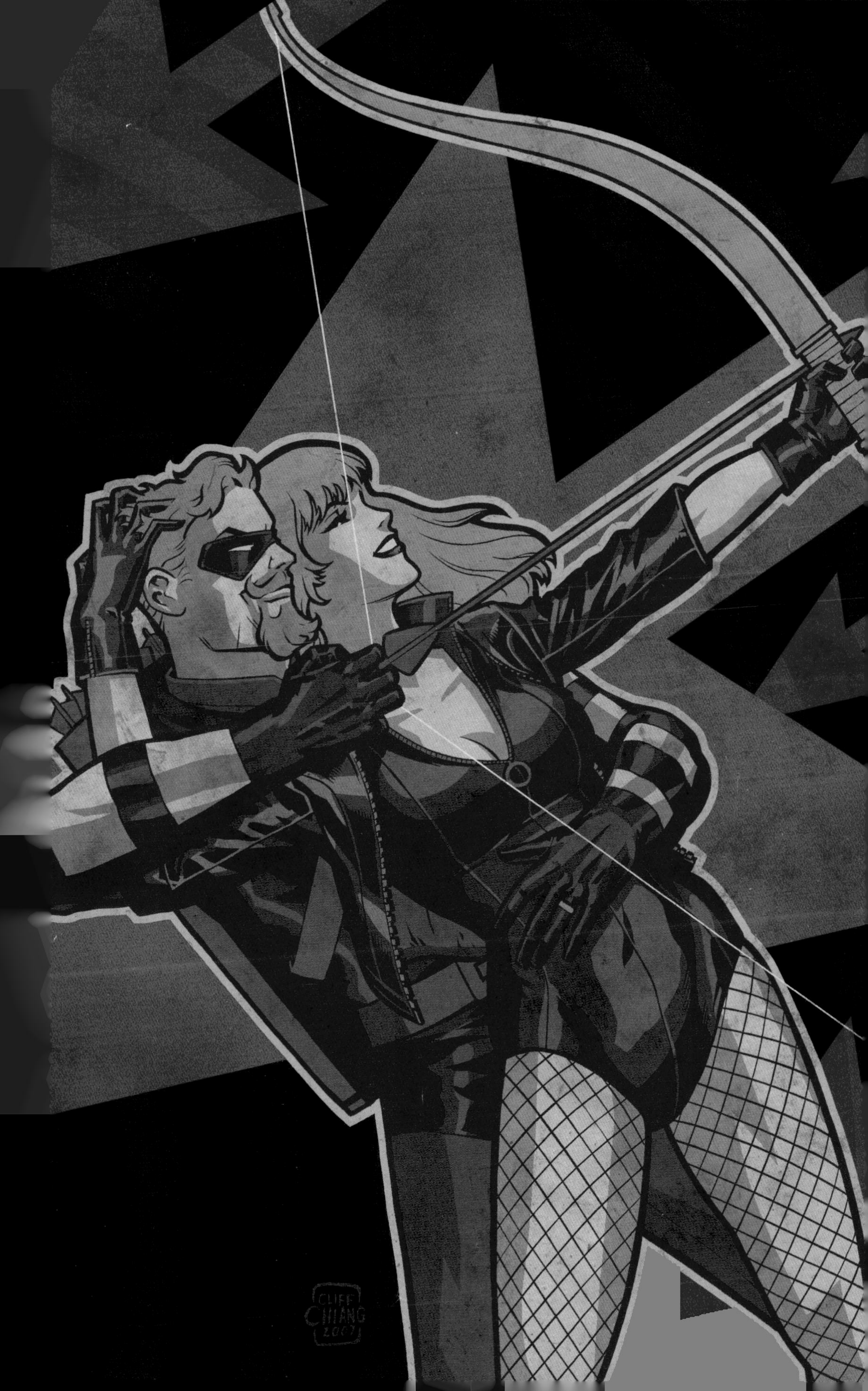
CLIFF CHIANG 2007

DEAD AGAIN PART ONE: HERE COMES THE BRIDE

Story: **Judd Winick**   *Art:* **Cliff Chiang**   *Color:* **Trish Mulvihill**

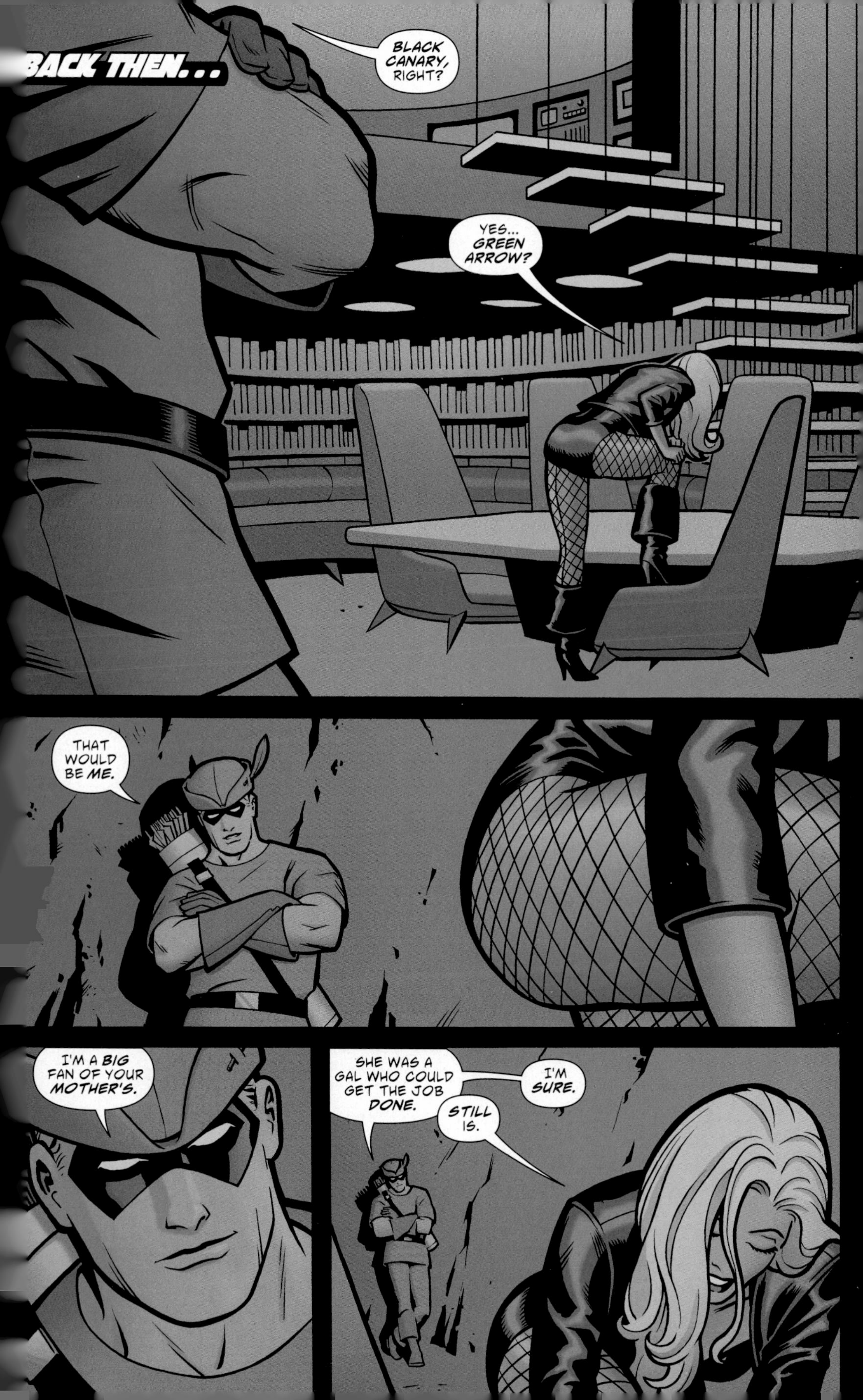
BACK THEN...
BLACK CANARY, RIGHT?
YES... GREEN ARROW?
THAT WOULD BE ME.
I'M A BIG FAN OF YOUR MOTHER'S.
SHE WAS A GAL WHO COULD GET THE JOB DONE.
I'M SURE.
STILL IS.

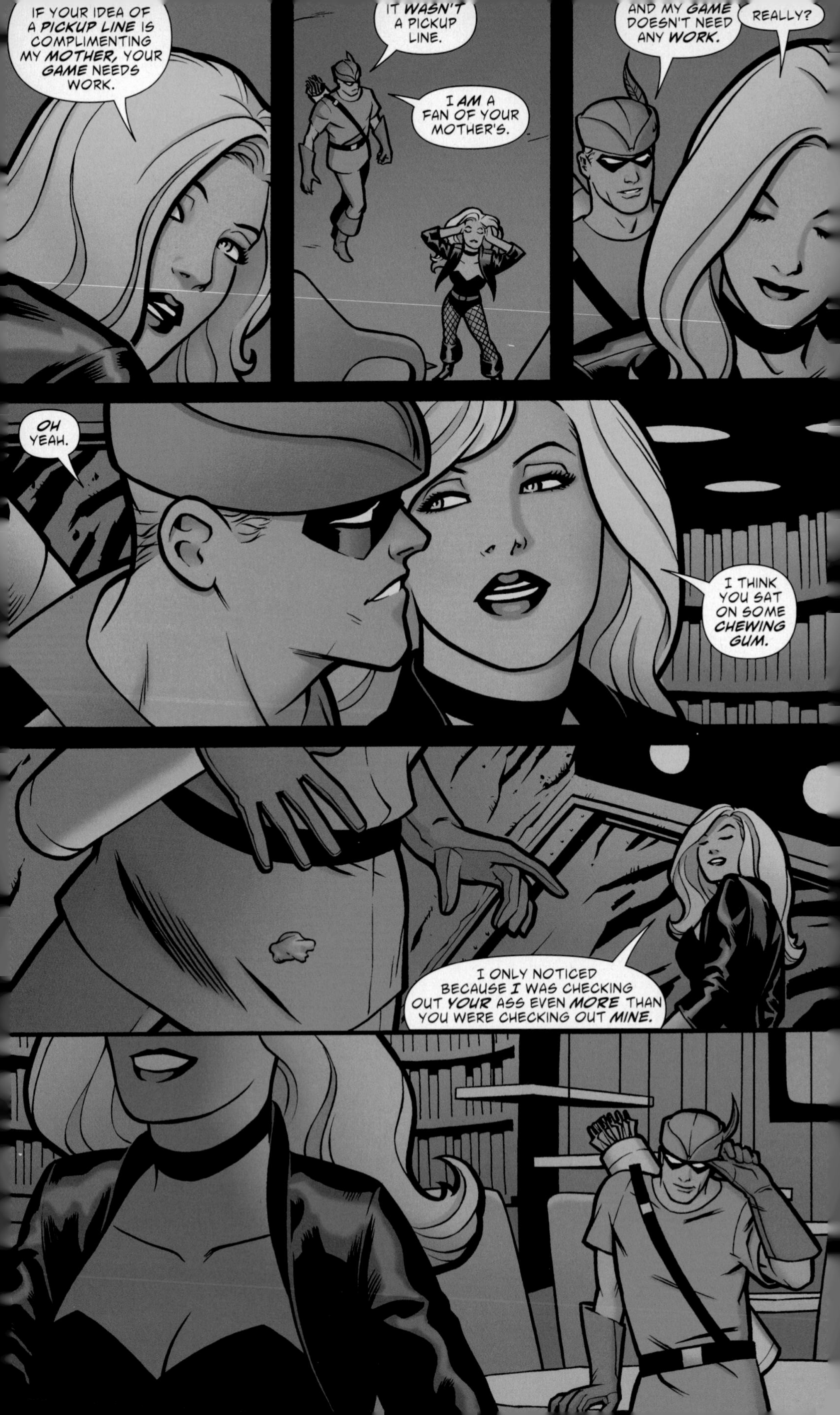
IF YOUR IDEA OF A PICKUP LINE IS COMPLIMENTING MY MOTHER, YOUR GAME NEEDS WORK.
IT WASN'T A PICKUP LINE.
I AM A FAN OF YOUR MOTHER'S.
AND MY GAME DOESN'T NEED ANY WORK.
REALLY?
OH YEAH.
I THINK YOU SAT ON SOME CHEWING GUM.
I ONLY NOTICED BECAUSE I WAS CHECKING OUT YOUR ASS EVEN MORE THAN YOU WERE CHECKING OUT MINE.

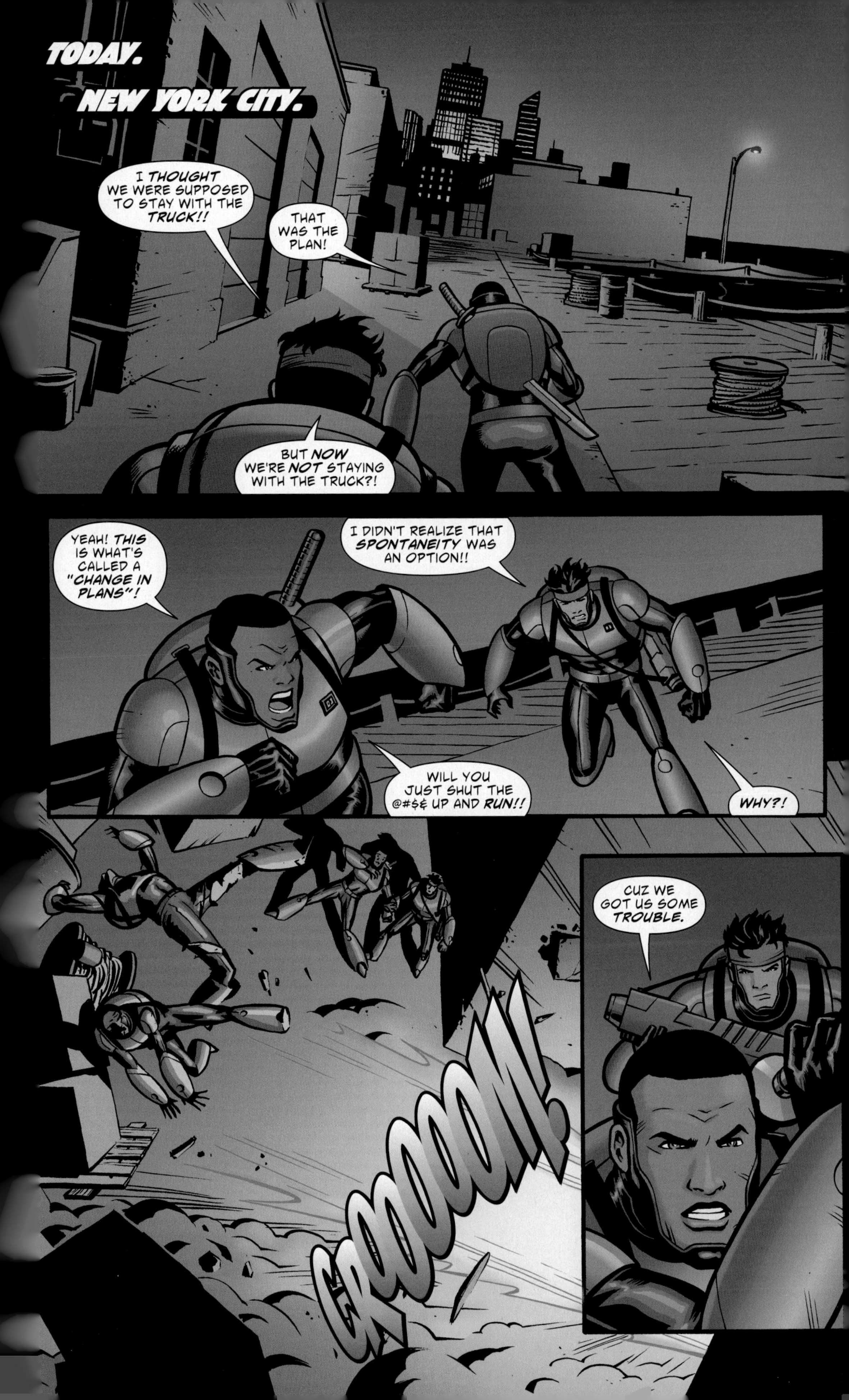
TODAY.
NEW YORK CITY.
I THOUGHT WE WERE SUPPOSED TO STAY WITH THE TRUCK!!
THAT WAS THE PLAN!
BUT NOW WE'RE NOT STAYING WITH THE TRUCK?!
YEAH! THIS IS WHAT'S CALLED A "CHANGE IN PLANS"!
I DIDN'T REALIZE THAT SPONTANEITY WAS AN OPTION!!
WILL YOU JUST SHUT THE @#$& UP AND RUN!!
WHY?!
CUZ WE GOT US SOME TROUBLE.
GROOOOOM!

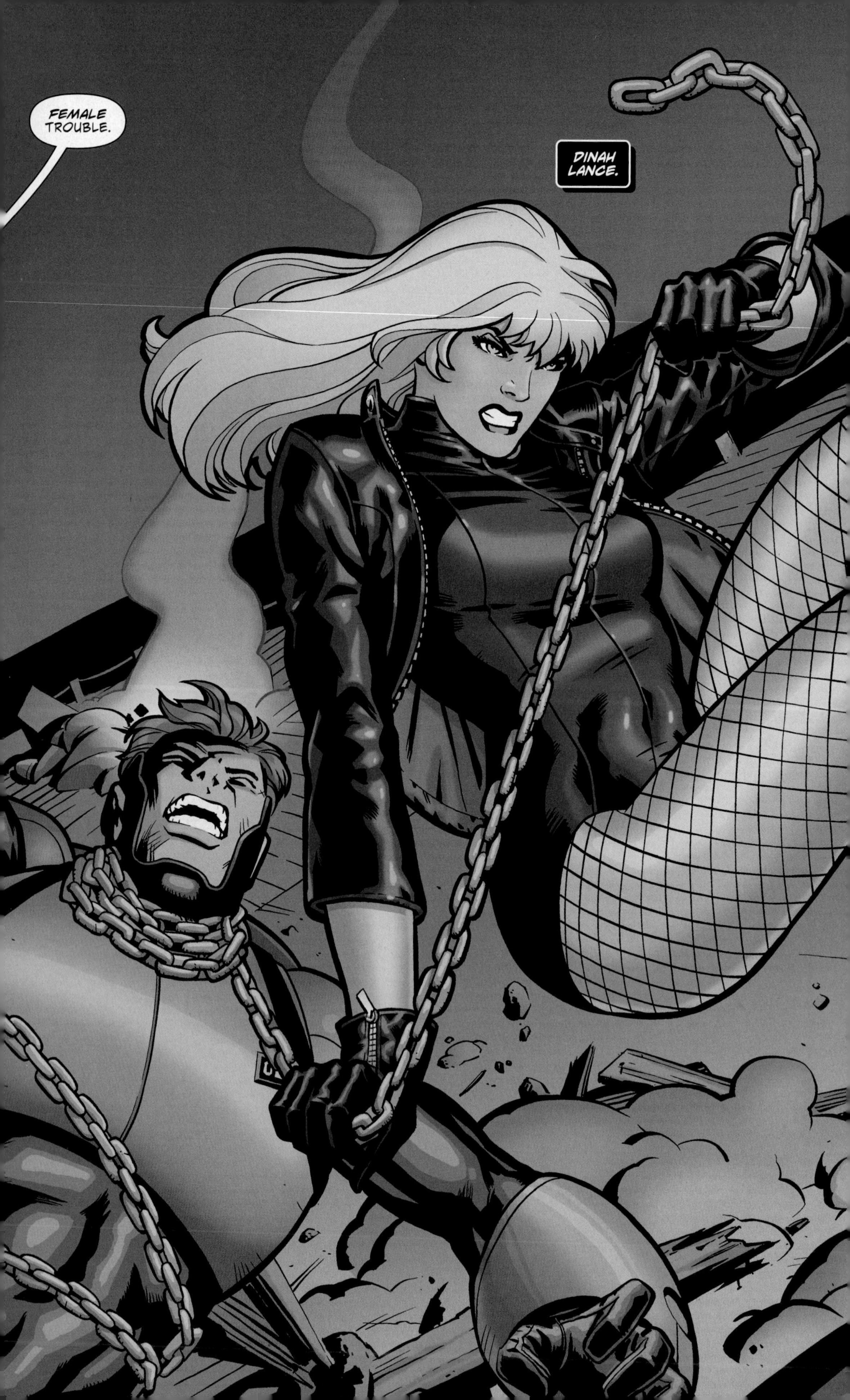
FEMALE TROUBLE.
DINAH LANCE.

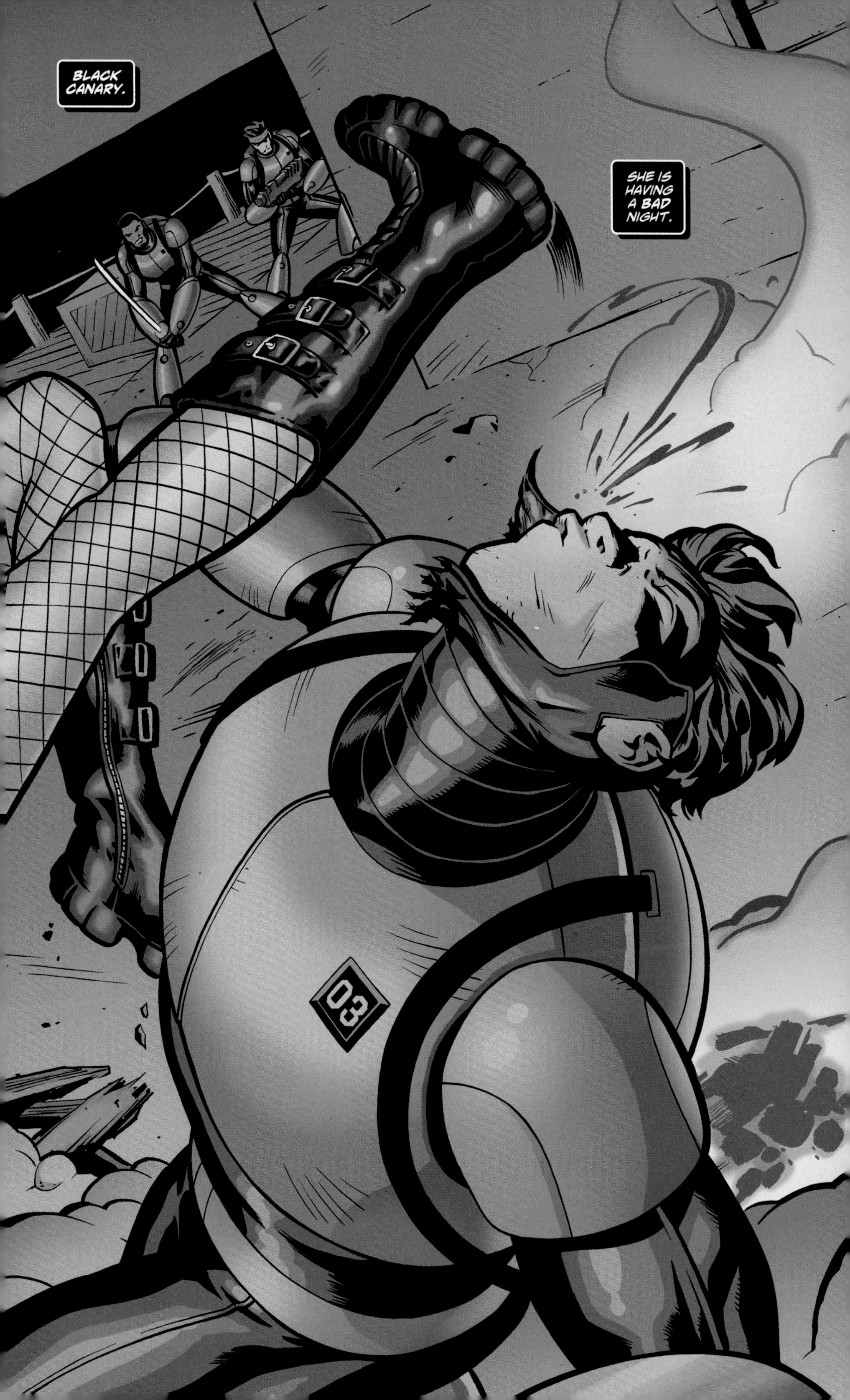
BLACK CANARY.
SHE IS HAVING A BAD NIGHT.

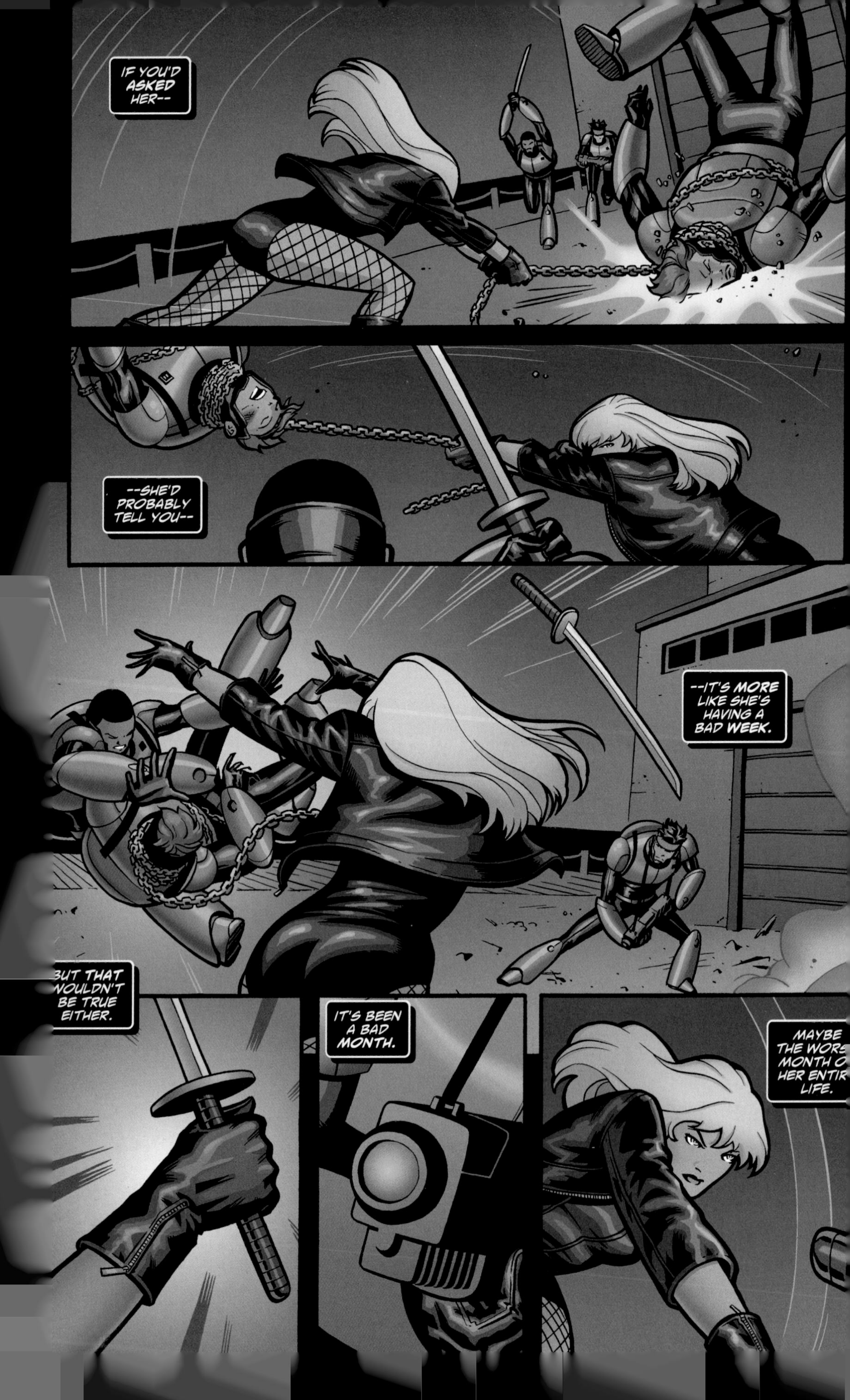
IF YOU'D ASKED HER--
--SHE'D PROBABLY TELL YOU--
--IT'S MORE LIKE SHE'S HAVING A BAD WEEK.
UT THAT OULDN'T BE TRUE EITHER.
IT'S BEEN A BAD MONTH.
MAYBE THE WORS MONTH O HER ENTIR LIFE.

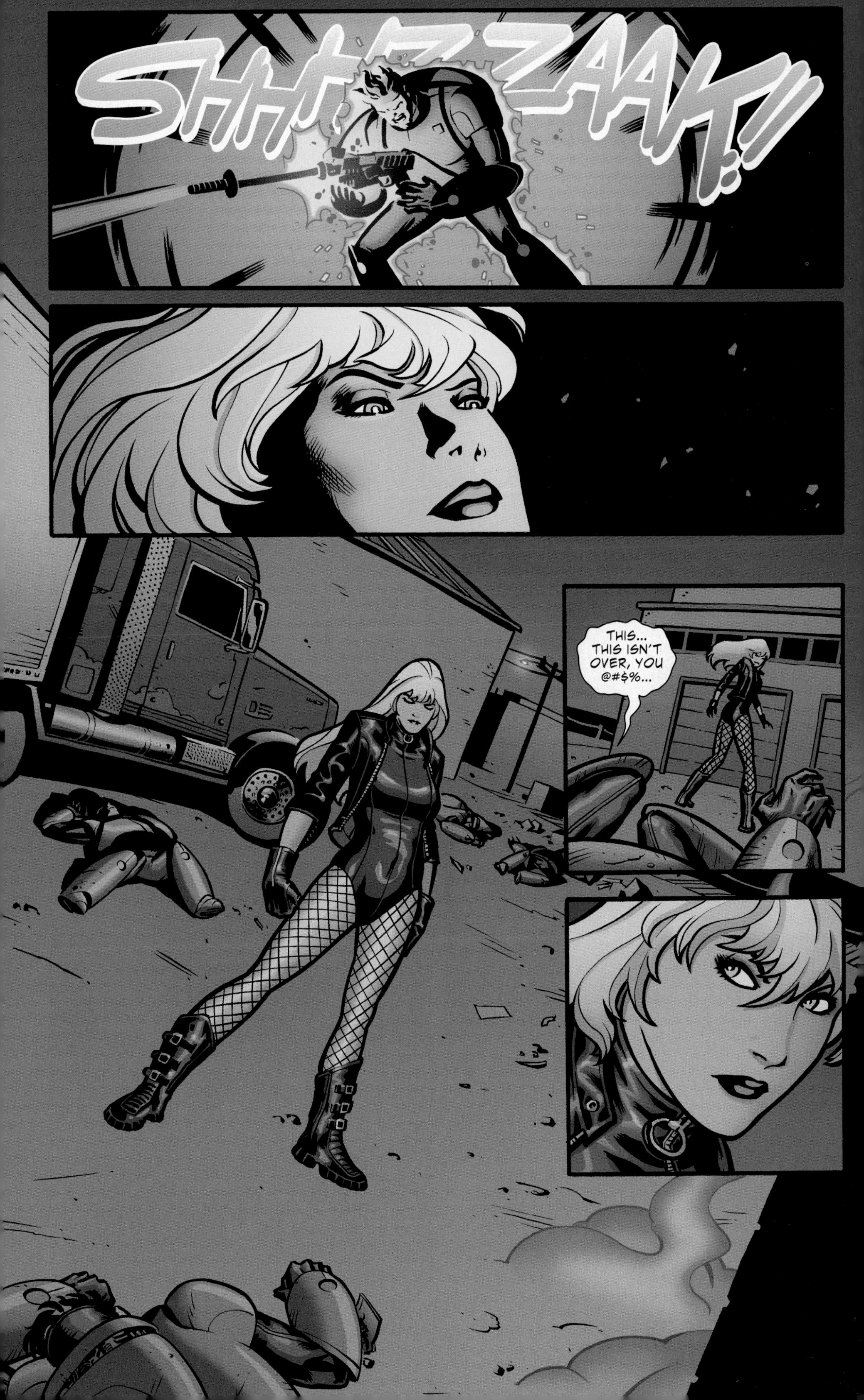
SHHHZZZAAAK!!
THIS... THIS ISN'T OVER, YOU @#$%...

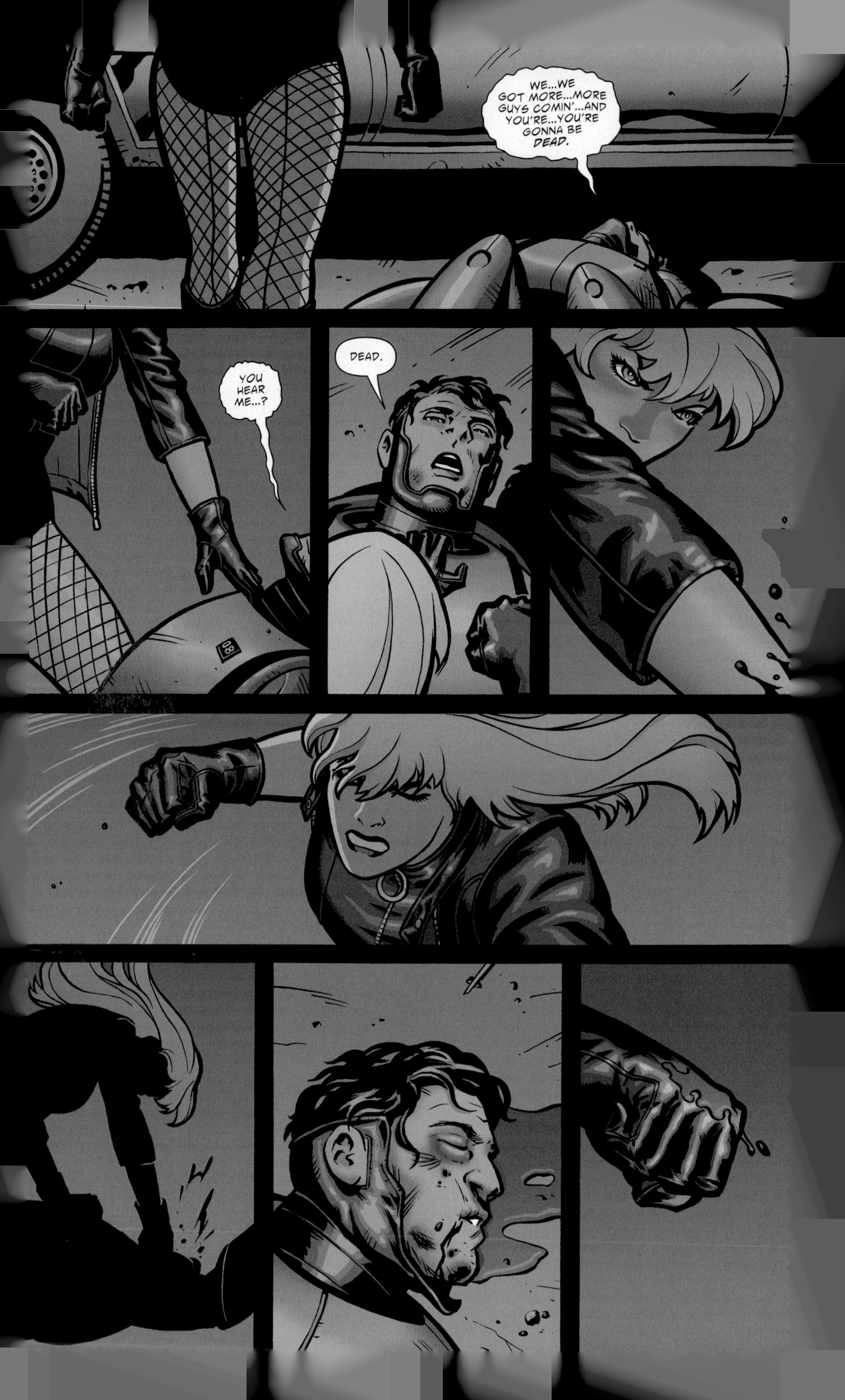
WE...WE GOT MORE...MORE GUYS COMIN'...AND YOU'RE...YOU'RE GONNA BE DEAD.
YOU HEAR ME...?
DEAD.

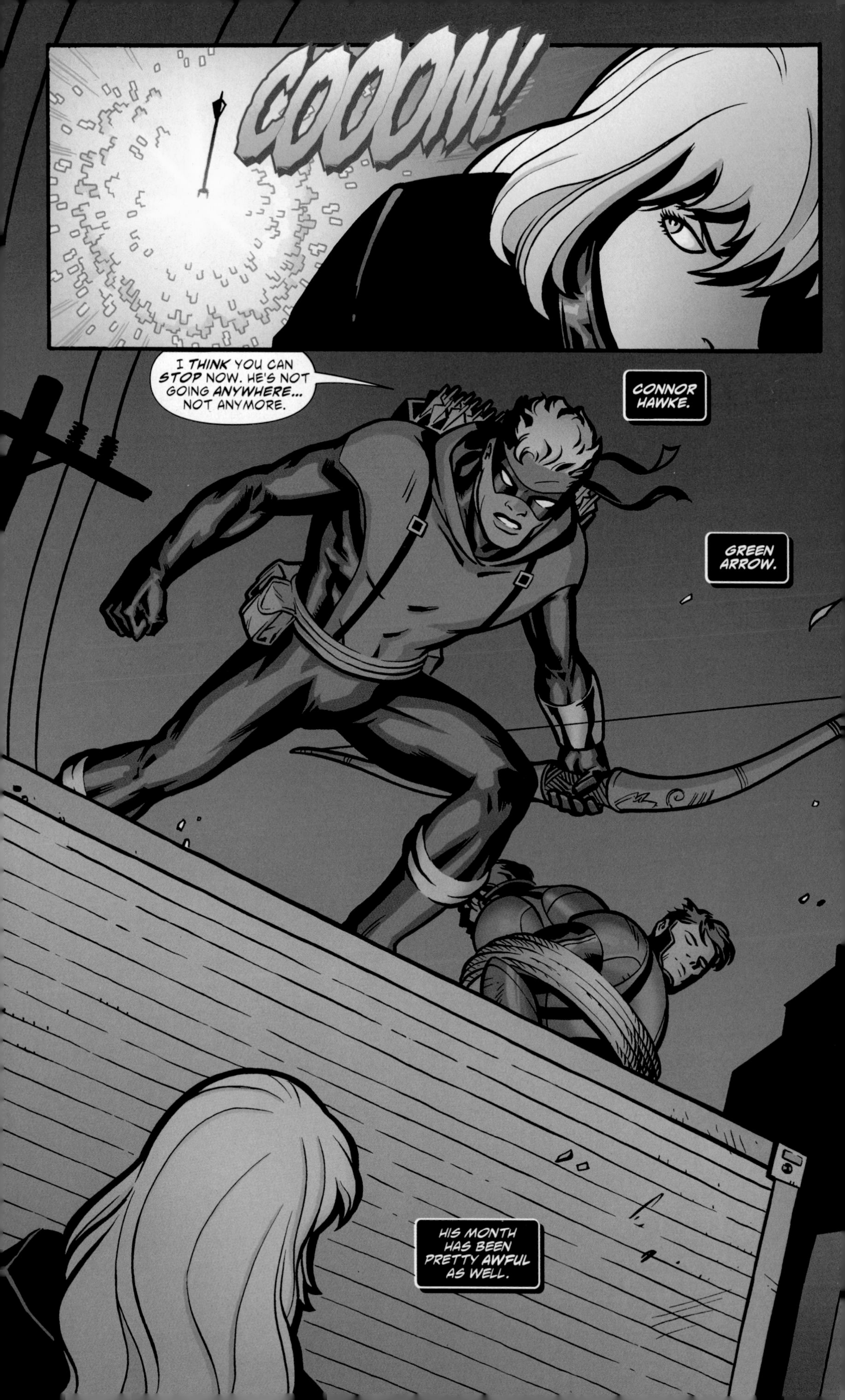
COOOM!
I THINK YOU CAN STOP NOW. HE'S NOT GOING ANYWHERE... NOT ANYMORE.
CONNOR HAWKE.
GREEN ARROW.
HIS MONTH HAS BEEN PRETTY AWFUL AS WELL.

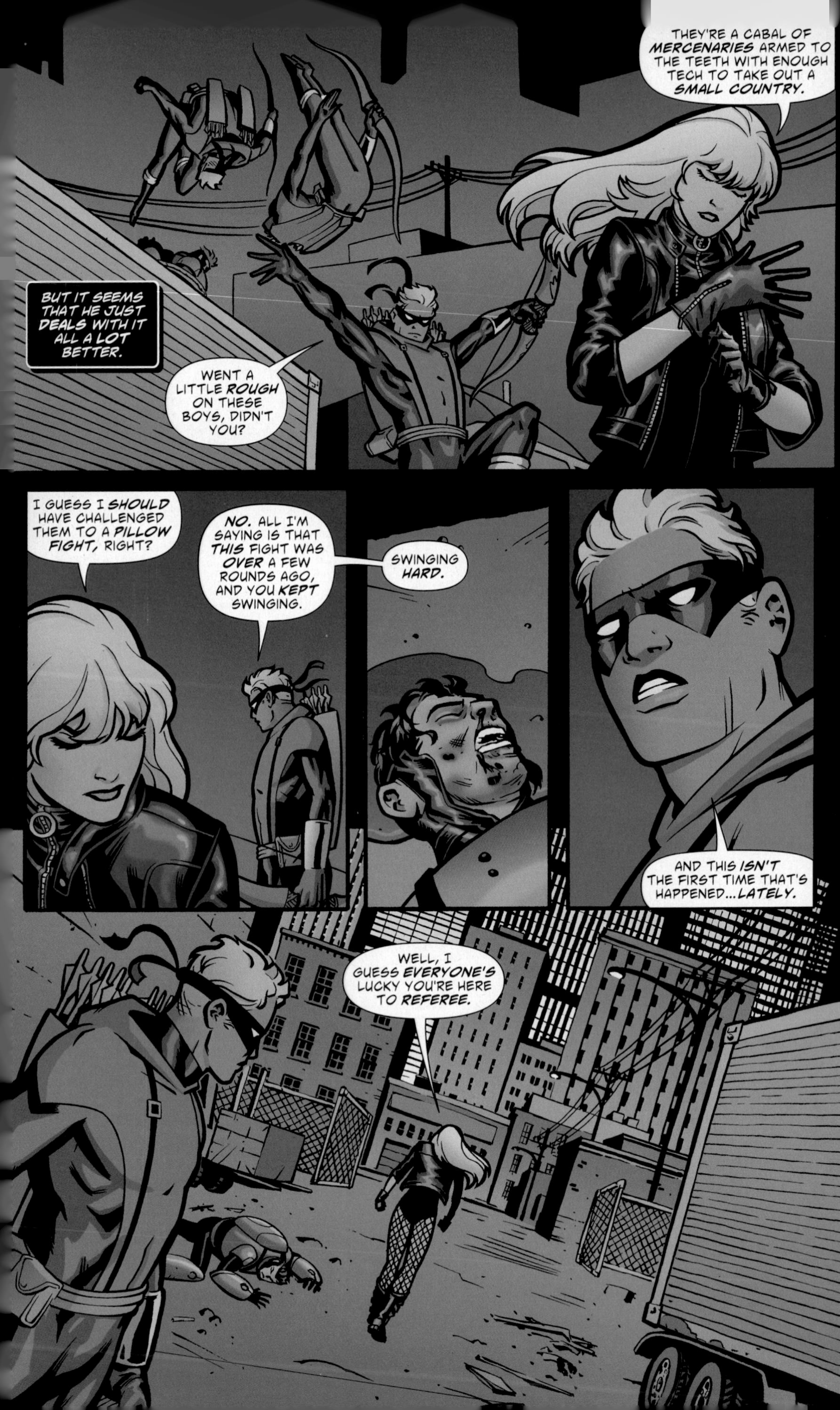
THEY'RE A CABAL OF MERCENARIES ARMED TO THE TEETH WITH ENOUGH TECH TO TAKE OUT A SMALL COUNTRY.
BUT IT SEEMS THAT HE JUST DEALS WITH IT ALL A LOT BETTER.
WENT A LITTLE ROUGH ON THESE BOYS, DIDN'T YOU?
I GUESS I SHOULD HAVE CHALLENGED THEM TO A PILLOW FIGHT, RIGHT?
NO. ALL I'M SAYING IS THAT THIS FIGHT WAS OVER A FEW ROUNDS AGO, AND YOU KEPT SWINGING.
SWINGING HARD.
AND THIS ISN'T THE FIRST TIME THAT'S HAPPENED...LATELY.
WELL, I GUESS EVERYONE'S LUCKY YOU'RE HERE TO REFEREE.

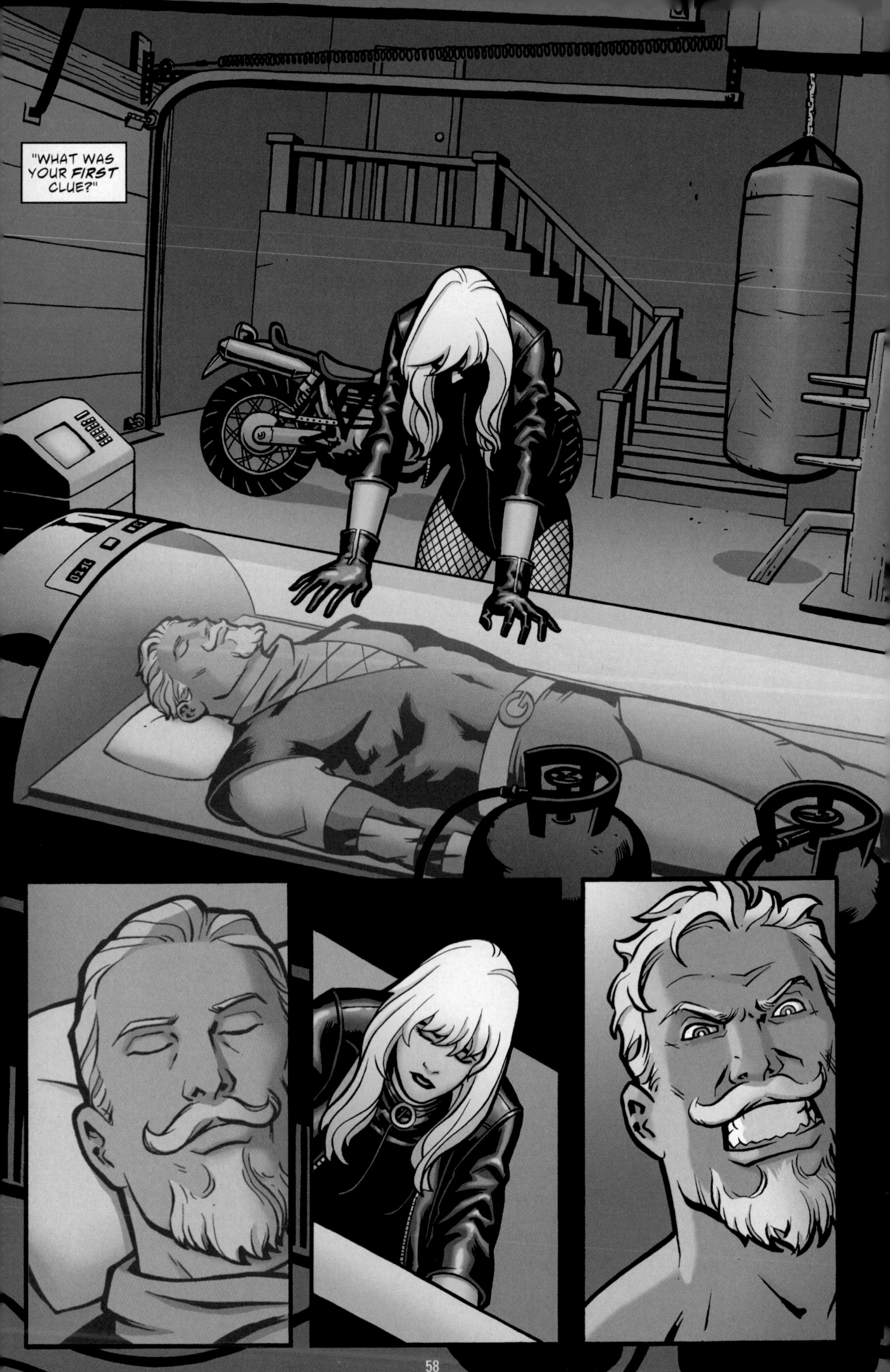
"WHAT WAS YOUR FIRST CLUE?"

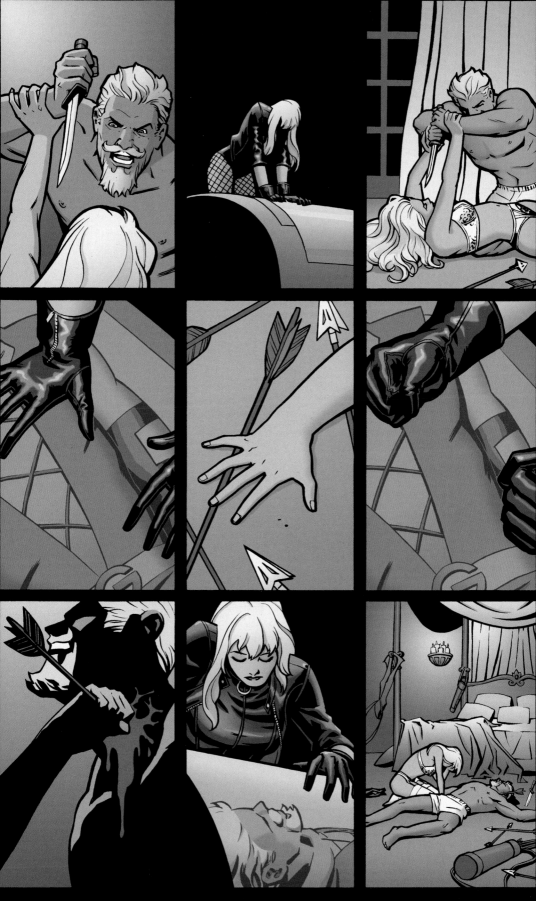

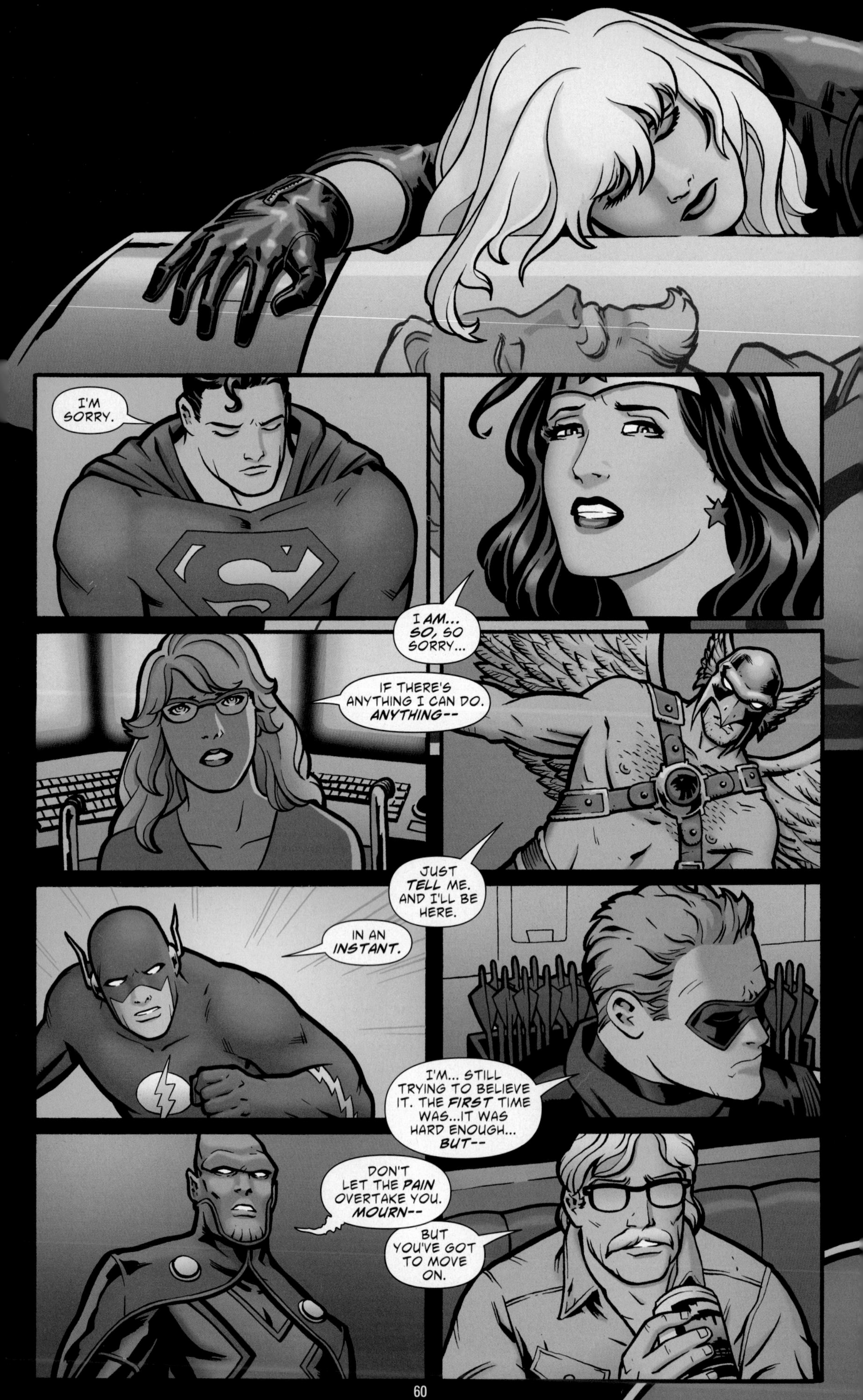
I'M SORRY.
I AM... SO, SO SORRY...
IF THERE'S ANYTHING I CAN DO. ANYTHING--
JUST TELL ME. AND I'LL BE HERE.
IN AN INSTANT.
I'M... STILL TRYING TO BELIEVE IT. THE FIRST TIME WAS...IT WAS HARD ENOUGH... BUT--
DON'T LET THE PAIN OVERTAKE YOU. MOURN--
BUT YOU'VE GOT TO MOVE ON.

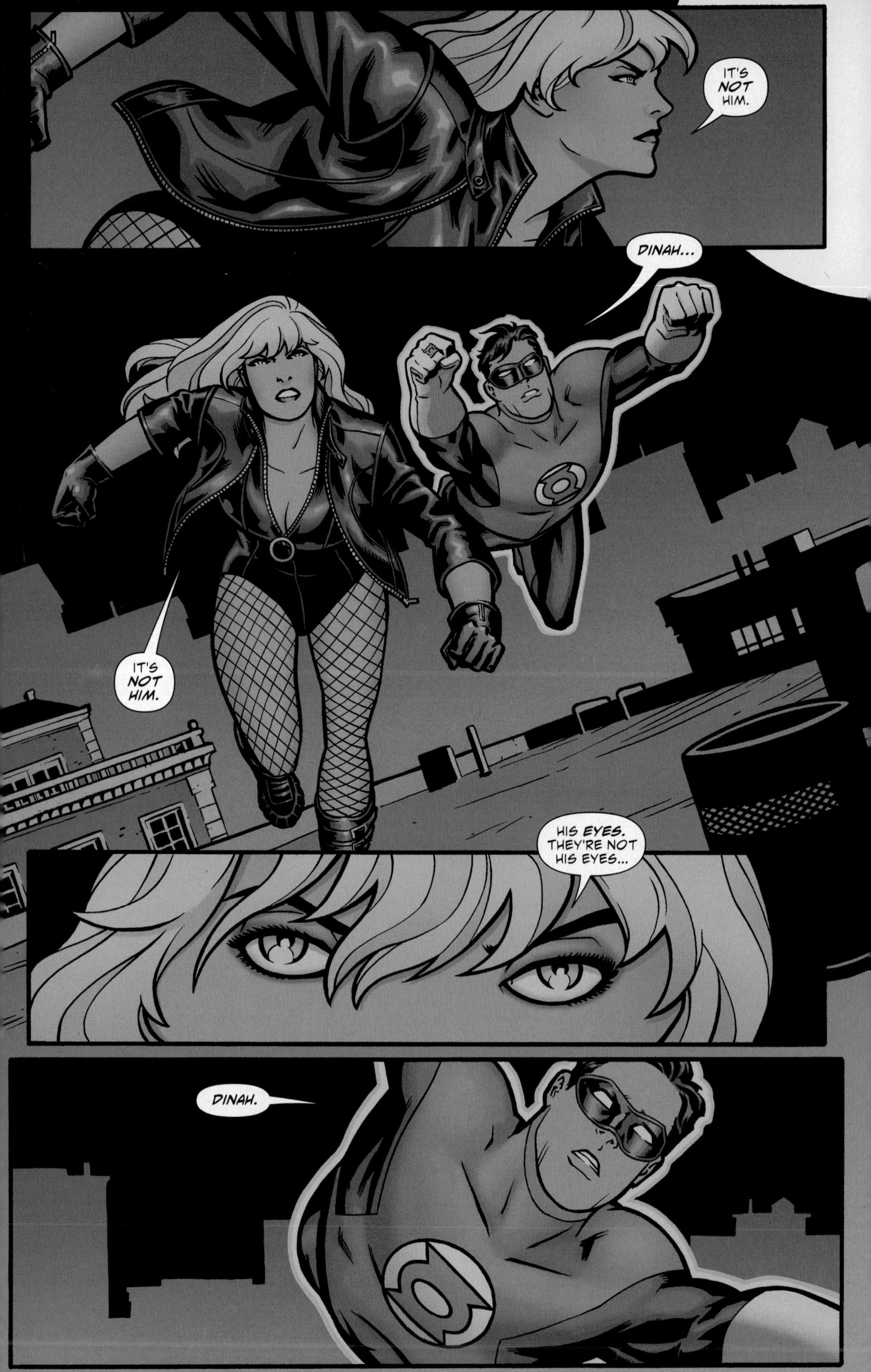
IT'S NOT HIM.
DINAH...
IT'S NOT HIM.
HIS EYES. THEY'RE NOT HIS EYES...
DINAH.

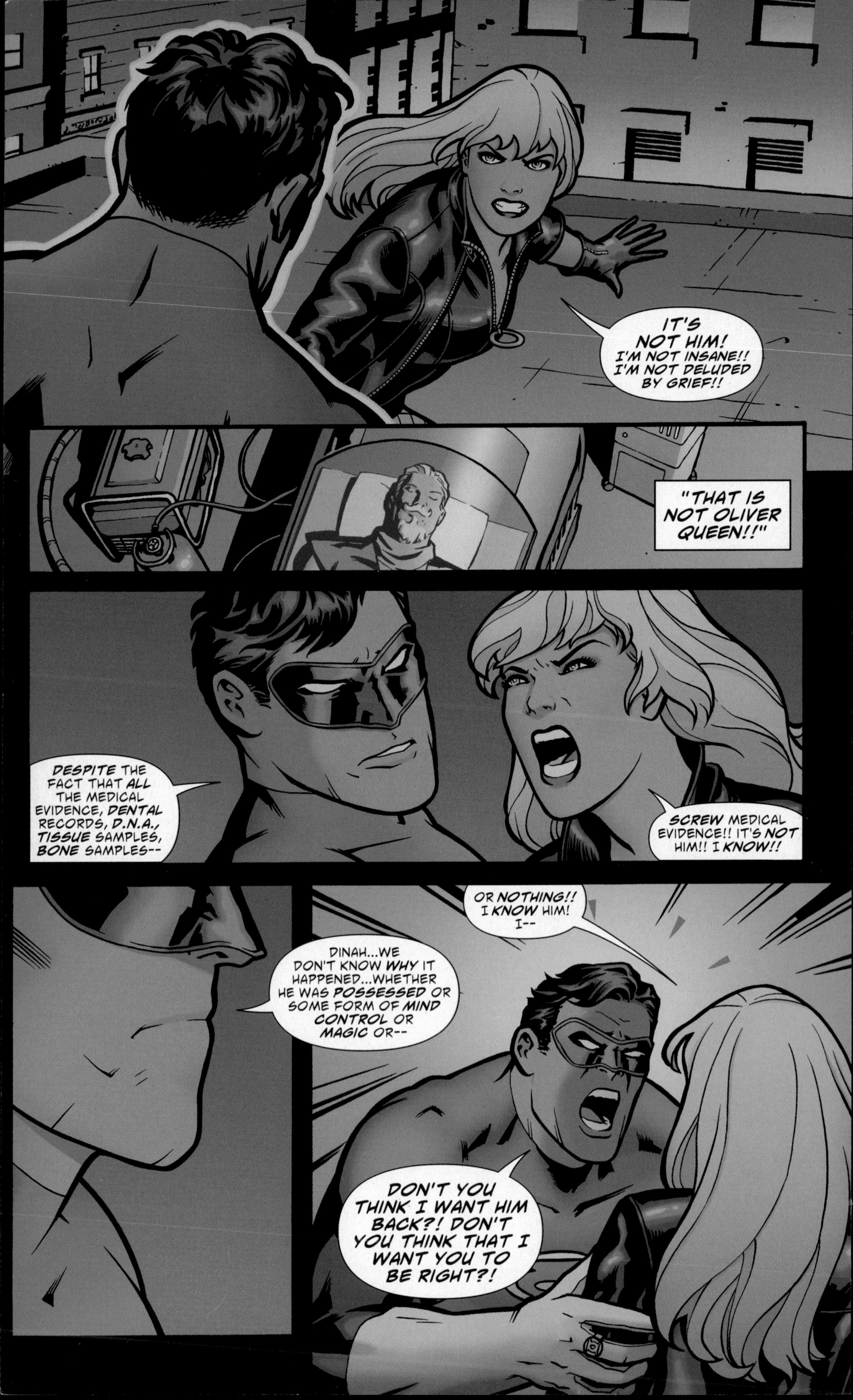
IT'S NOT HIM! I'M NOT INSANE!! I'M NOT DELUDED BY GRIEF!!
"THAT IS NOT OLIVER QUEEN!!"
DESPITE THE FACT THAT ALL THE MEDICAL EVIDENCE, DENTAL RECORDS, D.N.A., TISSUE SAMPLES, BONE SAMPLES--
SCREW MEDICAL EVIDENCE!! IT'S NOT HIM!! I KNOW!!
DINAH...WE DON'T KNOW WHY IT HAPPENED...WHETHER HE WAS POSSESSED OR SOME FORM OF MIND CONTROL OR MAGIC OR--
OR NOTHING!! I KNOW HIM! I--
DON'T YOU THINK I WANT HIM BACK?! DON'T YOU THINK THAT I WANT YOU TO BE RIGHT?!

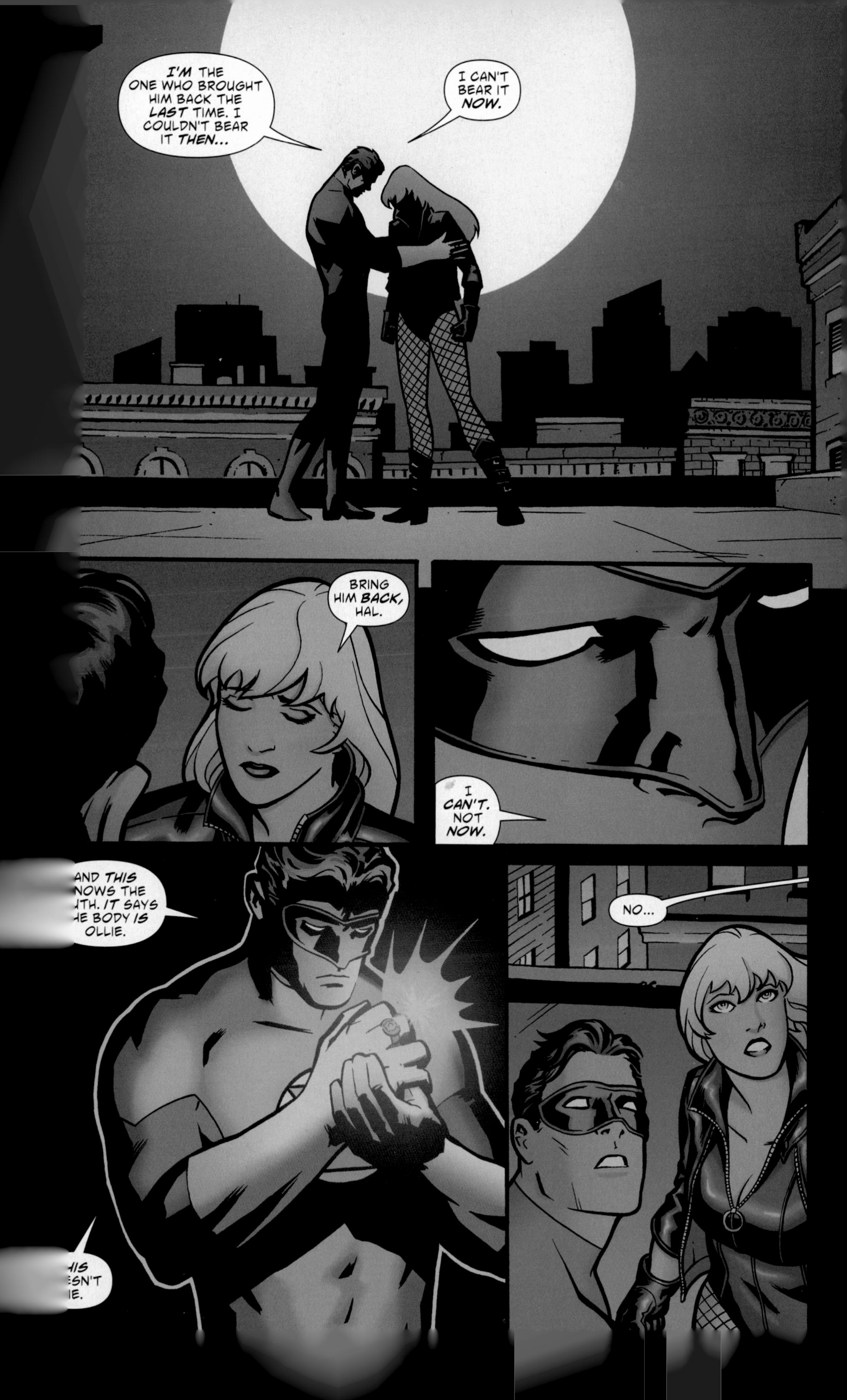
I'M THE ONE WHO BROUGHT HIM BACK THE LAST TIME. I COULDN'T BEAR IT THEN...
I CAN'T BEAR IT NOW.
BRING HIM BACK, HAL.
I CAN'T. NOT NOW.
AND THIS NOWS THE TH. IT SAYS E BODY IS OLLIE.
NO...
HIS ESN'T E.

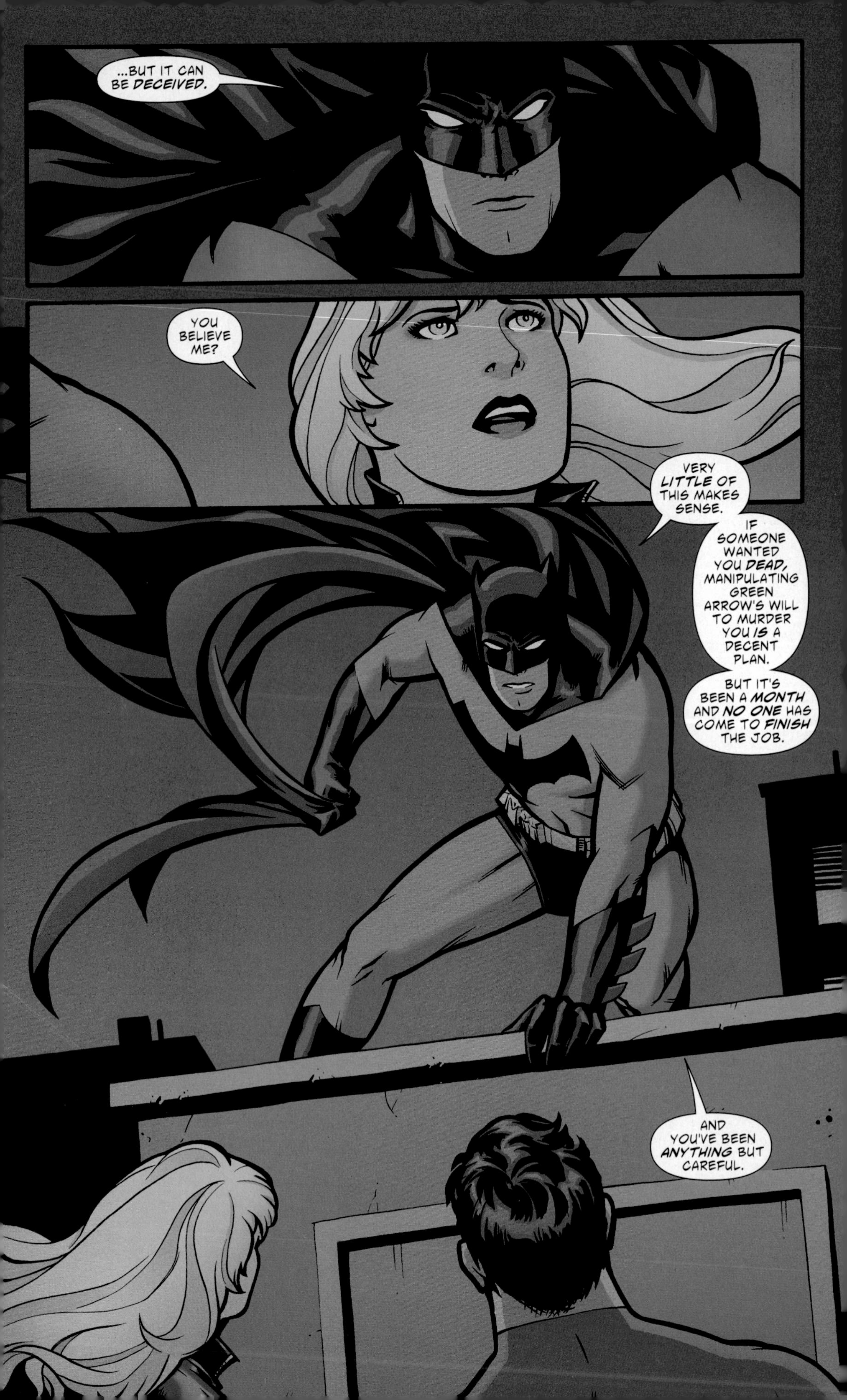
...BUT IT CAN BE *DECEIVED*.
YOU BELIEVE ME?
VERY *LITTLE* OF THIS MAKES SENSE.
IF SOMEONE WANTED YOU *DEAD*, MANIPULATING GREEN ARROW'S WILL TO MURDER YOU *IS* A DECENT PLAN.
BUT IT'S BEEN A *MONTH* AND *NO ONE* HAS COME TO *FINISH* THE JOB.
AND YOU'VE BEEN *ANYTHING* BUT CAREFUL.

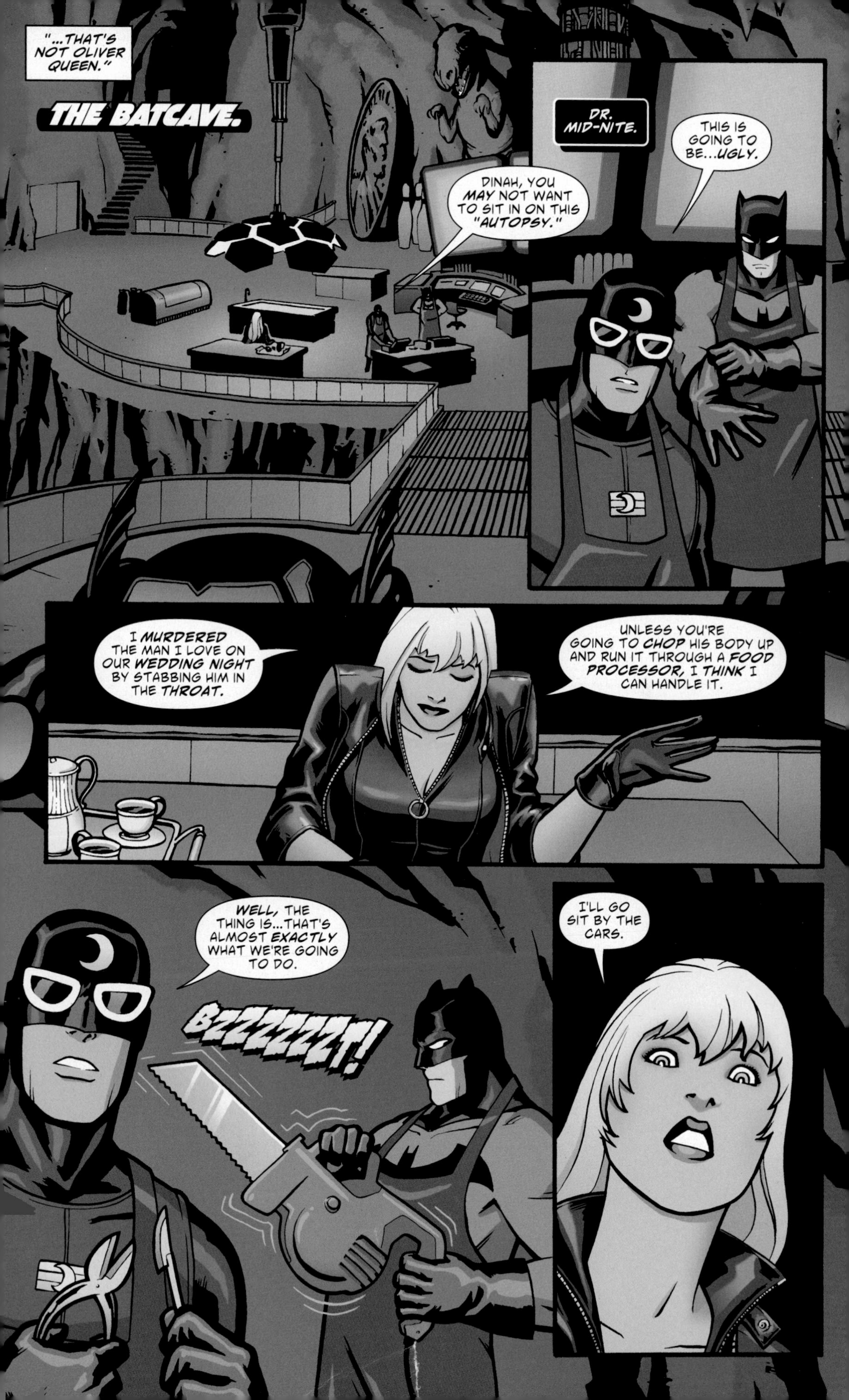
"...THAT'S NOT OLIVER QUEEN."
THE BATCAVE.
DR. MID-NITE.
DINAH, YOU MAY NOT WANT TO SIT IN ON THIS "AUTOPSY."
THIS IS GOING TO BE...UGLY.
I MURDERED THE MAN I LOVE ON OUR WEDDING NIGHT BY STABBING HIM IN THE THROAT.
UNLESS YOU'RE GOING TO CHOP HIS BODY UP AND RUN IT THROUGH A FOOD PROCESSOR, I THINK I CAN HANDLE IT.
WELL, THE THING IS...THAT'S ALMOST EXACTLY WHAT WE'RE GOING TO DO.
BZZZZZZZT!
I'LL GO SIT BY THE CARS.

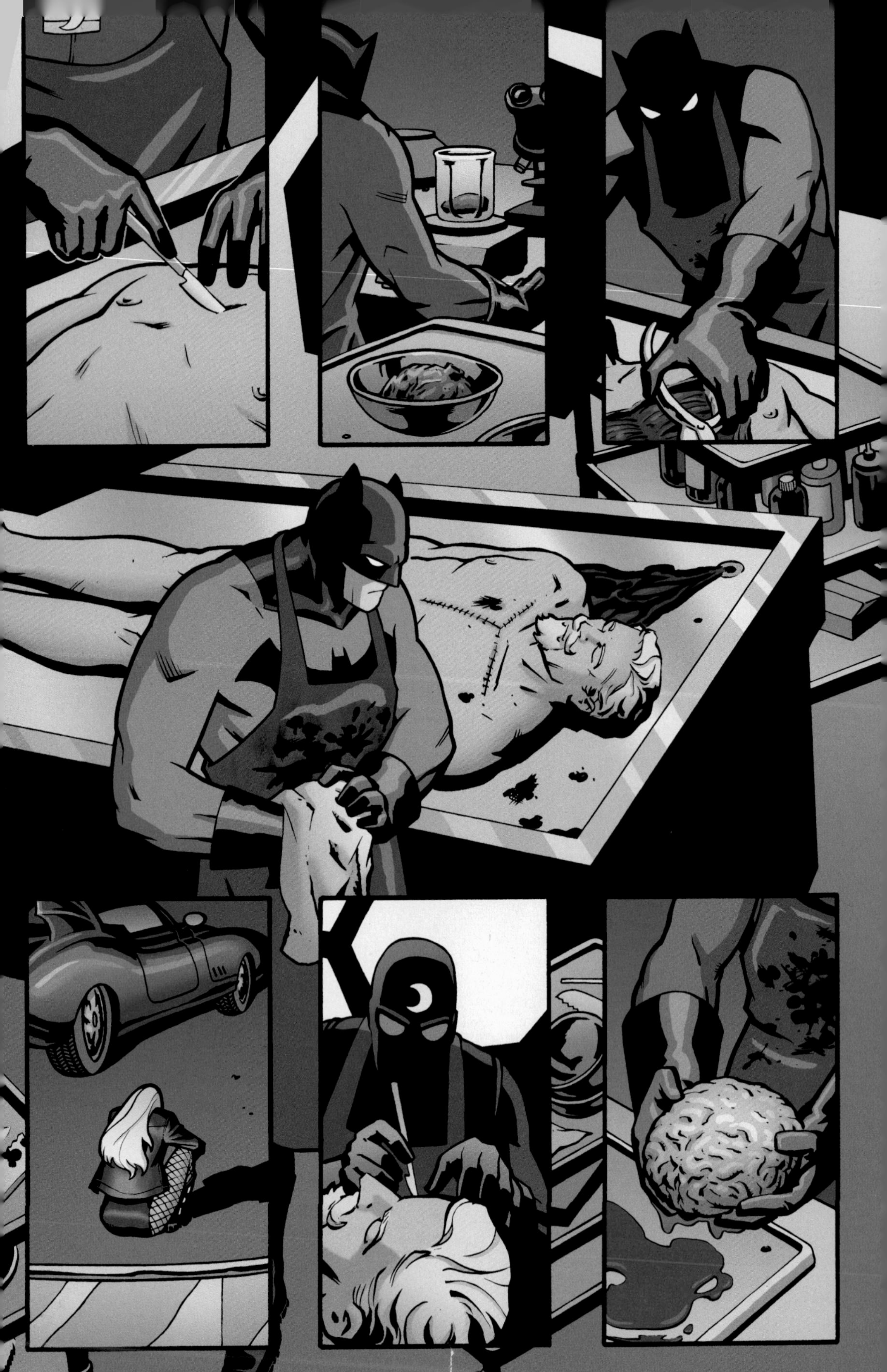

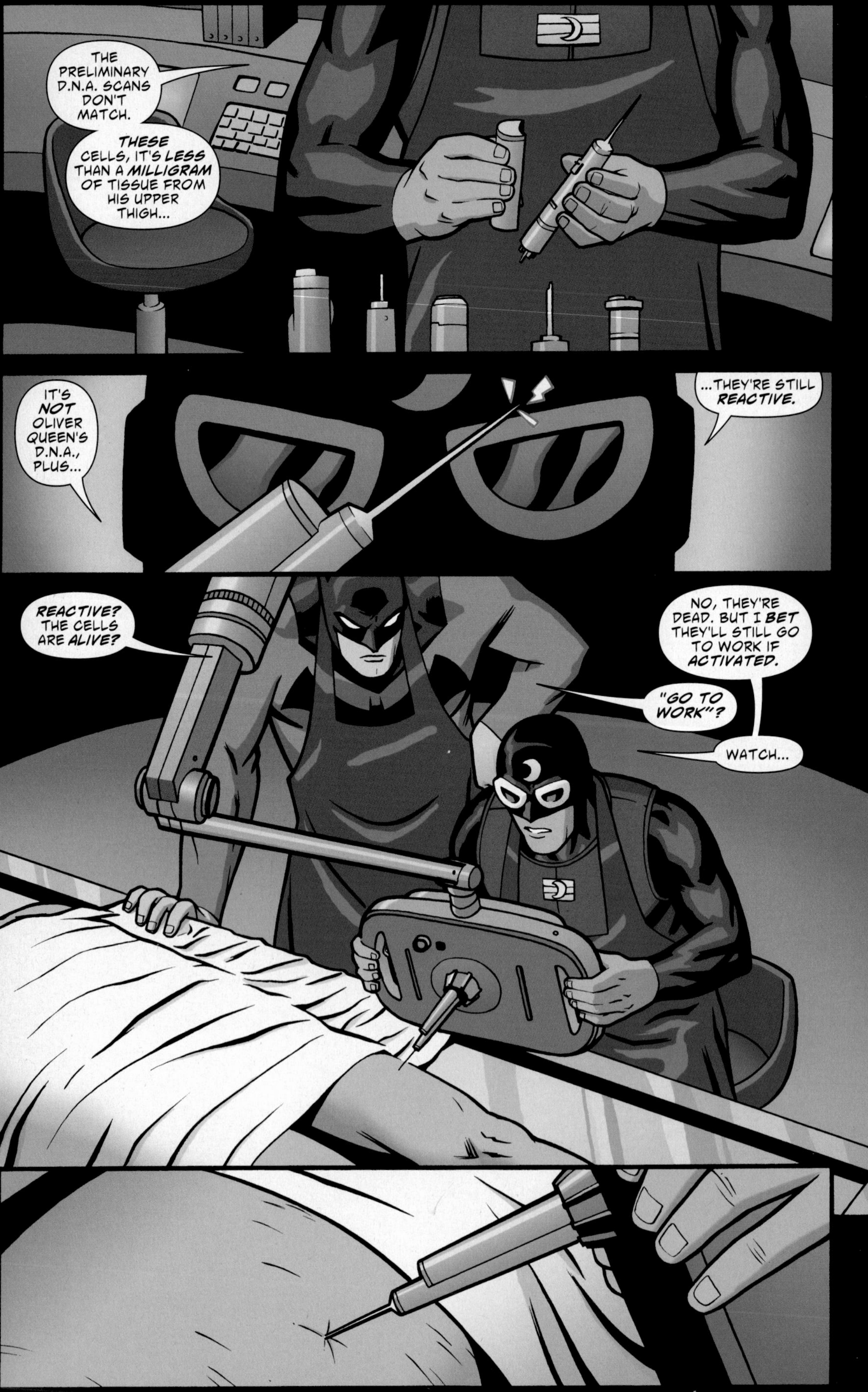
THE PRELIMINARY D.N.A. SCANS DON'T MATCH.
THESE CELLS, IT'S LESS THAN A MILLIGRAM OF TISSUE FROM HIS UPPER THIGH...
IT'S NOT OLIVER QUEEN'S D.N.A., PLUS...
...THEY'RE STILL REACTIVE.
REACTIVE? THE CELLS ARE ALIVE?
NO, THEY'RE DEAD. BUT I BET THEY'LL STILL GO TO WORK IF ACTIVATED.
"GO TO WORK"?
WATCH...

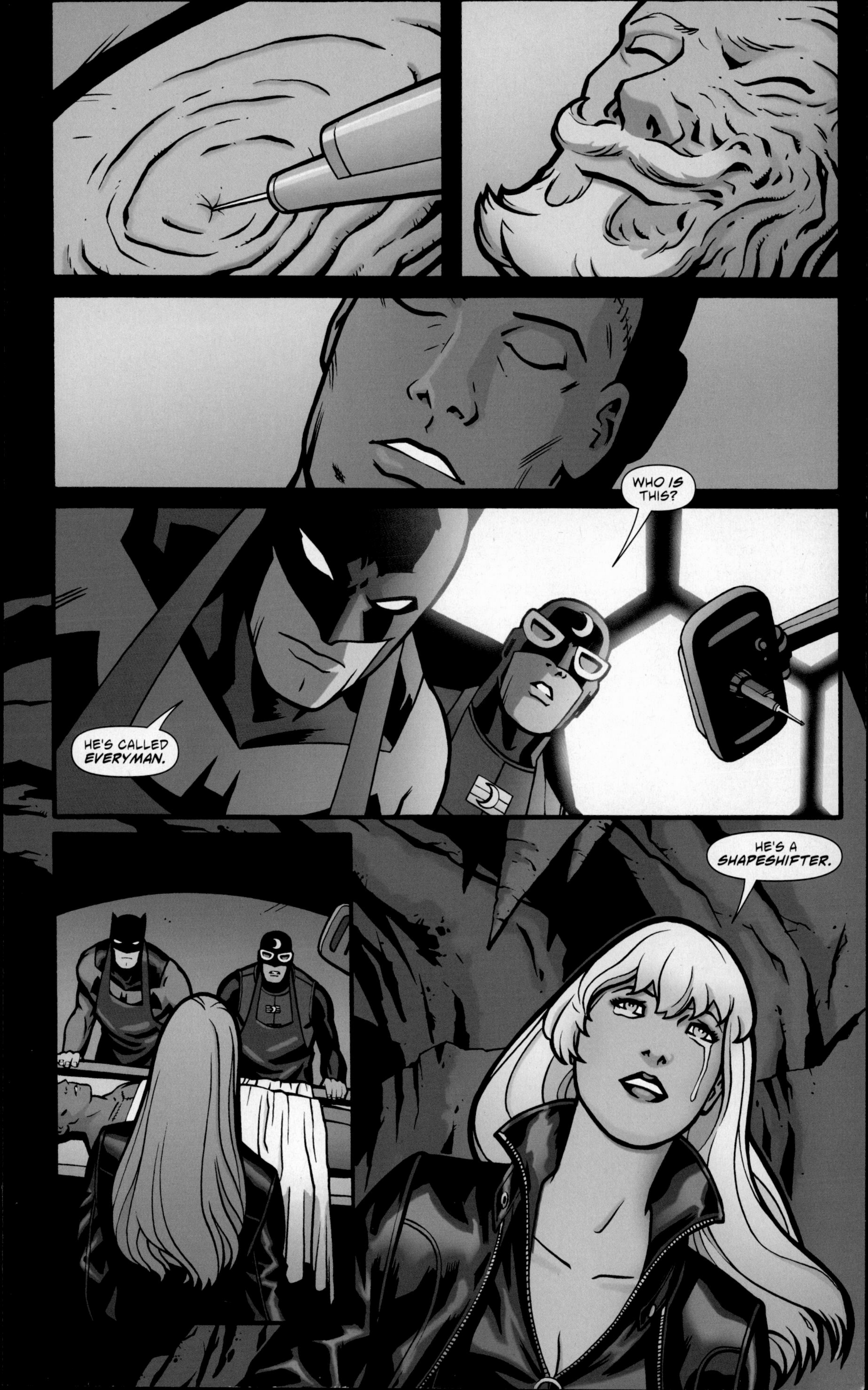
WHO IS THIS?
HE'S CALLED EVERYMAN.
HE'S A SHAPESHIFTER.

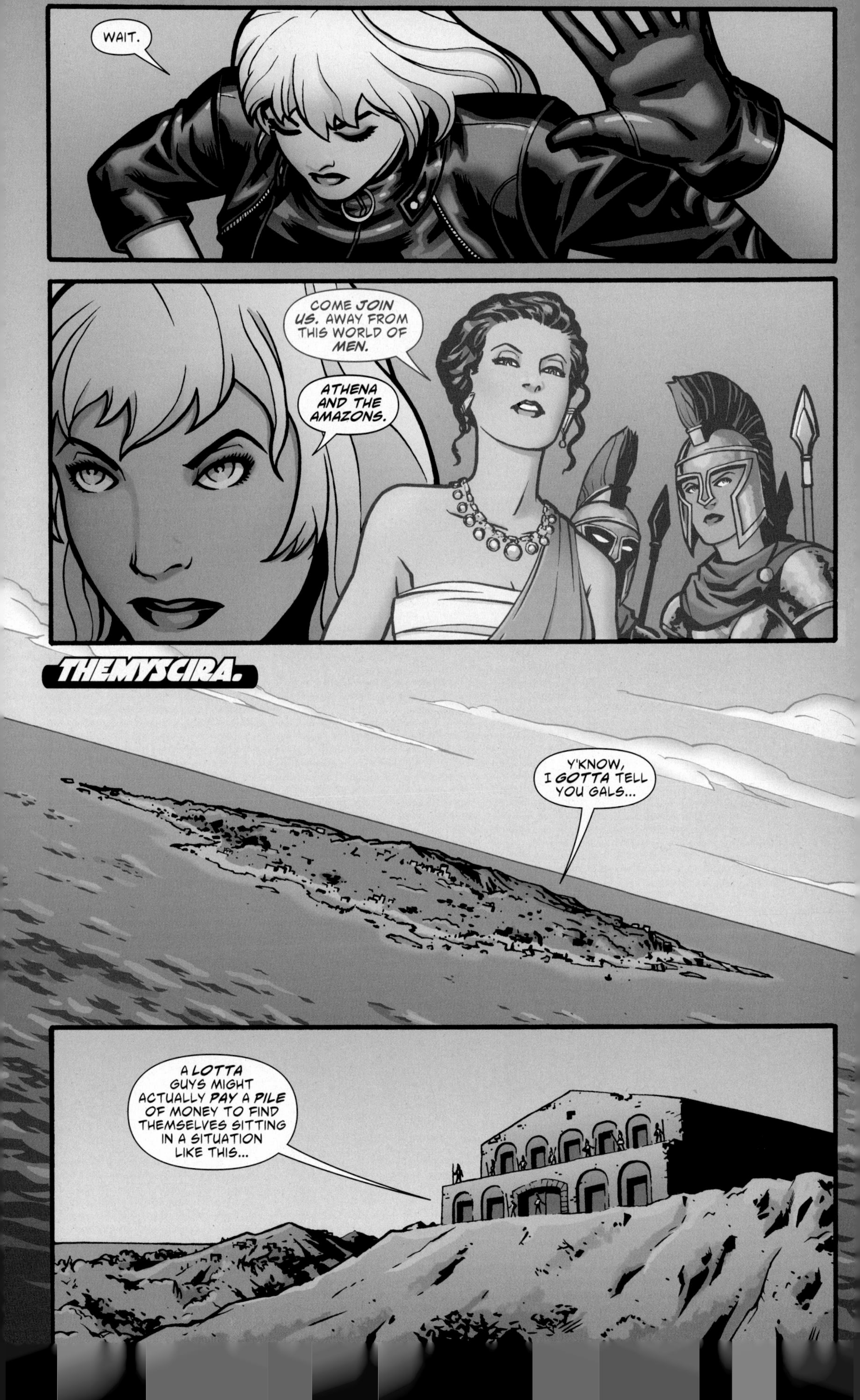
WAIT.
COME JOIN US. AWAY FROM THIS WORLD OF MEN.
ATHENA AND THE AMAZONS.
THEMYSCIRA.
Y'KNOW, I GOTTA TELL YOU GALS...
A LOTTA GUYS MIGHT ACTUALLY PAY A PILE OF MONEY TO FIND THEMSELVES SITTING IN A SITUATION LIKE THIS...

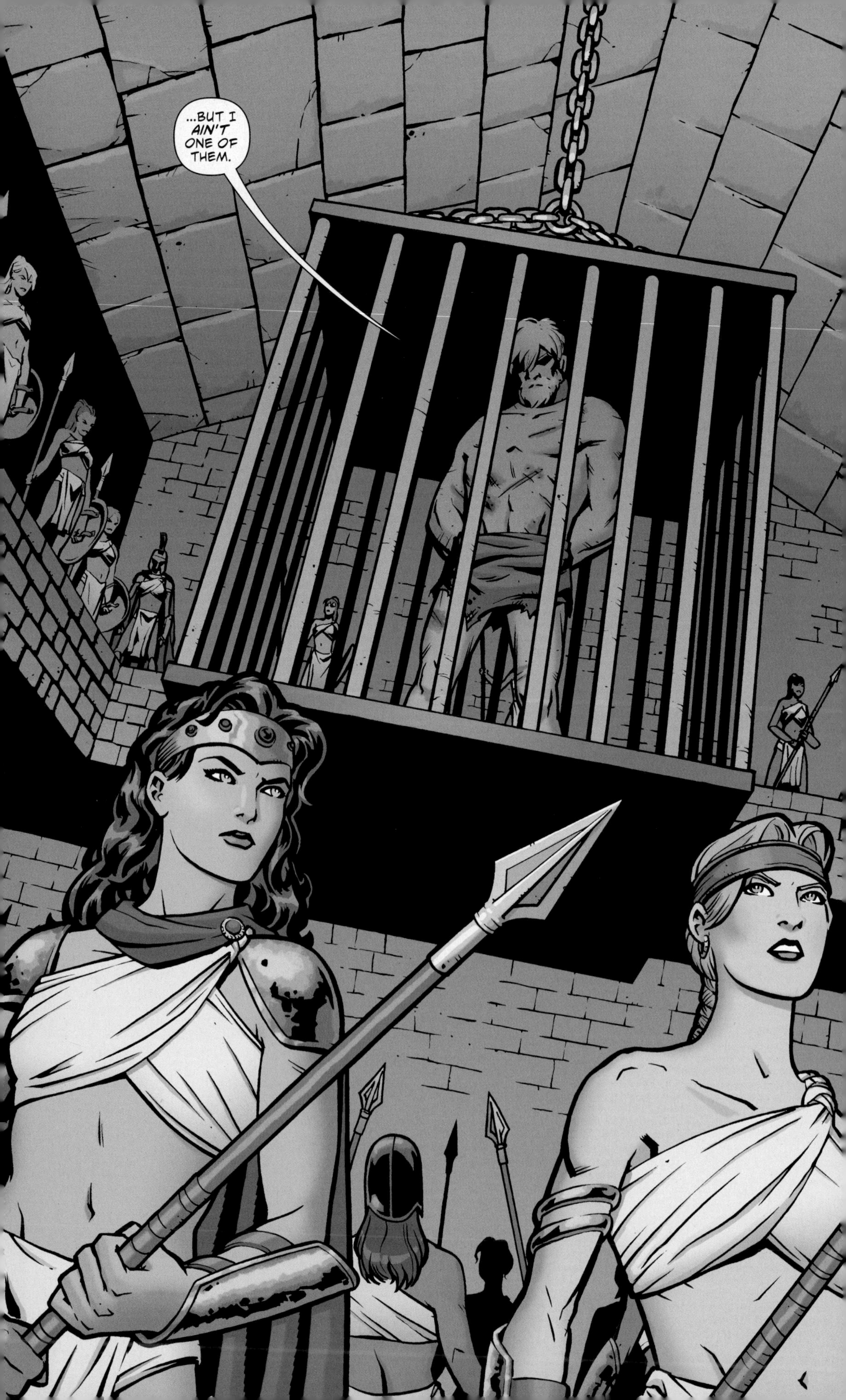
...BUT I AIN'T ONE OF THEM.

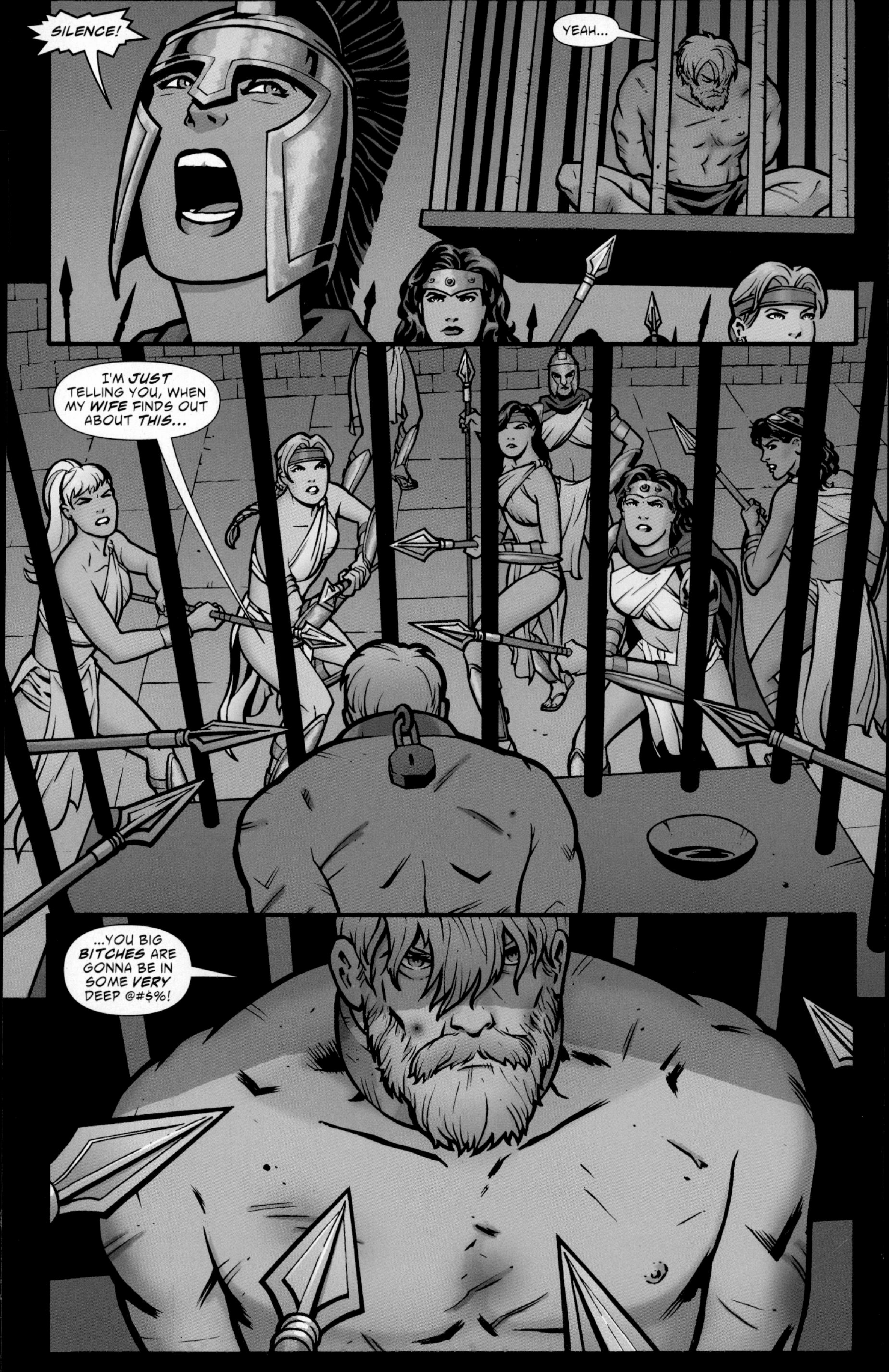
SILENCE!
YEAH...
I'M JUST TELLING YOU, WHEN MY WIFE FINDS OUT ABOUT THIS...
...YOU BIG BITCHES ARE GONNA BE IN SOME VERY DEEP @#$%!

GREEN ARROW AND BLACK CANARY #2 *Cliff Chiang*

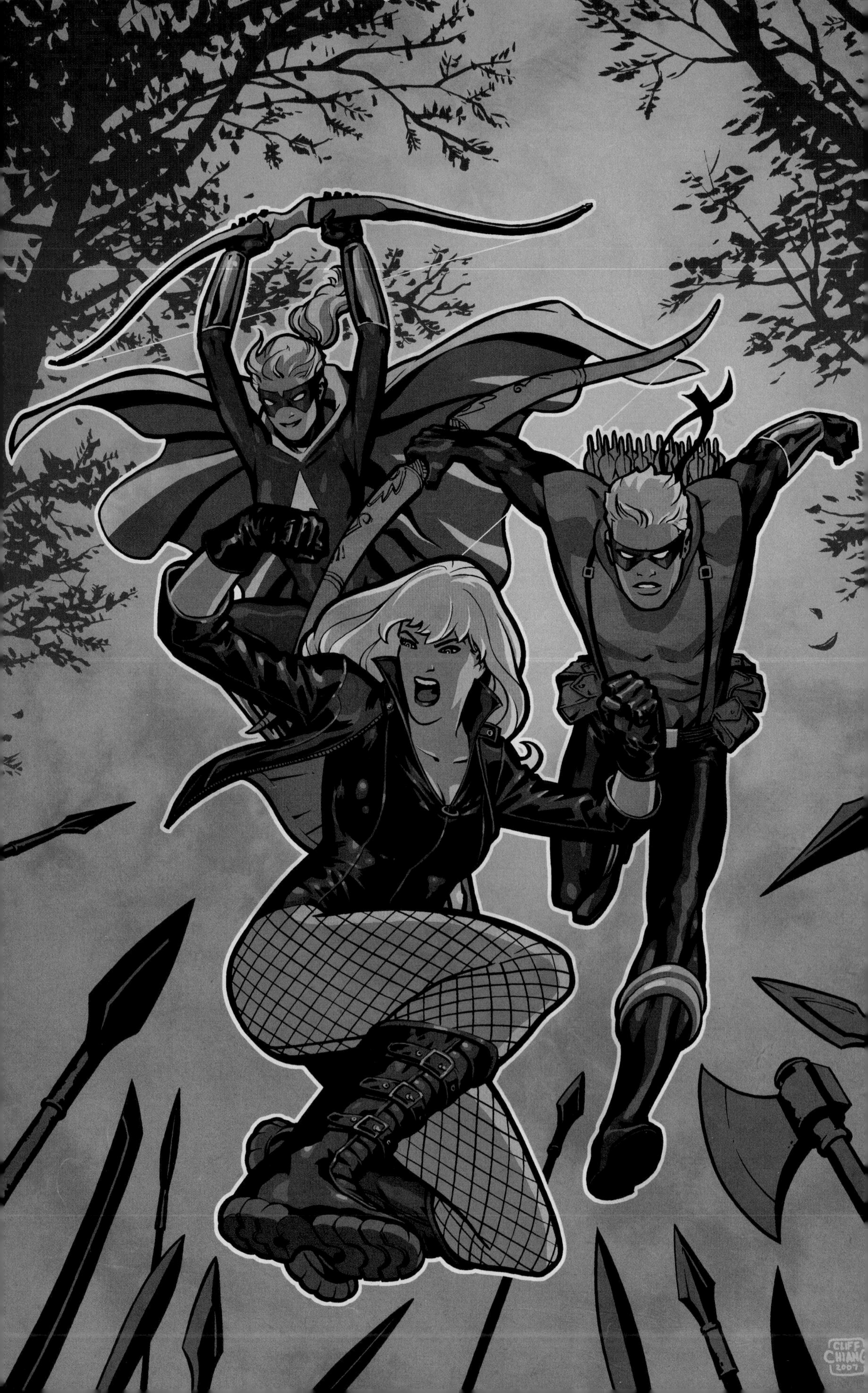
CLIFF CHIANG 2007

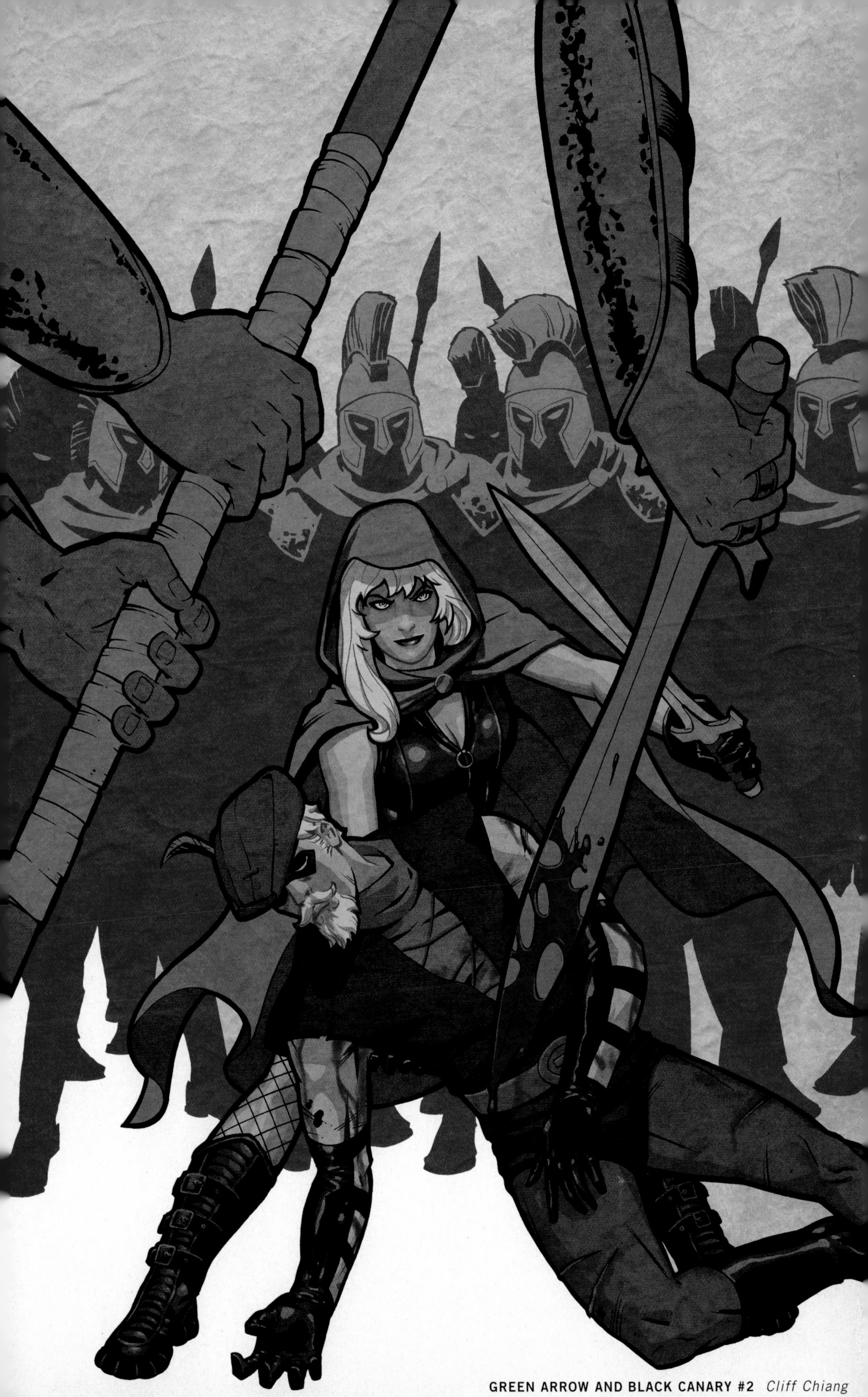

GREEN ARROW AND BLACK CANARY #2 *Cliff Chiang*

DEAD AGAIN PART TWO: THE NAKED AND THE *NOT-QUITE-SO*-DEAD

Story: **Judd Winick**   *Art:* **Cliff Chiang**   *Color:* **Trish Mulvihill**

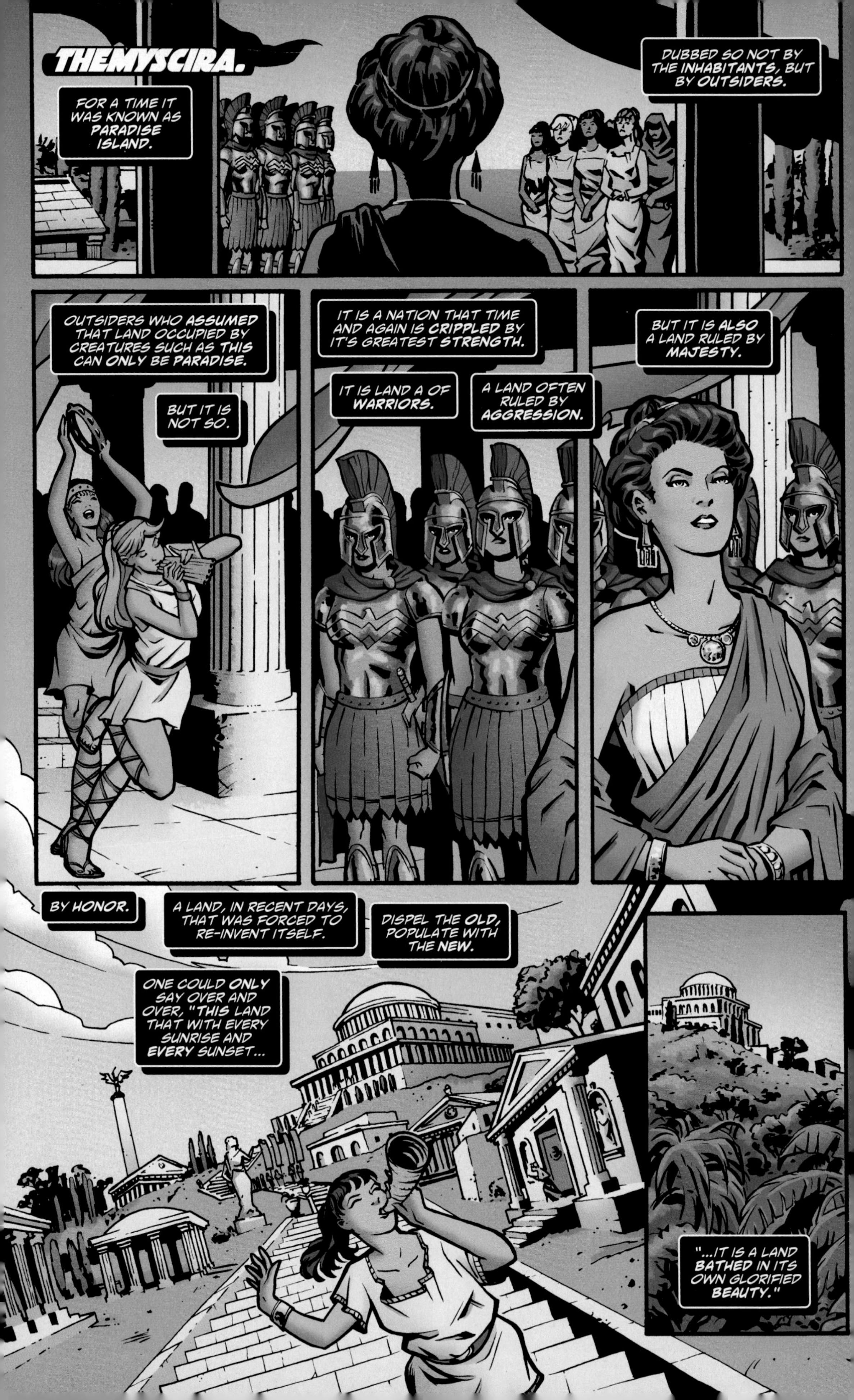
THEMYSCIRA.
FOR A TIME IT WAS KNOWN AS PARADISE ISLAND.
DUBBED SO NOT BY THE INHABITANTS, BUT BY OUTSIDERS.
OUTSIDERS WHO ASSUMED THAT LAND OCCUPIED BY CREATURES SUCH AS THIS CAN ONLY BE PARADISE.
BUT IT IS NOT SO.
IT IS A NATION THAT TIME AND AGAIN IS CRIPPLED BY IT'S GREATEST STRENGTH.
IT IS LAND A OF WARRIORS.
A LAND OFTEN RULED BY AGGRESSION.
BUT IT IS ALSO A LAND RULED BY MAJESTY.
BY HONOR.
A LAND, IN RECENT DAYS, THAT WAS FORCED TO RE-INVENT ITSELF.
DISPEL THE OLD, POPULATE WITH THE NEW.
ONE COULD ONLY SAY OVER AND OVER, "THIS LAND THAT WITH EVERY SUNRISE AND EVERY SUNSET...
"...IT IS A LAND BATHED IN ITS OWN GLORIFIED BEAUTY."

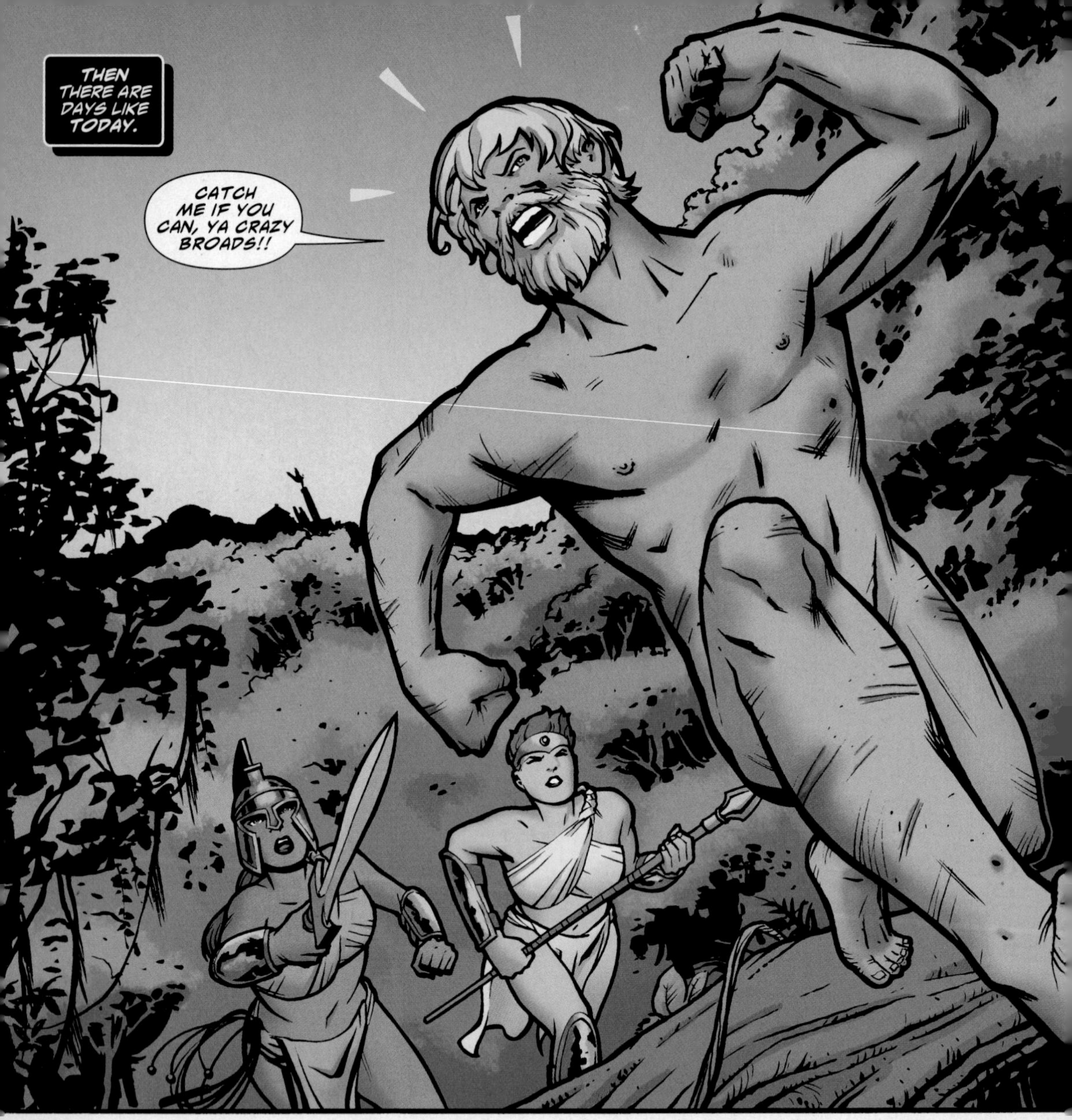
THEN THERE ARE DAYS LIKE TODAY.
CATCH ME IF YOU CAN, YA CRAZY BROADS!!

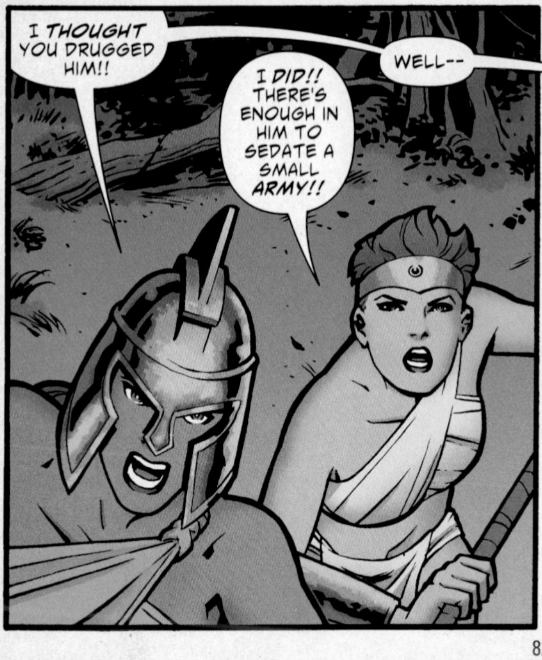
I THOUGHT YOU DRUGGED HIM!!
I DID!! THERE'S ENOUGH IN HIM TO SEDATE A SMALL ARMY!!
WELL--

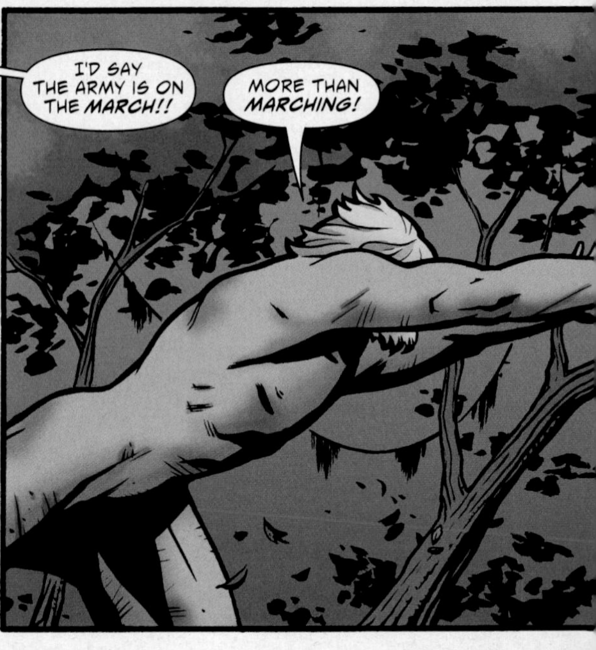
I'D SAY THE ARMY IS ON THE MARCH!!
MORE THAN MARCHING!

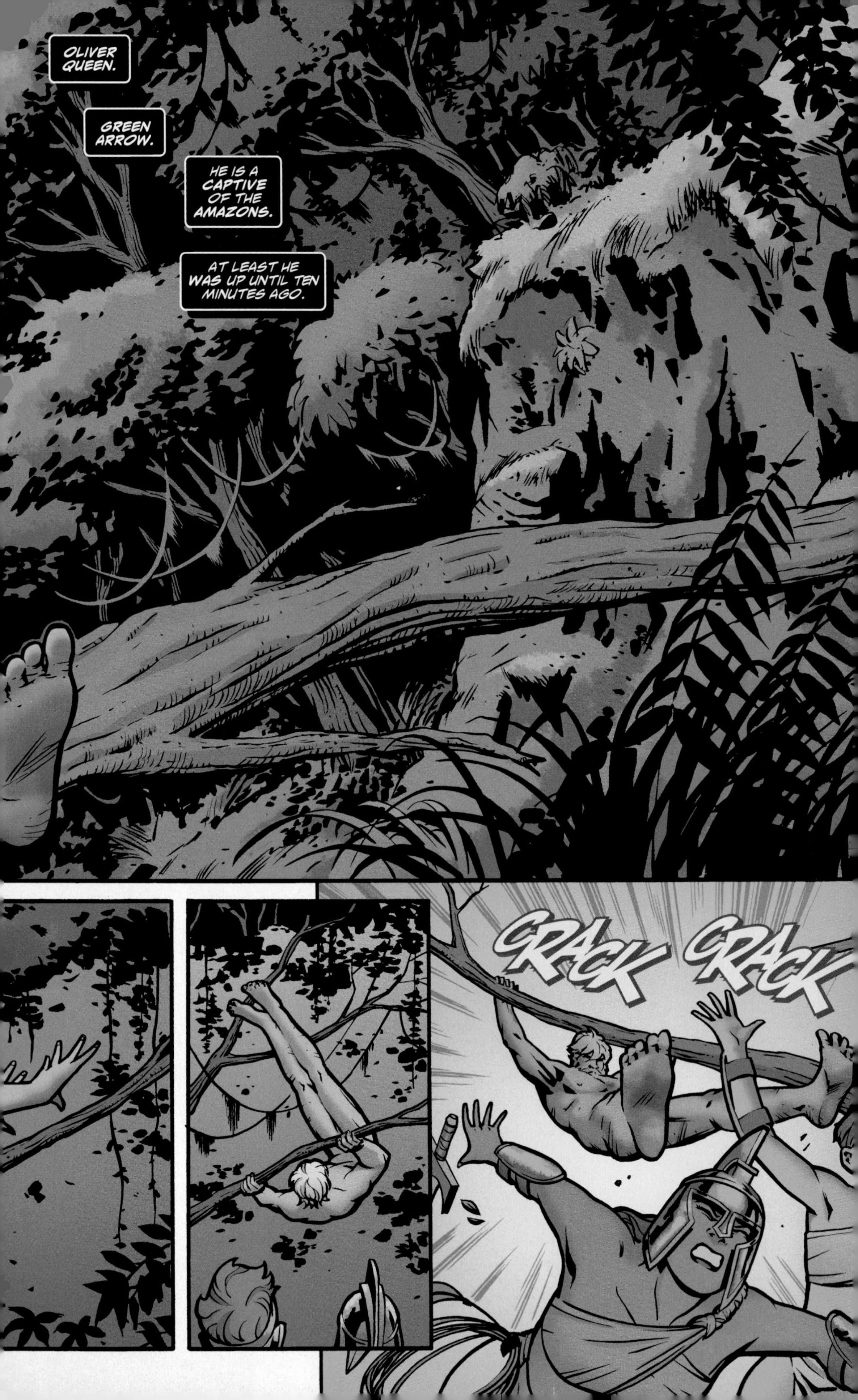

OLIVER QUEEN.
GREEN ARROW.
HE IS A CAPTIVE OF THE AMAZONS.
AT LEAST HE WAS UP UNTIL TEN MINUTES AGO.
CRACK CRACK

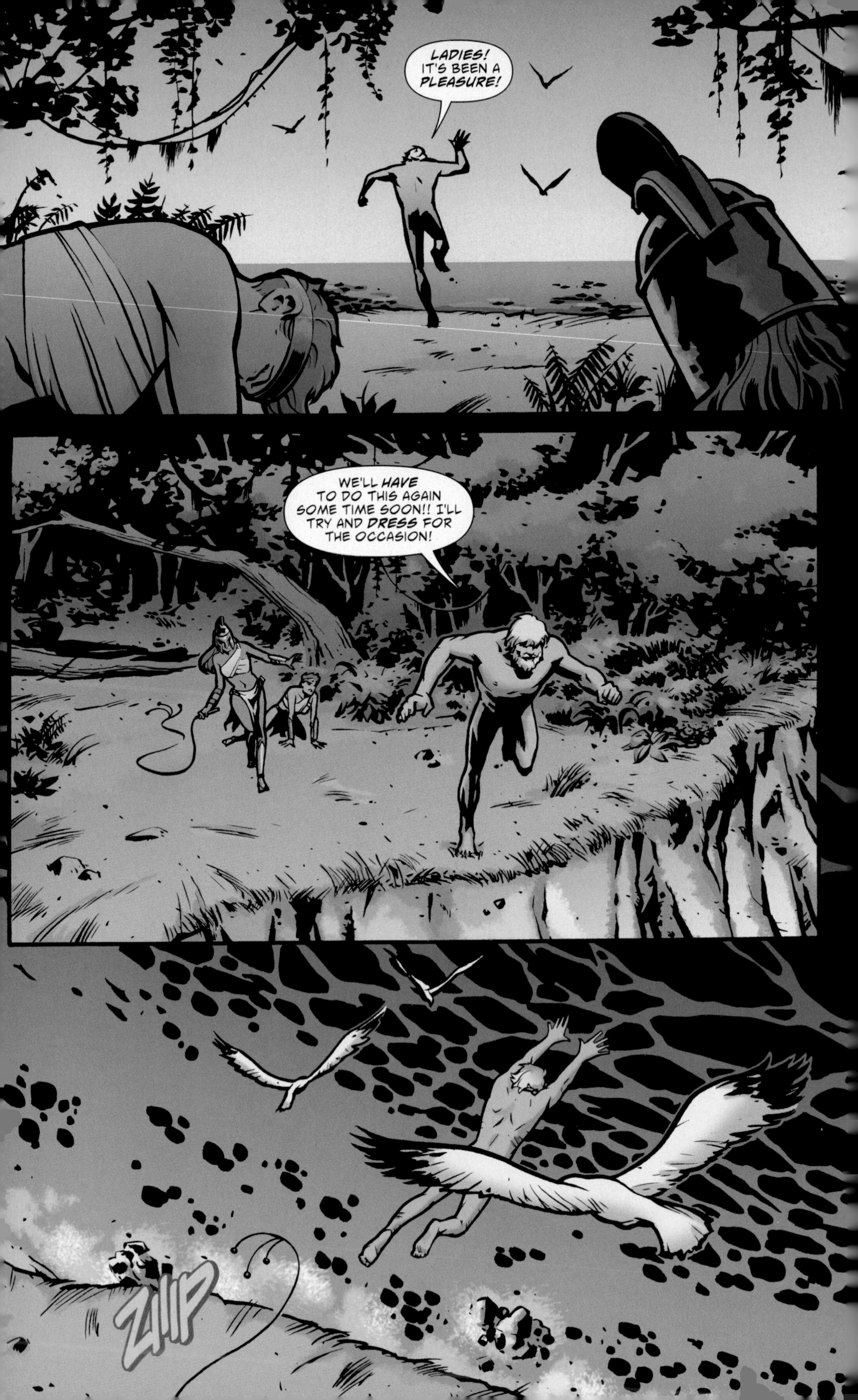
LADIES! IT'S BEEN A PLEASURE!
WE'LL HAVE TO DO THIS AGAIN SOME TIME SOON!! I'LL TRY AND DRESS FOR THE OCCASION!
ZIIIP

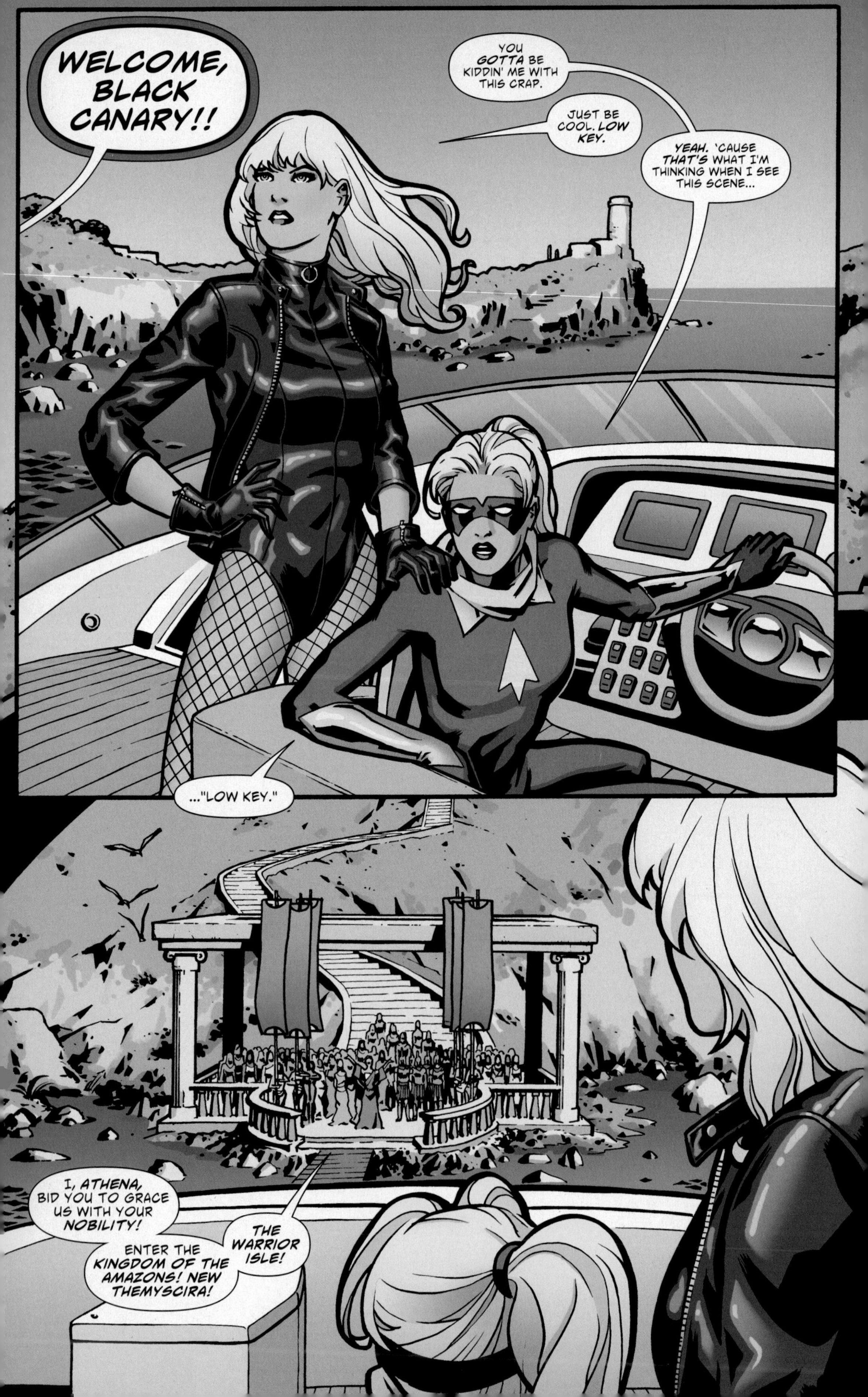
WELCOME, BLACK CANARY!!
YOU GOTTA BE KIDDIN' ME WITH THIS CRAP.
JUST BE COOL. LOW KEY.
YEAH. 'CAUSE THAT'S WHAT I'M THINKING WHEN I SEE THIS SCENE...
..."LOW KEY."
I, ATHENA, BID YOU TO GRACE US WITH YOUR NOBILITY!
ENTER THE KINGDOM OF THE AMAZONS! NEW THEMYSCIRA!
THE WARRIOR ISLE!

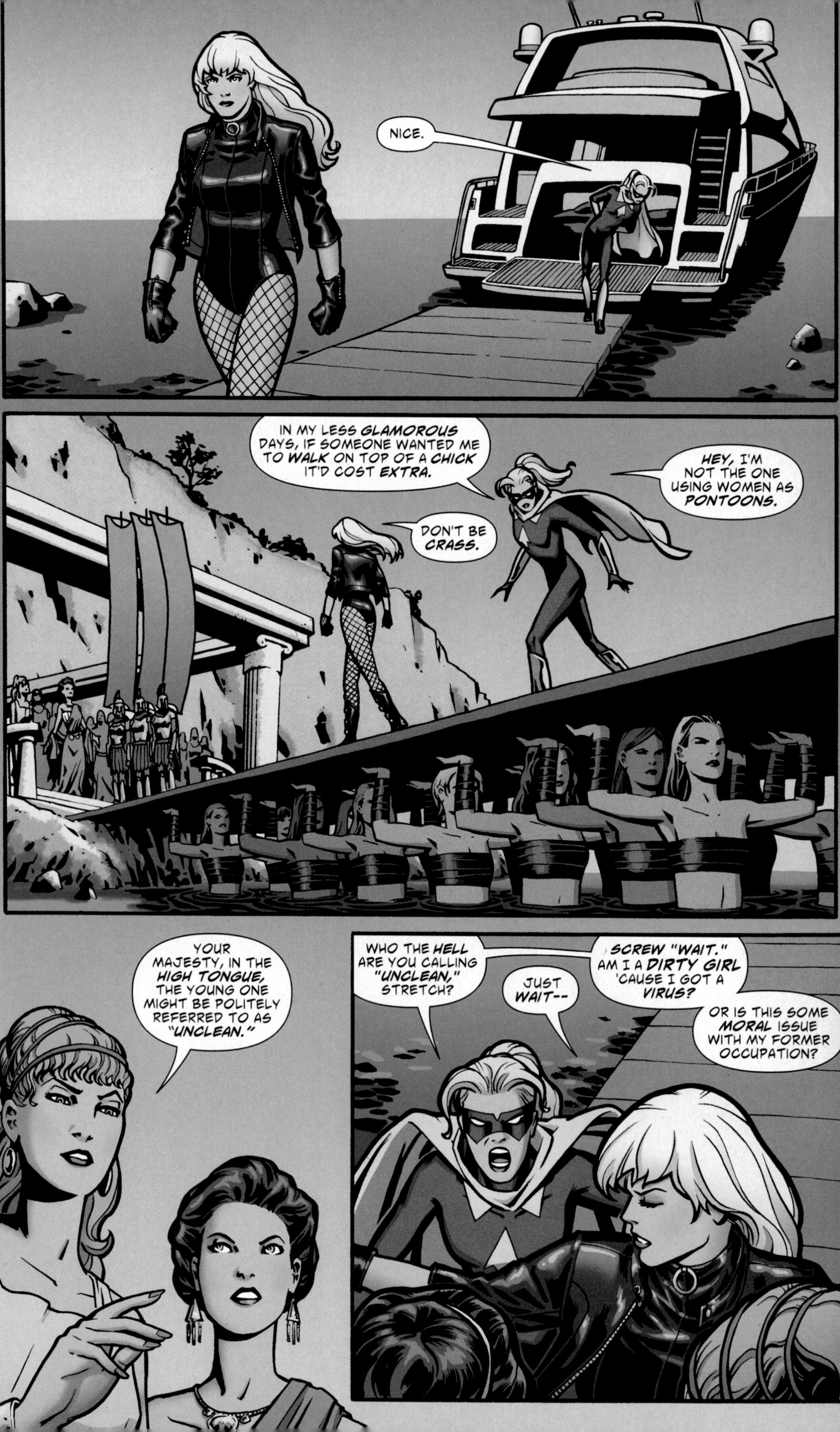
NICE.
IN MY LESS GLAMOROUS DAYS, IF SOMEONE WANTED ME TO WALK ON TOP OF A CHICK IT'D COST EXTRA.
HEY, I'M NOT THE ONE USING WOMEN AS PONTOONS.
DON'T BE CRASS.
YOUR MAJESTY, IN THE HIGH TONGUE, THE YOUNG ONE MIGHT BE POLITELY REFERRED TO AS "UNCLEAN."
WHO THE HELL ARE YOU CALLING "UNCLEAN," STRETCH?
JUST WAIT--
SCREW "WAIT." AM I A DIRTY GIRL 'CAUSE I GOT A VIRUS?
OR IS THIS SOME MORAL ISSUE WITH MY FORMER OCCUPATION?

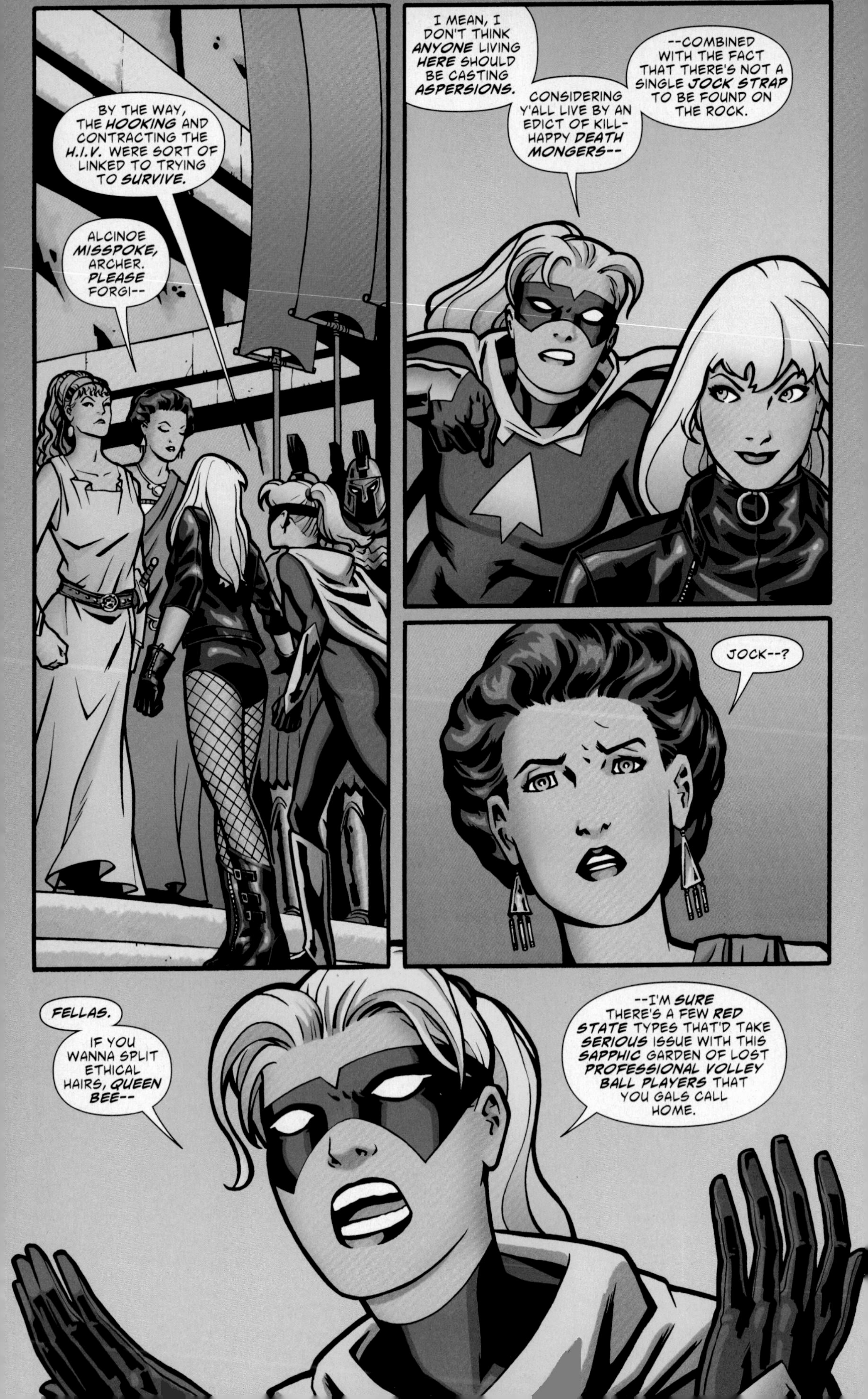
BY THE WAY, THE HOOKING AND CONTRACTING THE H.I.V. WERE SORT OF LINKED TO TRYING TO SURVIVE.
ALCINOE MISSPOKE, ARCHER. PLEASE FORGI--
I MEAN, I DON'T THINK ANYONE LIVING HERE SHOULD BE CASTING ASPERSIONS.
CONSIDERING Y'ALL LIVE BY AN EDICT OF KILL-HAPPY DEATH MONGERS--
--COMBINED WITH THE FACT THAT THERE'S NOT A SINGLE JOCK STRAP TO BE FOUND ON THE ROCK.
JOCK--?
FELLAS.
IF YOU WANNA SPLIT ETHICAL HAIRS, QUEEN BEE--
--I'M SURE THERE'S A FEW RED STATE TYPES THAT'D TAKE SERIOUS ISSUE WITH THIS SAPPHIC GARDEN OF LOST PROFESSIONAL VOLLEY BALL PLAYERS THAT YOU GALS CALL HOME.

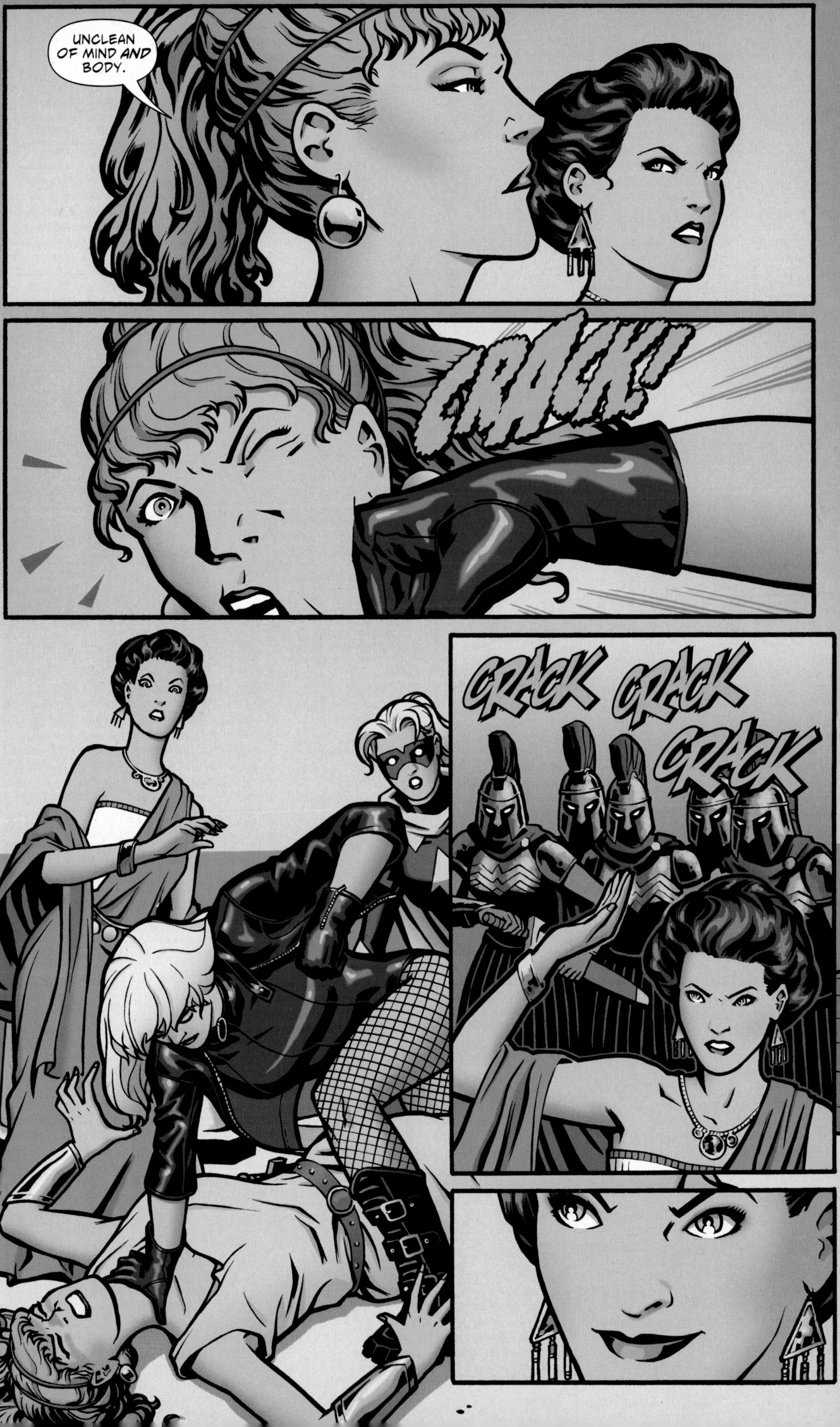
UNCLEAN OF MIND AND BODY.
CRACK!
CRACK CRACK CRACK

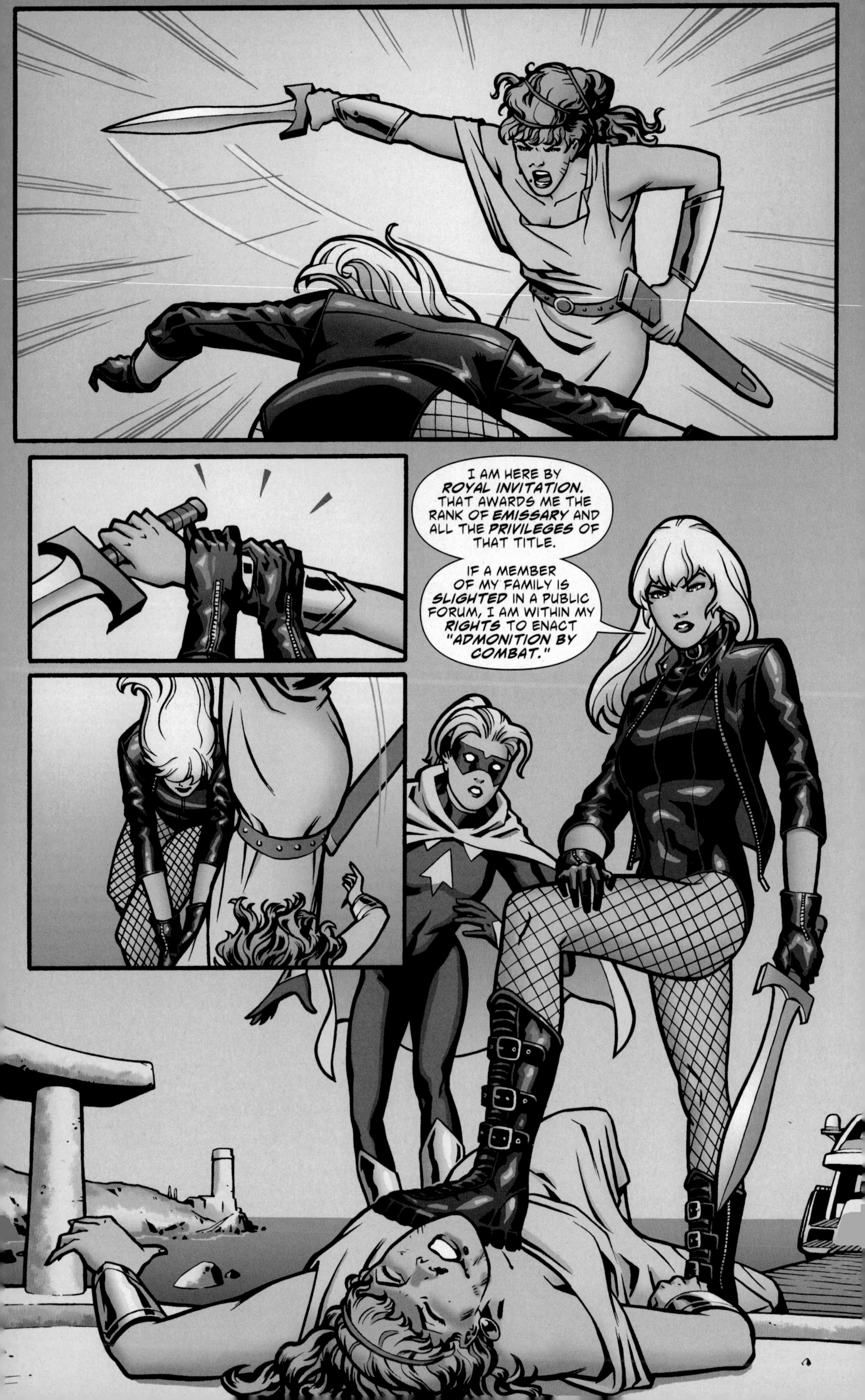
I AM HERE BY ROYAL INVITATION. THAT AWARDS ME THE RANK OF EMISSARY AND ALL THE PRIVILEGES OF THAT TITLE.
IF A MEMBER OF MY FAMILY IS SLIGHTED IN A PUBLIC FORUM, I AM WITHIN MY RIGHTS TO ENACT "ADMONITION BY COMBAT."

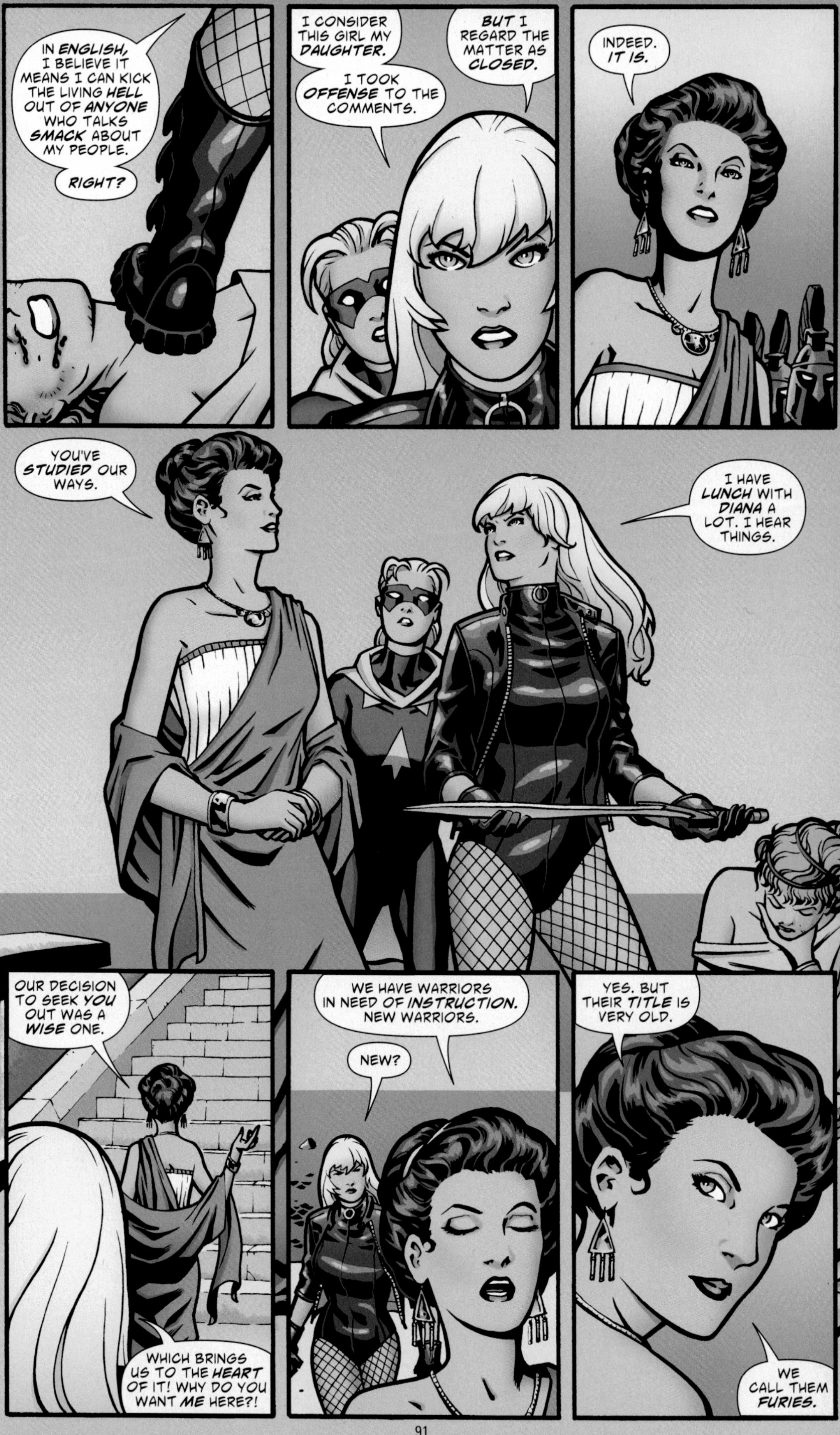

IN ENGLISH, I BELIEVE IT MEANS I CAN KICK THE LIVING HELL OUT OF ANYONE WHO TALKS SMACK ABOUT MY PEOPLE.
RIGHT?
I CONSIDER THIS GIRL MY DAUGHTER.
I TOOK OFFENSE TO THE COMMENTS.
BUT I REGARD THE MATTER AS CLOSED.
INDEED. IT IS.
YOU'VE STUDIED OUR WAYS.
I HAVE LUNCH WITH DIANA A LOT. I HEAR THINGS.
OUR DECISION TO SEEK YOU OUT WAS A WISE ONE.
WHICH BRINGS US TO THE HEART OF IT! WHY DO YOU WANT ME HERE?!
WE HAVE WARRIORS IN NEED OF INSTRUCTION. NEW WARRIORS.
NEW?
YES. BUT THEIR TITLE IS VERY OLD.
WE CALL THEM FURIES.

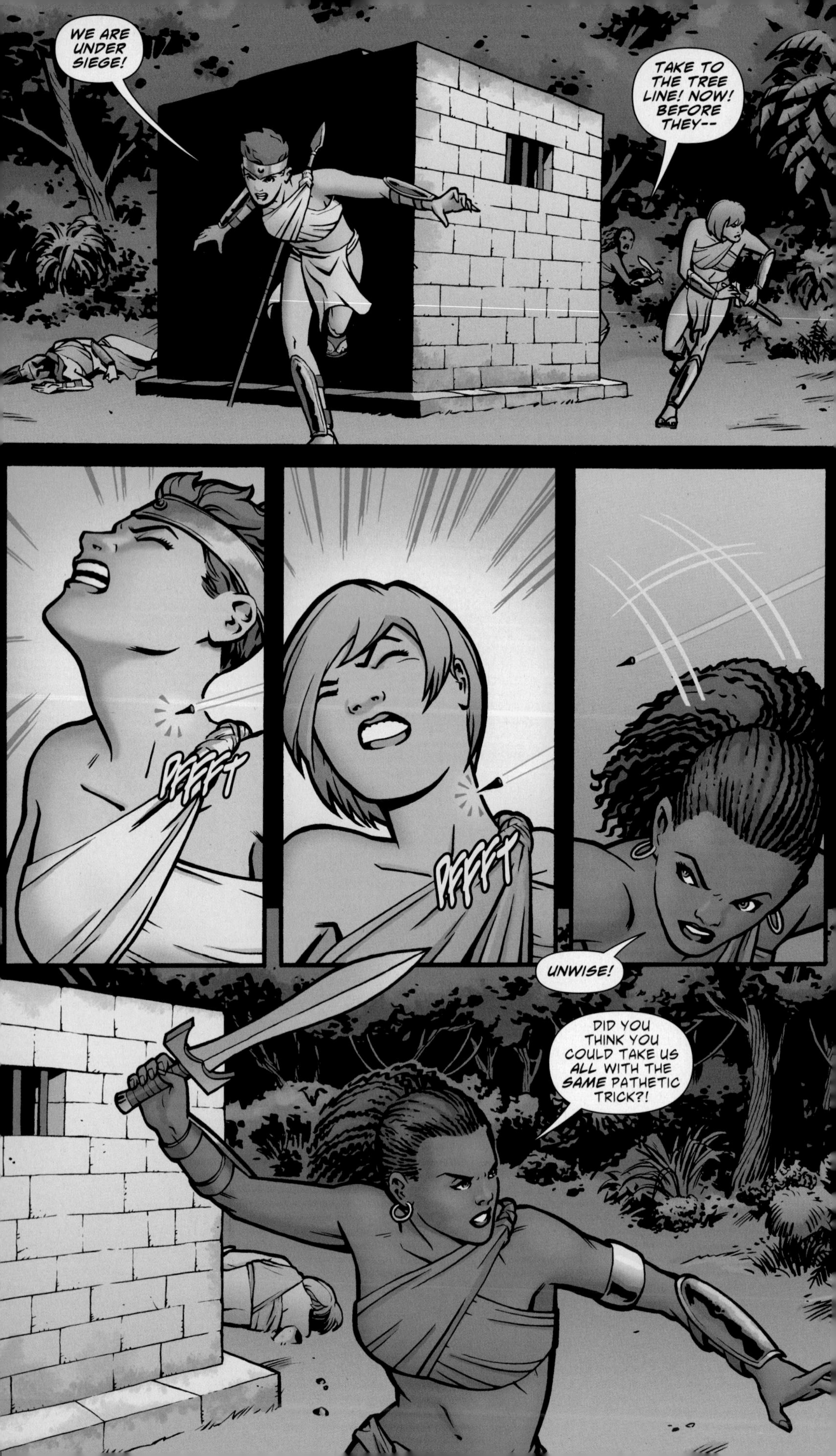
WE ARE UNDER SIEGE!
TAKE TO THE TREE LINE! NOW! BEFORE THEY--
PFFFT
PFFFT
UNWISE!
DID YOU THINK YOU COULD TAKE US ALL WITH THE SAME PATHETIC TRICK?!

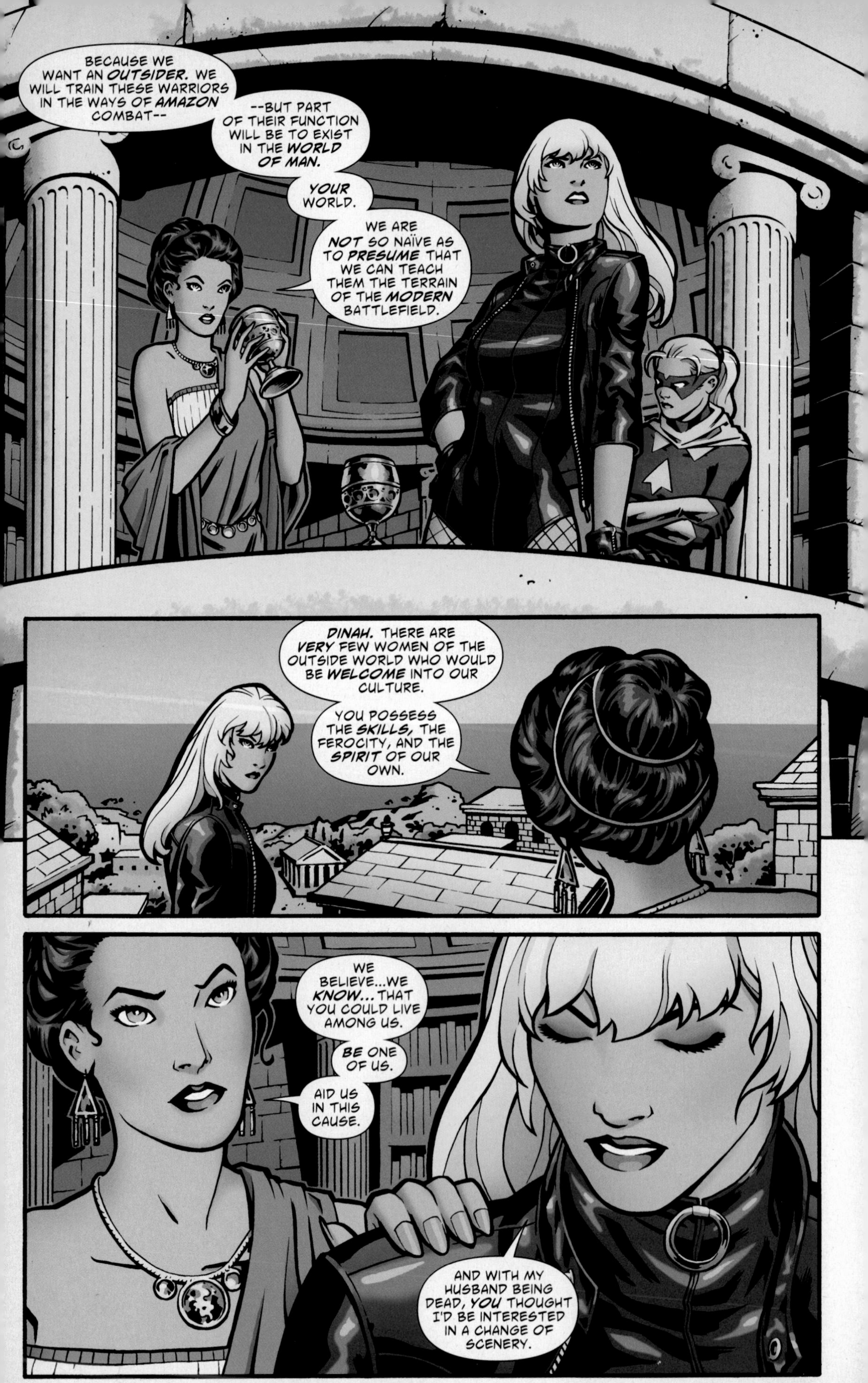
BECAUSE WE WANT AN OUTSIDER. WE WILL TRAIN THESE WARRIORS IN THE WAYS OF AMAZON COMBAT--
--BUT PART OF THEIR FUNCTION WILL BE TO EXIST IN THE WORLD OF MAN.
YOUR WORLD.
WE ARE NOT SO NAÏVE AS TO PRESUME THAT WE CAN TEACH THEM THE TERRAIN OF THE MODERN BATTLEFIELD.
DINAH. THERE ARE VERY FEW WOMEN OF THE OUTSIDE WORLD WHO WOULD BE WELCOME INTO OUR CULTURE.
YOU POSSESS THE SKILLS, THE FEROCITY, AND THE SPIRIT OF OUR OWN.
WE BELIEVE...WE KNOW... THAT YOU COULD LIVE AMONG US.
BE ONE OF US.
AID US IN THIS CAUSE.
AND WITH MY HUSBAND BEING DEAD, YOU THOUGHT I'D BE INTERESTED IN A CHANGE OF SCENERY.

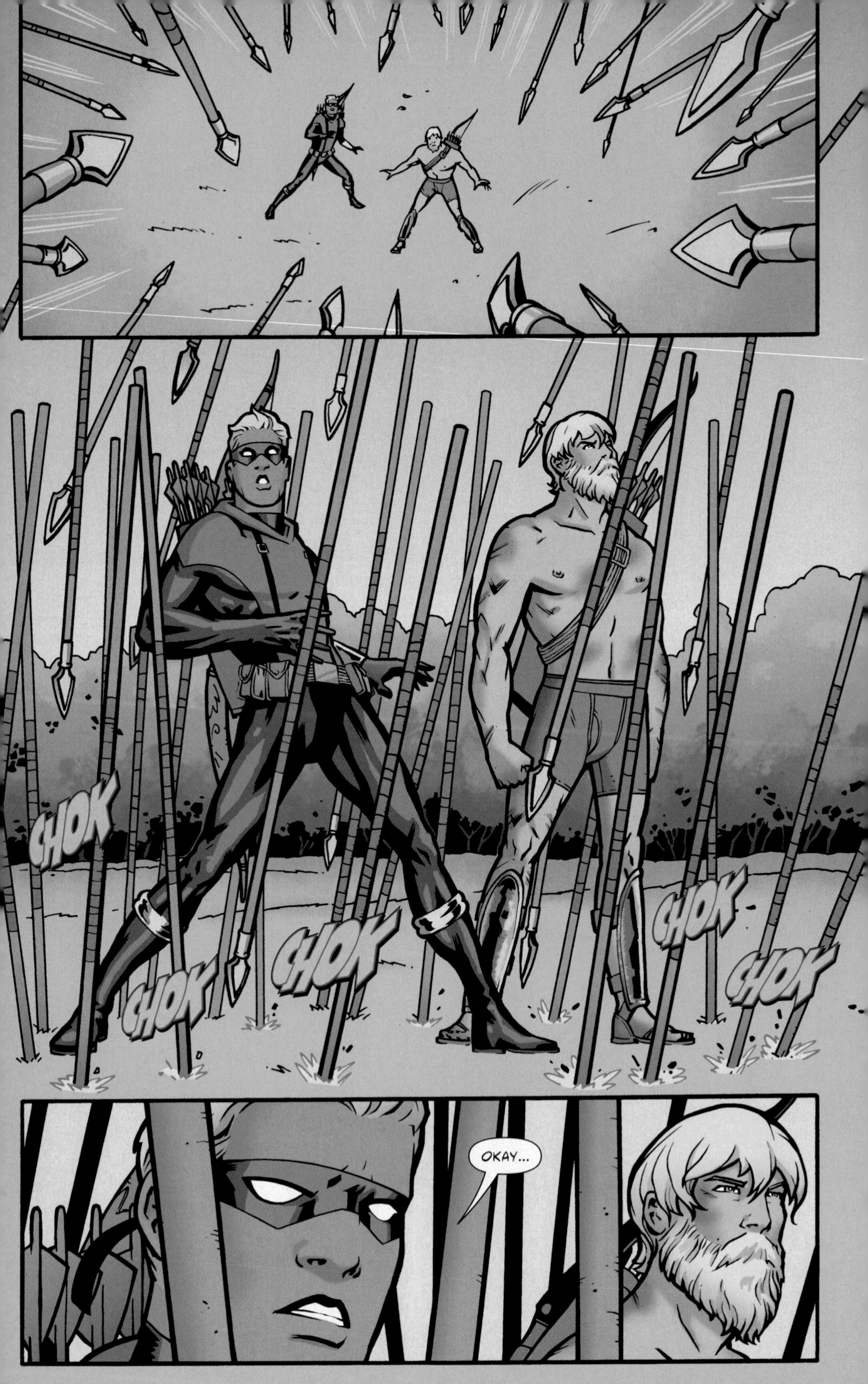
CHOK
CHOK
CHOK
CHOK
CHOK
OKAY...

GREEN ARROW AND BLACK CANARY #3 *Cliff Chiang*

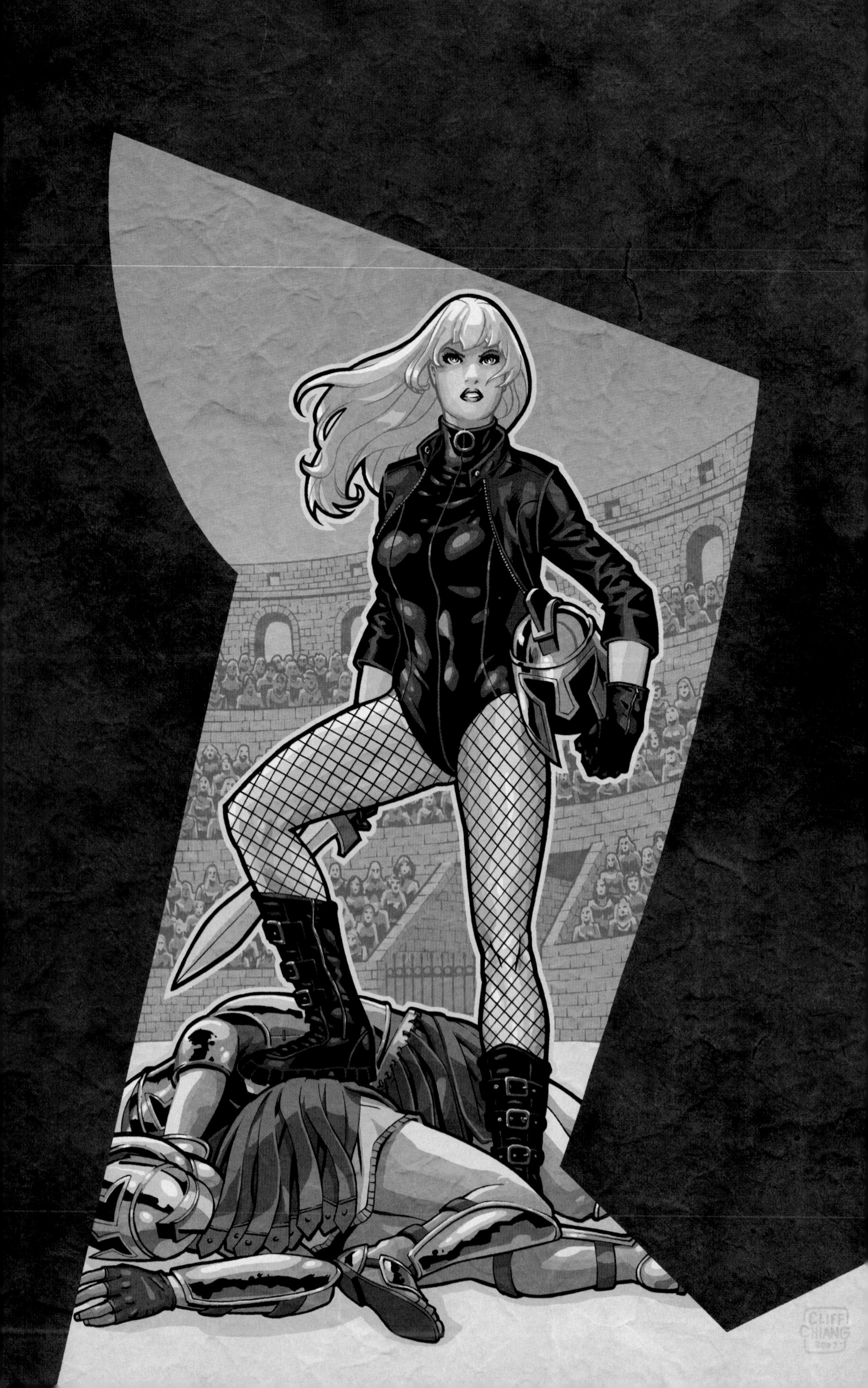
CLIFF CHIANG 2007

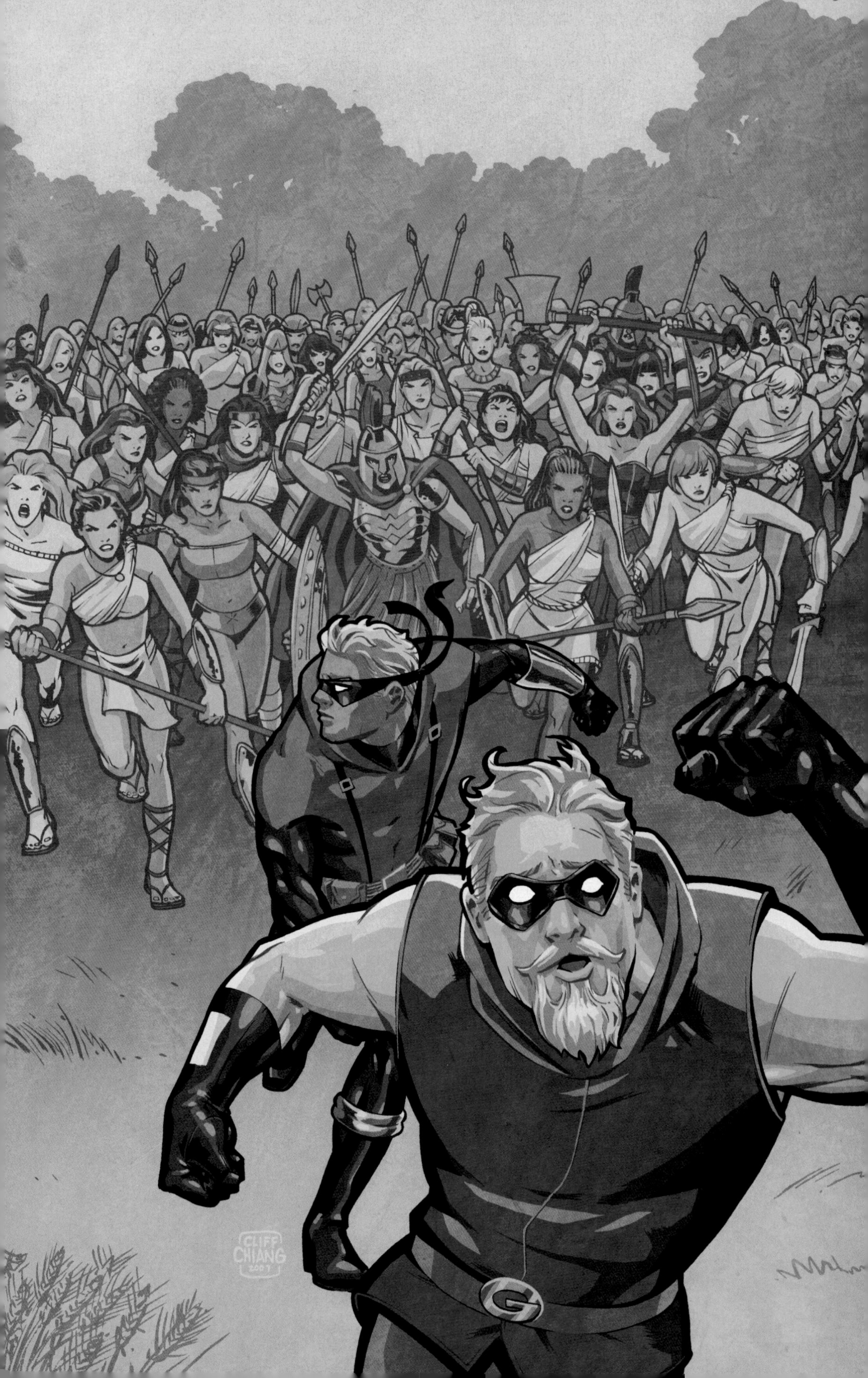
CLIFF
CHIANG
2007

DEAD AGAIN PART THREE: HIT AND RUN, RUN, RUN!

Story: **Judd Winick**   *Art:* **Cliff Chiang**   *Color:* **Trish Mulvihill**

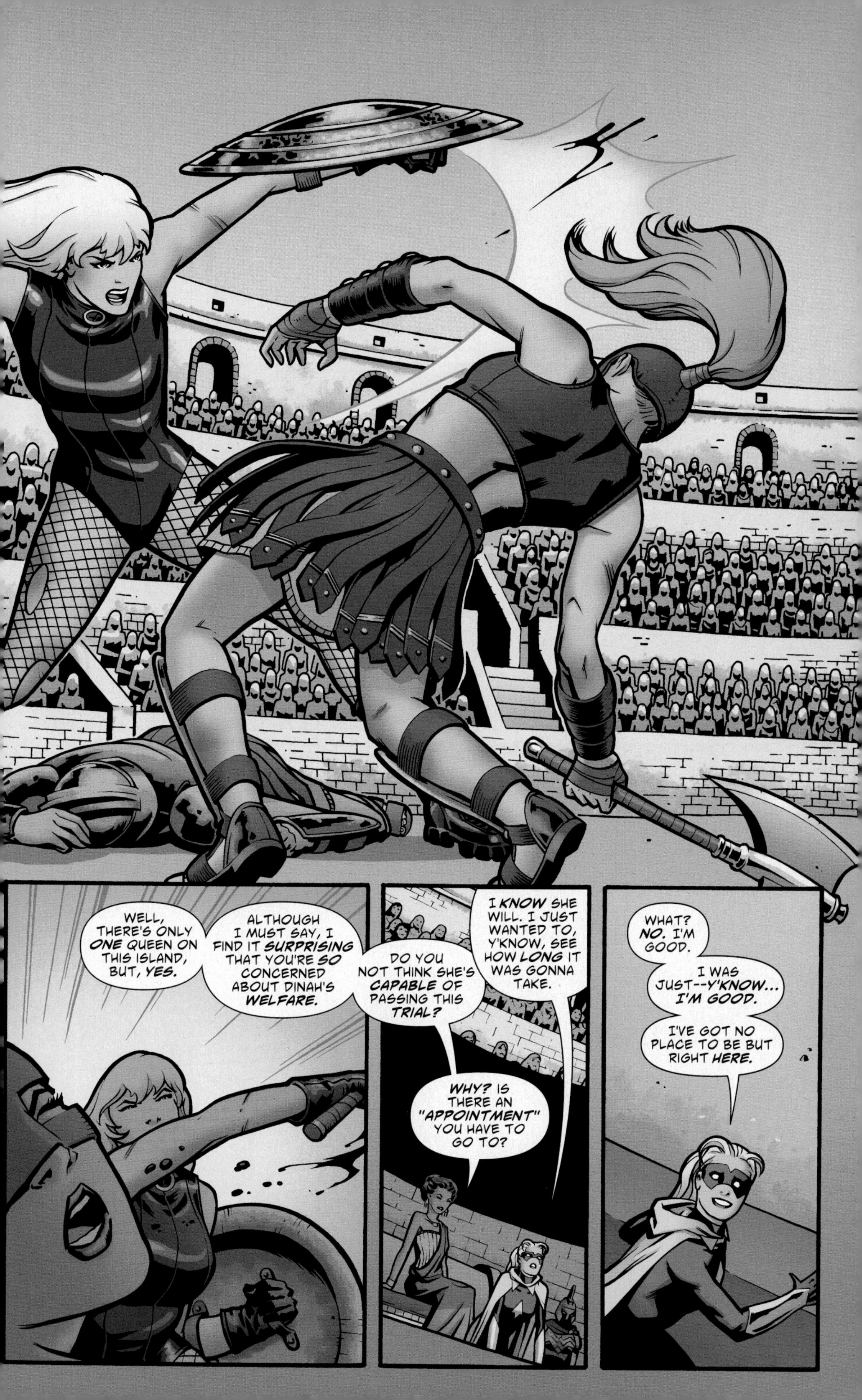
WELL, THERE'S ONLY ONE QUEEN ON THIS ISLAND, BUT, YES.
ALTHOUGH I MUST SAY, I FIND IT SURPRISING THAT YOU'RE SO CONCERNED ABOUT DINAH'S WELFARE.
I KNOW SHE WILL. I JUST WANTED TO, Y'KNOW, SEE HOW LONG IT WAS GONNA TAKE.
DO YOU NOT THINK SHE'S CAPABLE OF PASSING THIS TRIAL?
WHY? IS THERE AN "APPOINTMENT" YOU HAVE TO GO TO?
WHAT? NO. I'M GOOD.
I WAS JUST--Y'KNOW... I'M GOOD.
I'VE GOT NO PLACE TO BE BUT RIGHT HERE.

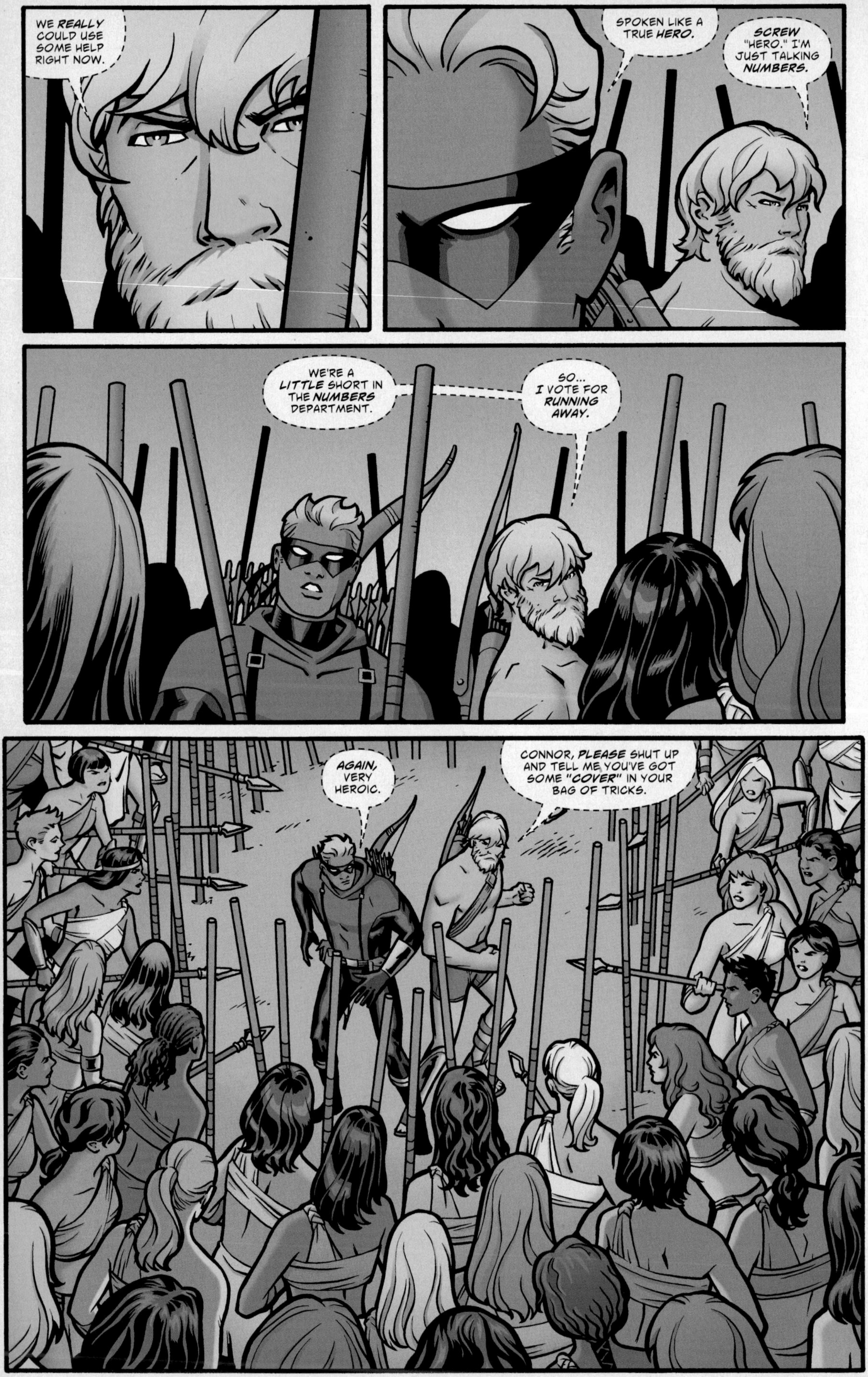
WE REALLY COULD USE SOME HELP RIGHT NOW.
SPOKEN LIKE A TRUE HERO.
SCREW "HERO." I'M JUST TALKING NUMBERS.
WE'RE A LITTLE SHORT IN THE NUMBERS DEPARTMENT.
SO... I VOTE FOR RUNNING AWAY.
AGAIN, VERY HEROIC.
CONNOR, PLEASE SHUT UP AND TELL ME YOU'VE GOT SOME "COVER" IN YOUR BAG OF TRICKS.

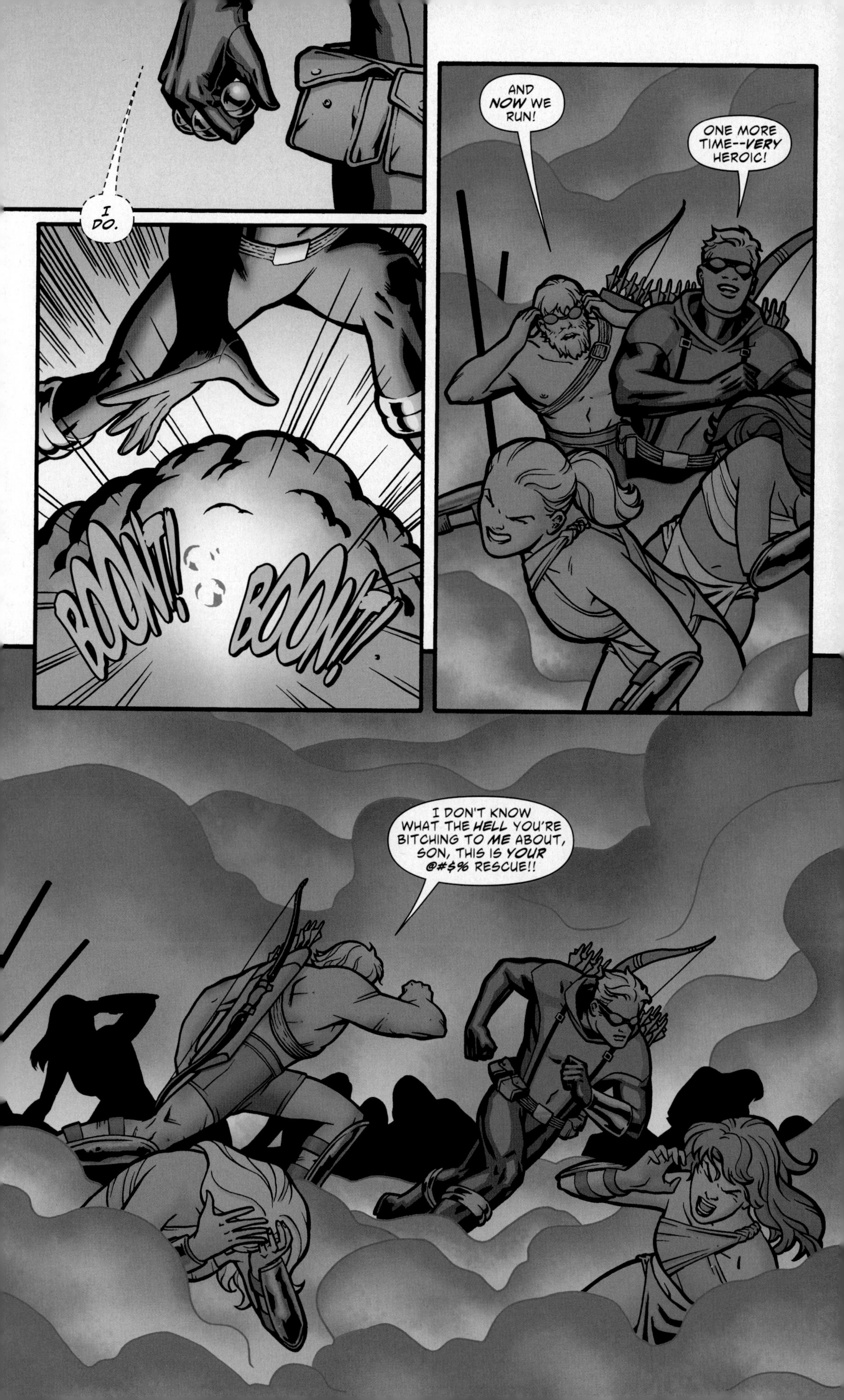

I DO.
BOOM!!
BOOM!!
AND NOW WE RUN!
ONE MORE TIME--VERY HEROIC!
I DON'T KNOW WHAT THE HELL YOU'RE BITCHING TO ME ABOUT, SON, THIS IS YOUR @#$% RESCUE!!

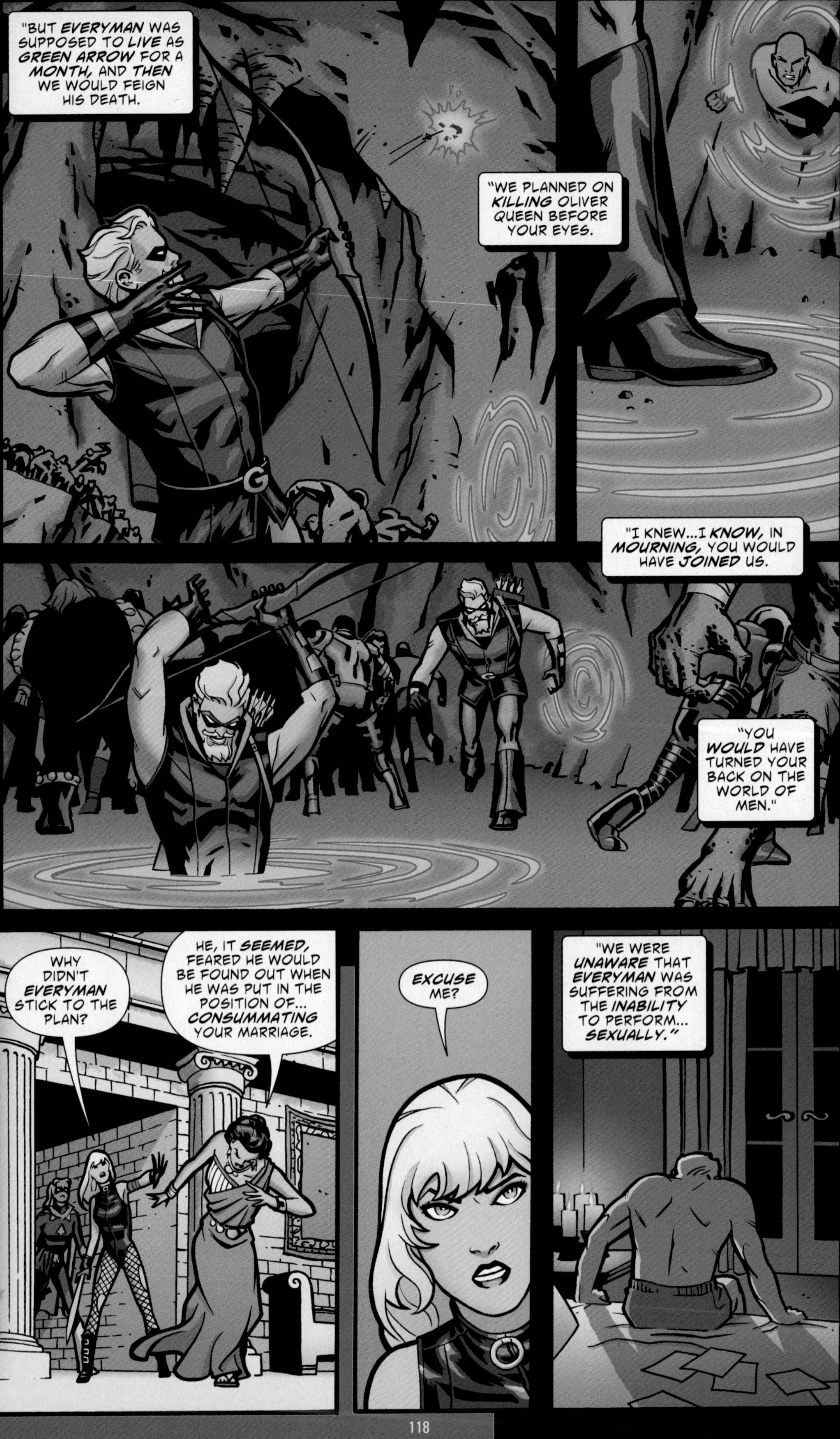

"BUT EVERYMAN WAS SUPPOSED TO LIVE AS GREEN ARROW FOR A MONTH, AND THEN WE WOULD FEIGN HIS DEATH.
"WE PLANNED ON KILLING OLIVER QUEEN BEFORE YOUR EYES.
"I KNEW...I KNOW, IN MOURNING, YOU WOULD HAVE JOINED US.
"YOU WOULD HAVE TURNED YOUR BACK ON THE WORLD OF MEN."
WHY DIDN'T EVERYMAN STICK TO THE PLAN?
HE, IT SEEMED, FEARED HE WOULD BE FOUND OUT WHEN HE WAS PUT IN THE POSITION OF... CONSUMMATING YOUR MARRIAGE.
EXCUSE ME?
"WE WERE UNAWARE THAT EVERYMAN WAS SUFFERING FROM THE INABILITY TO PERFORM... SEXUALLY."

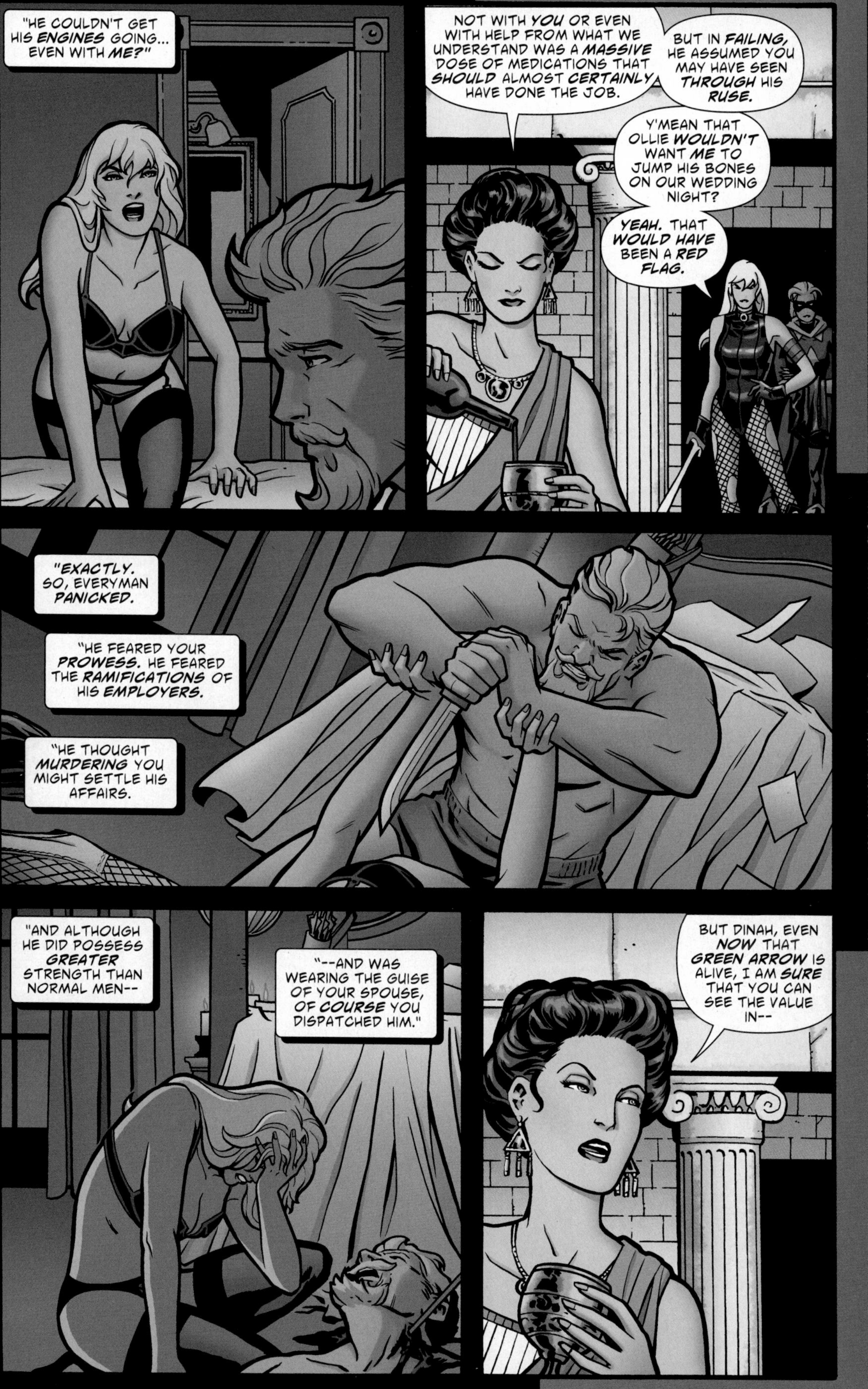
"HE COULDN'T GET HIS ENGINES GOING... EVEN WITH ME?"
NOT WITH YOU OR EVEN WITH HELP FROM WHAT WE UNDERSTAND WAS A MASSIVE DOSE OF MEDICATIONS THAT SHOULD ALMOST CERTAINLY HAVE DONE THE JOB.
BUT IN FAILING, HE ASSUMED YOU MAY HAVE SEEN THROUGH HIS RUSE.
Y'MEAN THAT OLLIE WOULDN'T WANT ME TO JUMP HIS BONES ON OUR WEDDING NIGHT?
YEAH. THAT WOULD HAVE BEEN A RED FLAG.
"EXACTLY. SO, EVERYMAN PANICKED.
"HE FEARED YOUR PROWESS. HE FEARED THE RAMIFICATIONS OF HIS EMPLOYERS.
"HE THOUGHT MURDERING YOU MIGHT SETTLE HIS AFFAIRS.
"AND ALTHOUGH HE DID POSSESS GREATER STRENGTH THAN NORMAL MEN--
"--AND WAS WEARING THE GUISE OF YOUR SPOUSE, OF COURSE YOU DISPATCHED HIM."
BUT DINAH, EVEN NOW THAT GREEN ARROW IS ALIVE, I AM SURE THAT YOU CAN SEE THE VALUE IN--

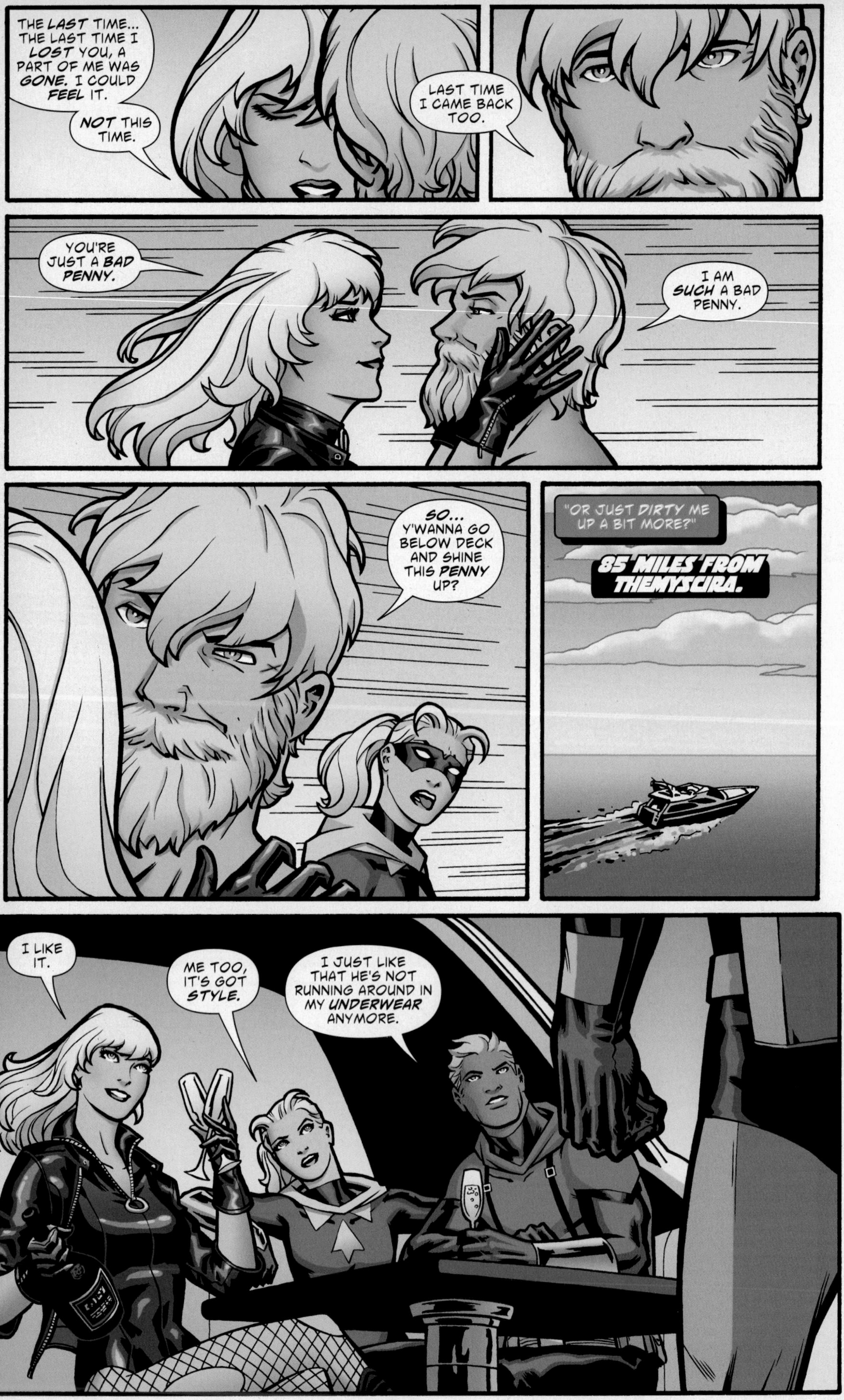
THE LAST TIME... THE LAST TIME I LOST YOU, A PART OF ME WAS GONE. I COULD FEEL IT.
NOT THIS TIME.
LAST TIME I CAME BACK TOO.
YOU'RE JUST A BAD PENNY.
I AM SUCH A BAD PENNY.
SO... Y'WANNA GO BELOW DECK AND SHINE THIS PENNY UP?
"OR JUST DIRTY ME UP A BIT MORE?"
85 MILES FROM THEMYSCIRA.
I LIKE IT.
ME TOO, IT'S GOT STYLE.
I JUST LIKE THAT HE'S NOT RUNNING AROUND IN MY UNDERWEAR ANYMORE.

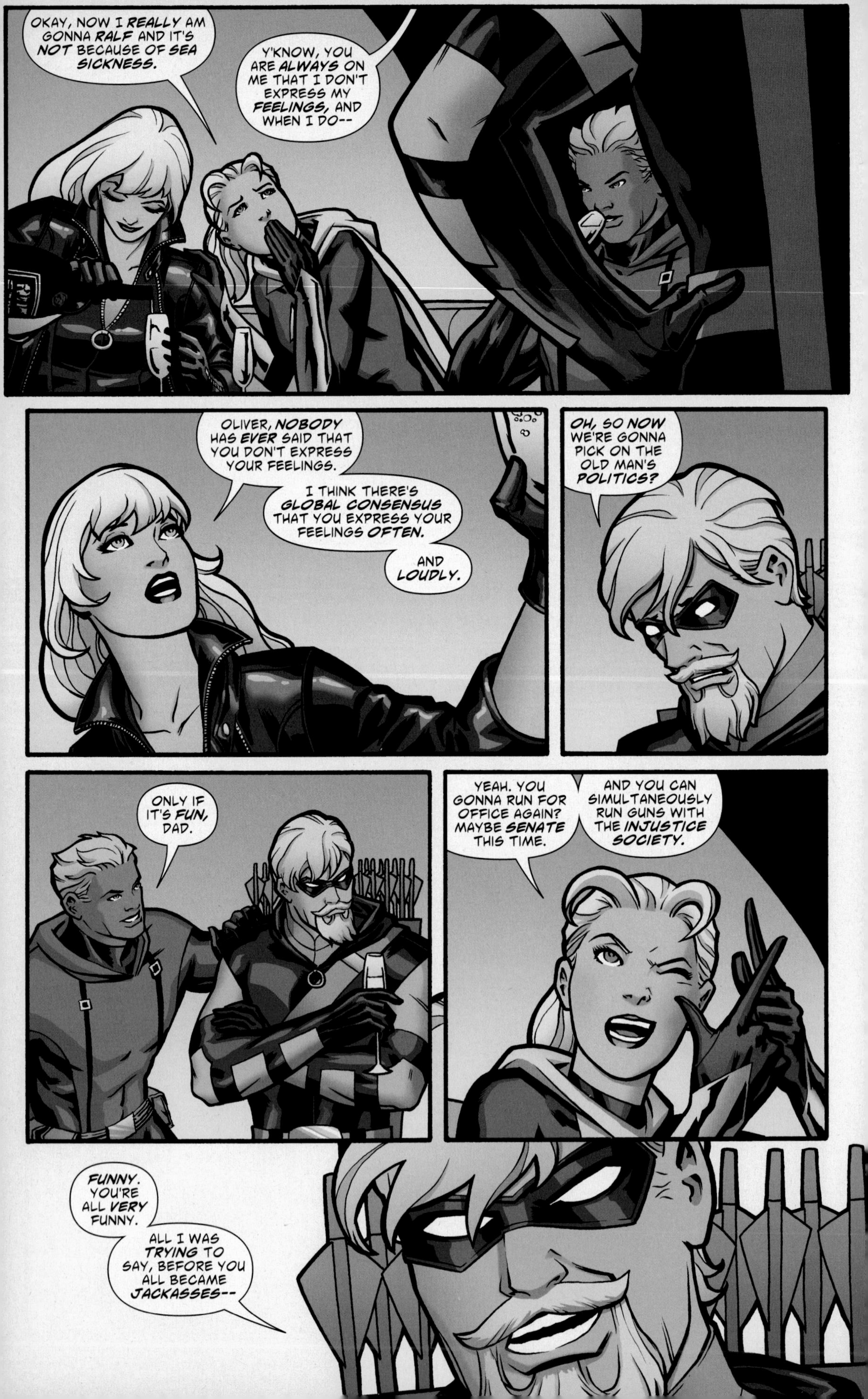
OKAY, NOW I REALLY AM GONNA RALF AND IT'S NOT BECAUSE OF SEA SICKNESS.
Y'KNOW, YOU ARE ALWAYS ON ME THAT I DON'T EXPRESS MY FEELINGS, AND WHEN I DO--
OLIVER, NOBODY HAS EVER SAID THAT YOU DON'T EXPRESS YOUR FEELINGS.
I THINK THERE'S GLOBAL CONSENSUS THAT YOU EXPRESS YOUR FEELINGS OFTEN.
AND LOUDLY.
OH, SO NOW WE'RE GONNA PICK ON THE OLD MAN'S POLITICS?
ONLY IF IT'S FUN, DAD.
YEAH. YOU GONNA RUN FOR OFFICE AGAIN? MAYBE SENATE THIS TIME.
AND YOU CAN SIMULTANEOUSLY RUN GUNS WITH THE INJUSTICE SOCIETY.
FUNNY. YOU'RE ALL VERY FUNNY.
ALL I WAS TRYING TO SAY, BEFORE YOU ALL BECAME JACKASSES--

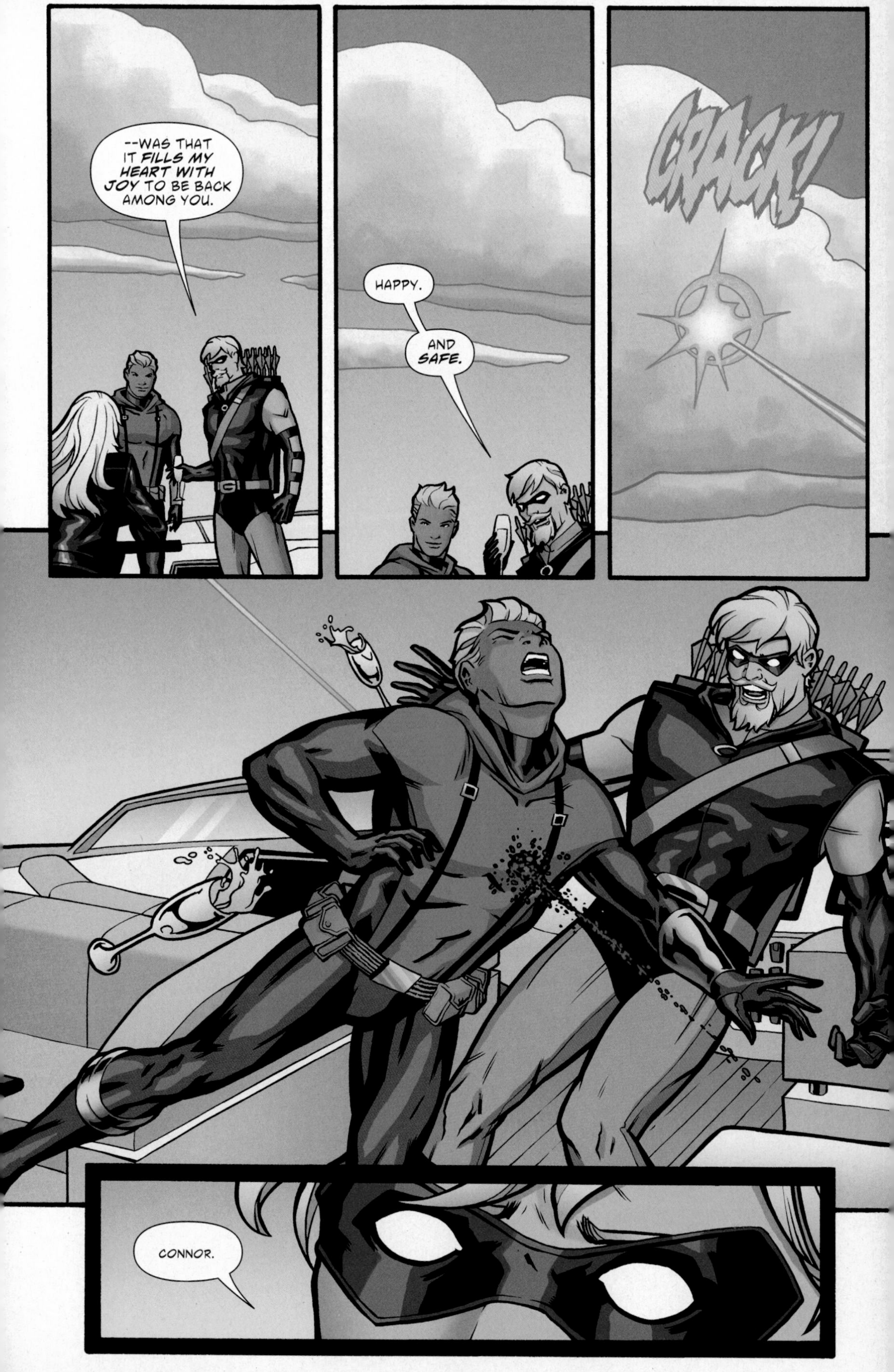
--WAS THAT IT FILLS MY HEART WITH JOY TO BE BACK AMONG YOU.
HAPPY.
AND SAFE.
CRACK!
CONNOR.

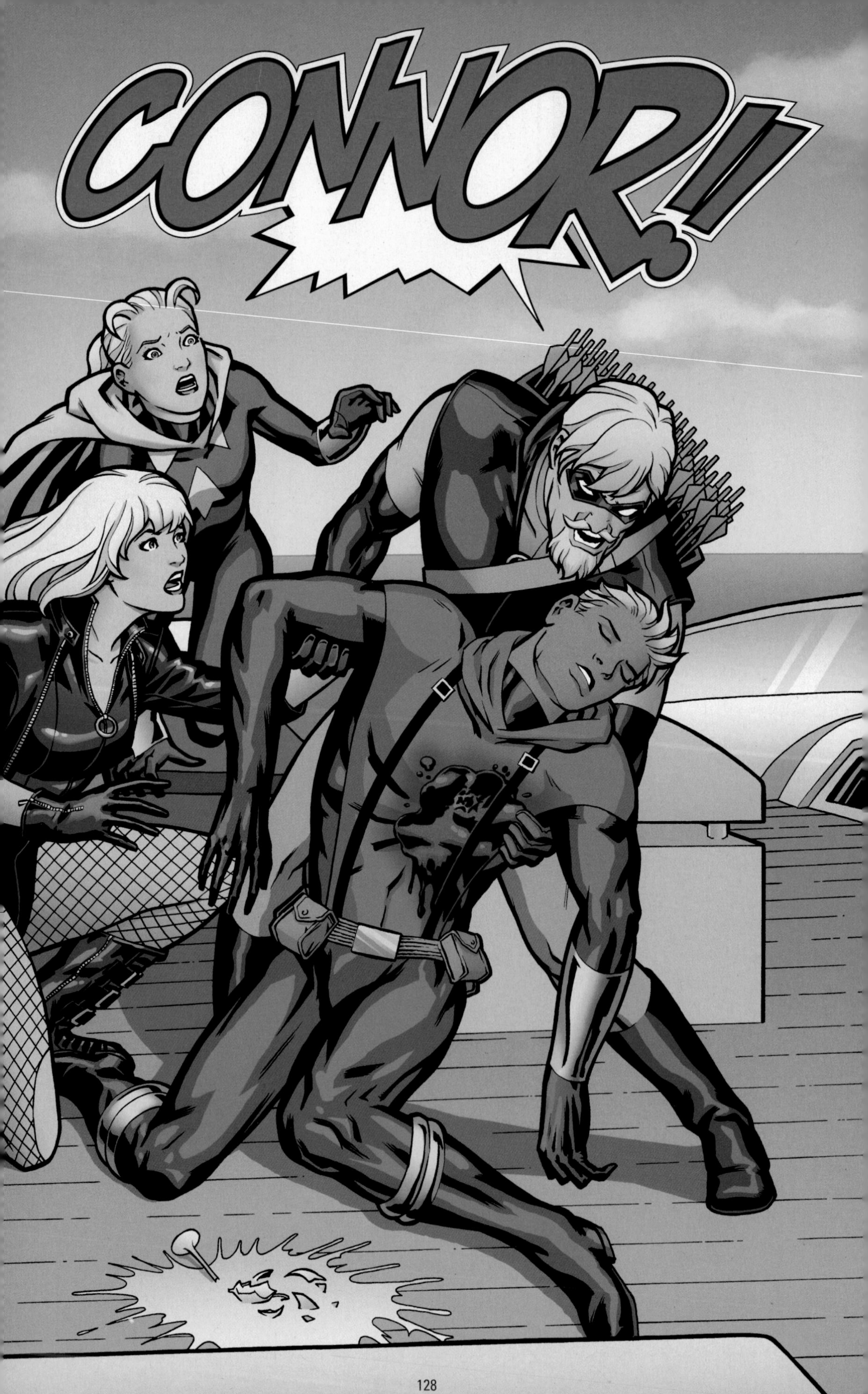
CONNOR!!

GREEN ARROW AND BLACK CANARY #4 *Cliff Chiang*

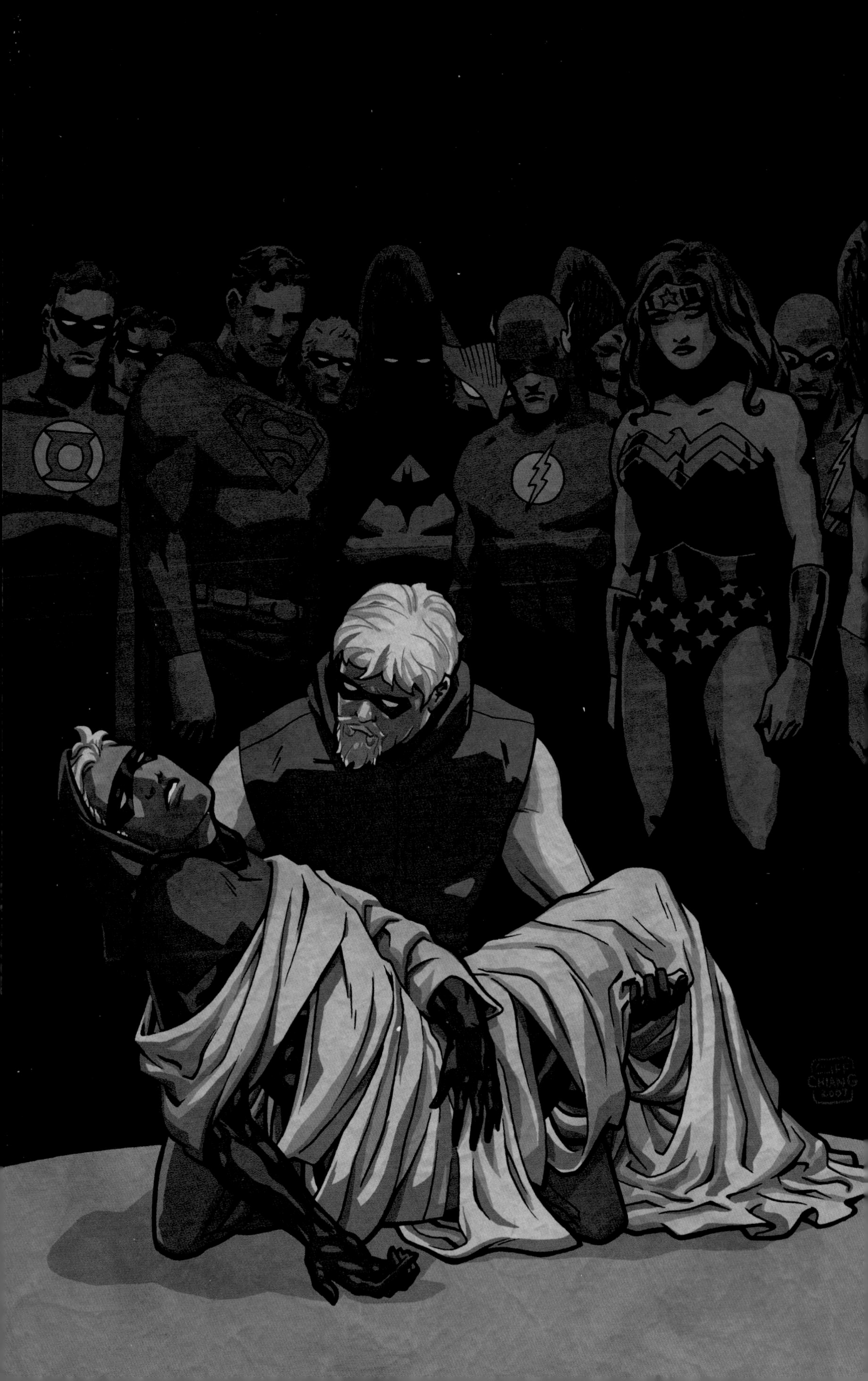
CHIANG

DEAD AGAIN CONCLUSION: PLEASE PLAY WHERE DADDY CAN SEE YOU.

Story: **Judd Winick** *Art:* **Cliff Chiang** *Color:* **Trish Mulvihill**

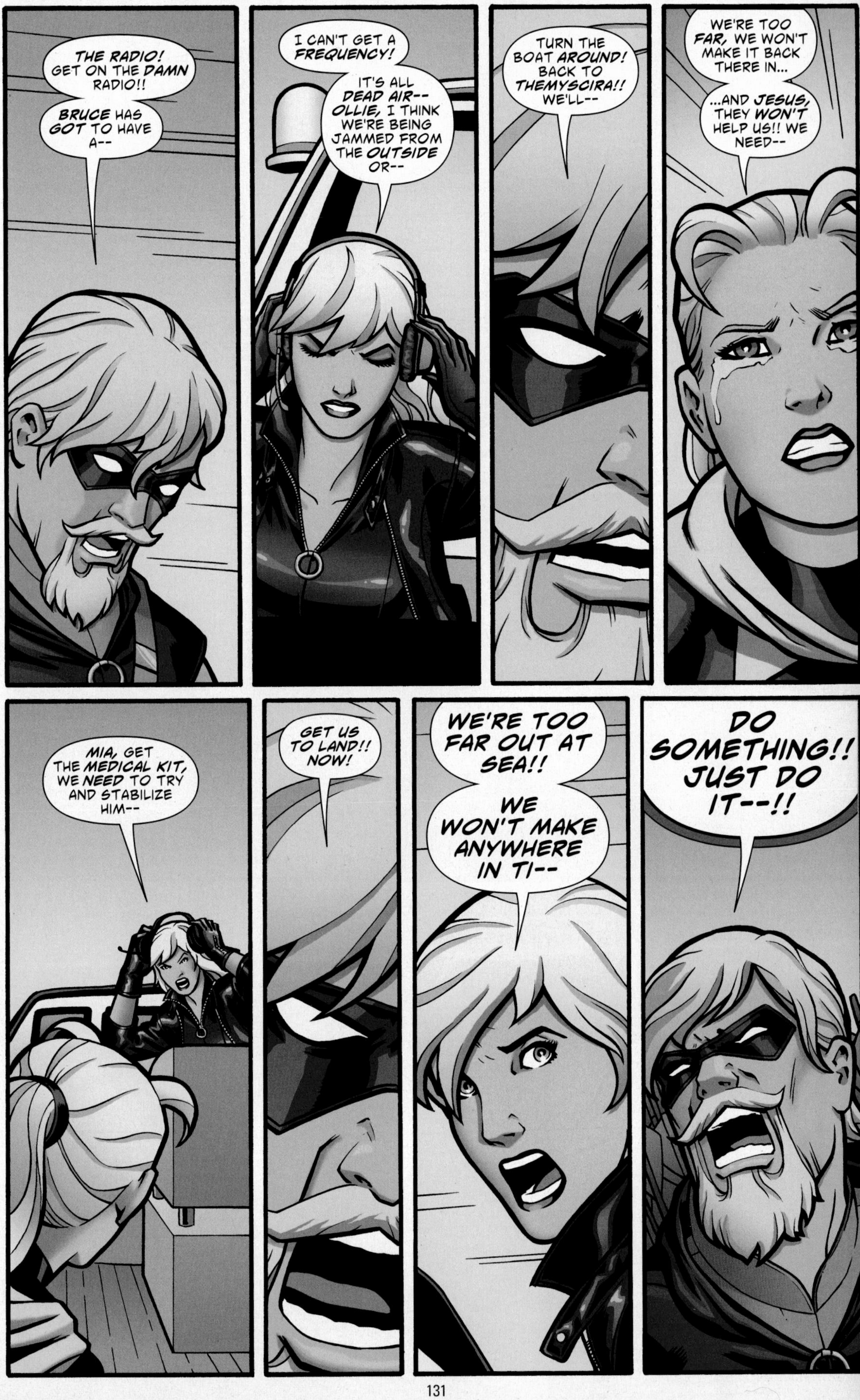
THE RADIO! GET ON THE DAMN RADIO!!
BRUCE HAS GOT TO HAVE A--
I CAN'T GET A FREQUENCY!
IT'S ALL DEAD AIR-- OLLIE, I THINK WE'RE BEING JAMMED FROM THE OUTSIDE OR--
TURN THE BOAT AROUND! BACK TO THEMYSCIRA!! WE'LL--
WE'RE TOO FAR, WE WON'T MAKE IT BACK THERE IN...
...AND JESUS, THEY WON'T HELP US!! WE NEED--
MIA, GET THE MEDICAL KIT, WE NEED TO TRY AND STABILIZE HIM--
GET US TO LAND!! NOW!
WE'RE TOO FAR OUT AT SEA!!
WE WON'T MAKE ANYWHERE IN TI--
DO SOMETHING!! JUST DO IT--!!

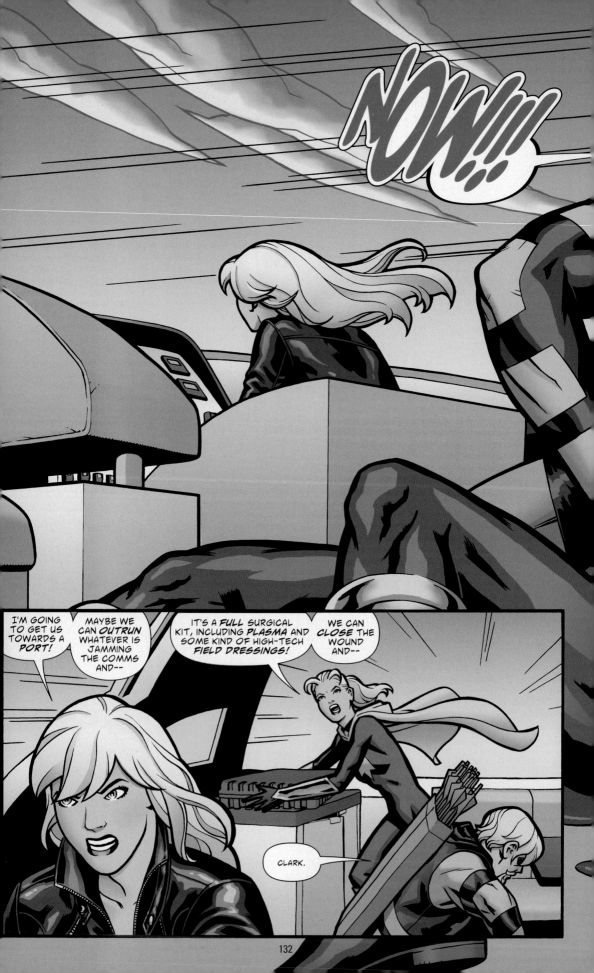

NOW!!!

I'M GOING TO GET US TOWARDS A PORT!

MAYBE WE CAN OUTRUN WHATEVER IS JAMMING THE COMMS AND--

IT'S A FULL SURGICAL KIT, INCLUDING PLASMA AND SOME KIND OF HIGH-TECH FIELD DRESSINGS!

WE CAN CLOSE THE WOUND AND--

CLARK.

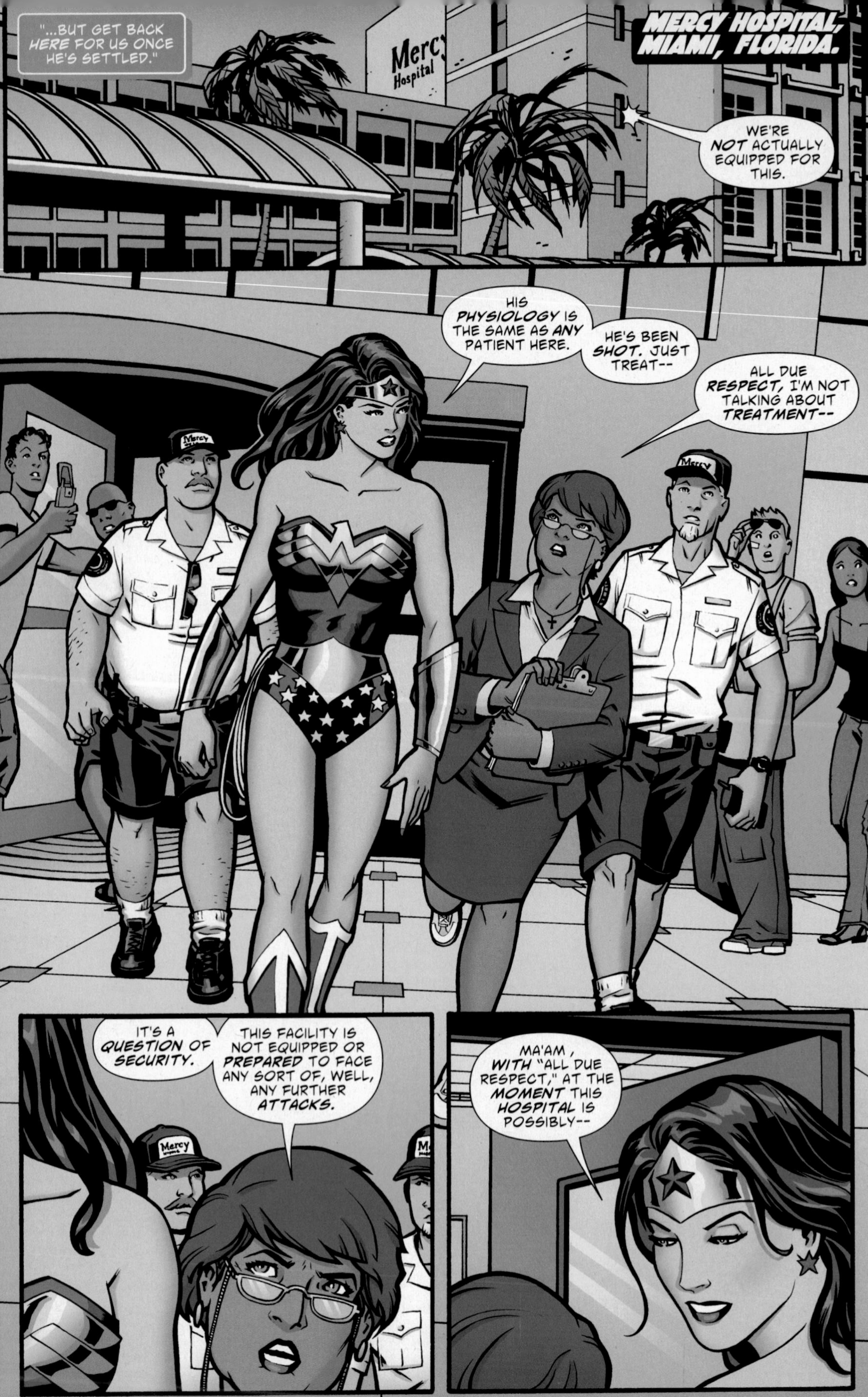
"...BUT GET BACK HERE FOR US ONCE HE'S SETTLED."
MERCY HOSPITAL, MIAMI, FLORIDA.
Mercy Hospital
WE'RE NOT ACTUALLY EQUIPPED FOR THIS.
HIS PHYSIOLOGY IS THE SAME AS ANY PATIENT HERE.
HE'S BEEN SHOT. JUST TREAT--
ALL DUE RESPECT, I'M NOT TALKING ABOUT TREATMENT--
Mercy
IT'S A QUESTION OF SECURITY.
THIS FACILITY IS NOT EQUIPPED OR PREPARED TO FACE ANY SORT OF, WELL, ANY FURTHER ATTACKS.
MA'AM, WITH "ALL DUE RESPECT," AT THE MOMENT THIS HOSPITAL IS POSSIBLY--

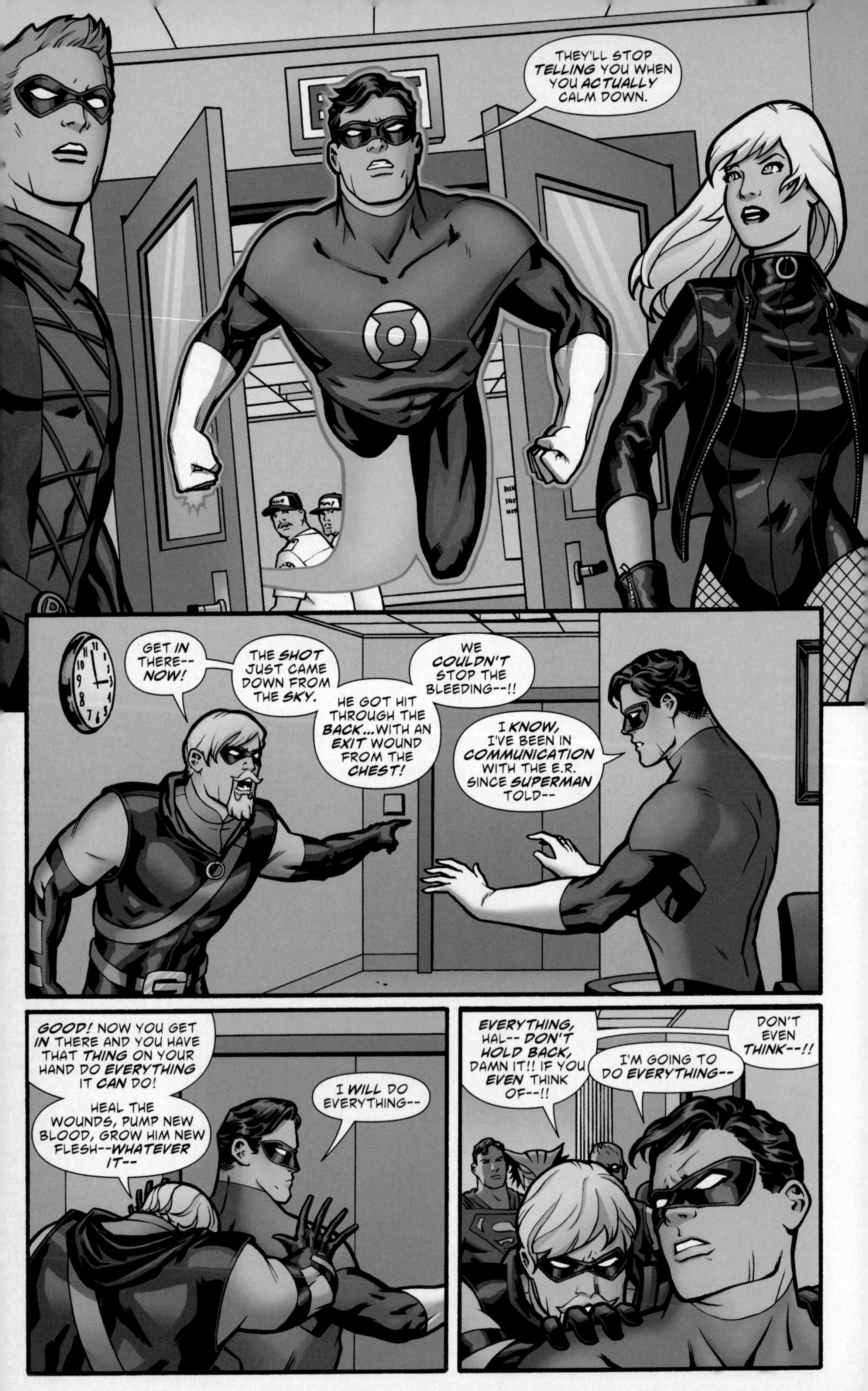
THEY'LL STOP TELLING YOU WHEN YOU ACTUALLY CALM DOWN.
GET IN THERE-- NOW!
THE SHOT JUST CAME DOWN FROM THE SKY.
HE GOT HIT THROUGH THE BACK...WITH AN EXIT WOUND FROM THE CHEST!
WE COULDN'T STOP THE BLEEDING--!!
I KNOW, I'VE BEEN IN COMMUNICATION WITH THE E.R. SINCE SUPERMAN TOLD--
GOOD! NOW YOU GET IN THERE AND YOU HAVE THAT THING ON YOUR HAND DO EVERYTHING IT CAN DO!
HEAL THE WOUNDS, PUMP NEW BLOOD, GROW HIM NEW FLESH--WHATEVER IT--
I WILL DO EVERYTHING--
EVERYTHING, HAL-- DON'T HOLD BACK, DAMN IT!! IF YOU EVEN THINK OF--!!
I'M GOING TO DO EVERYTHING--
DON'T EVEN THINK--!!

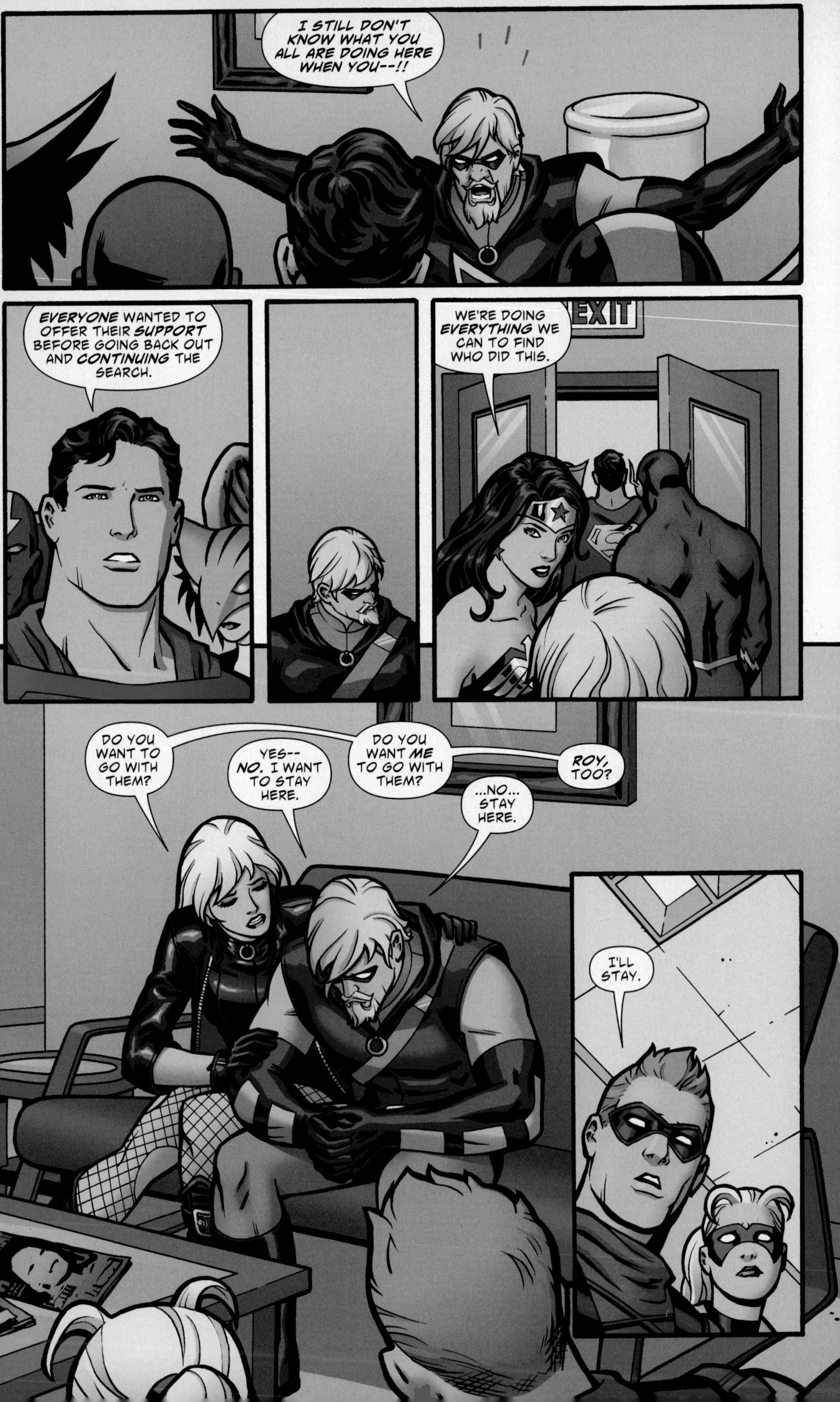
I STILL DON'T KNOW WHAT YOU ALL ARE DOING HERE WHEN YOU--!!
EVERYONE WANTED TO OFFER THEIR SUPPORT BEFORE GOING BACK OUT AND CONTINUING THE SEARCH.
WE'RE DOING EVERYTHING WE CAN TO FIND WHO DID THIS.
EXIT
DO YOU WANT TO GO WITH THEM?
YES-- NO. I WANT TO STAY HERE.
DO YOU WANT ME TO GO WITH THEM?
...NO... STAY HERE.
ROY, TOO?
I'LL STAY.

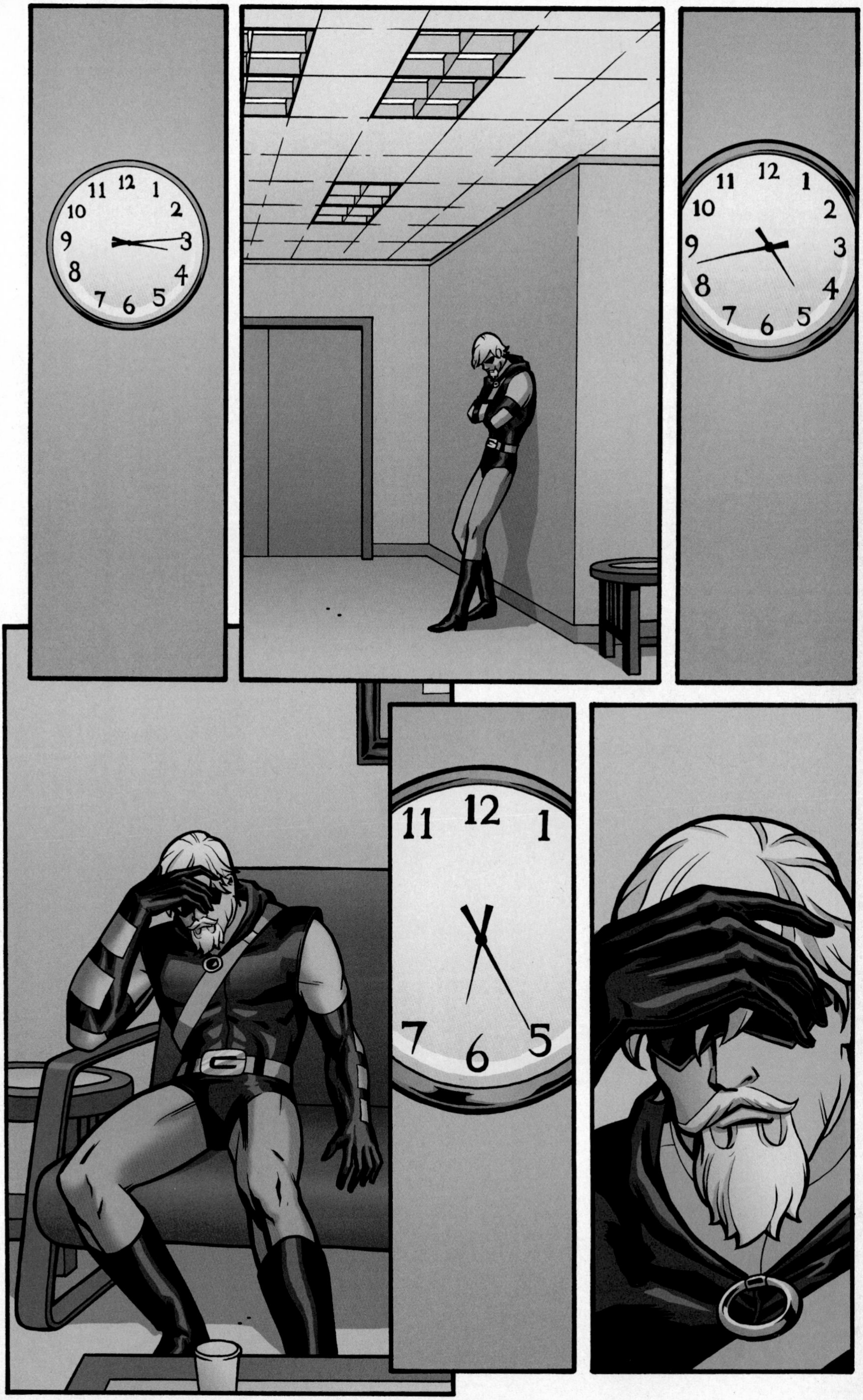

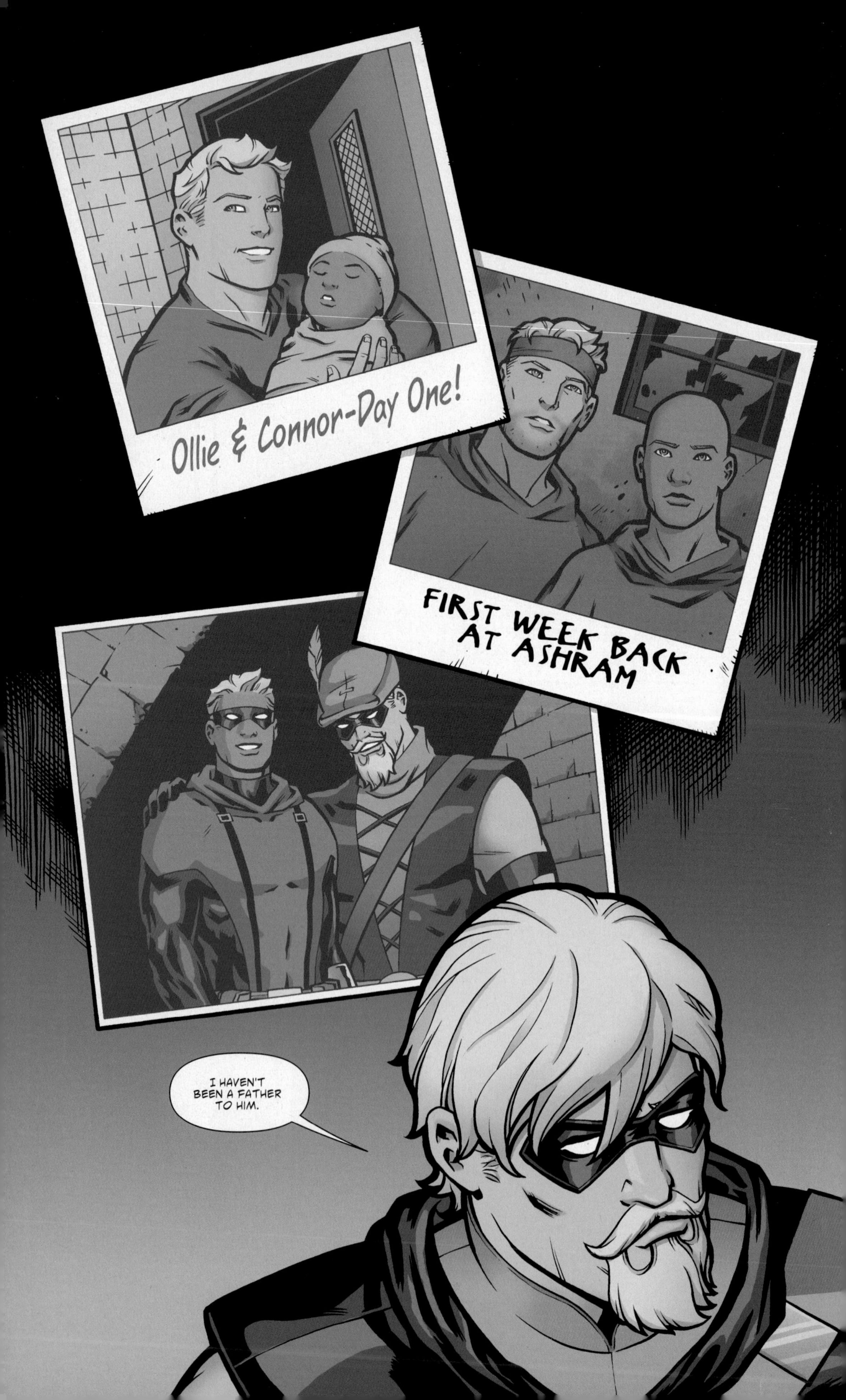
Ollie & Connor-Day One!
FIRST WEEK BACK AT ASHRAM
I HAVEN'T BEEN A FATHER TO HIM.

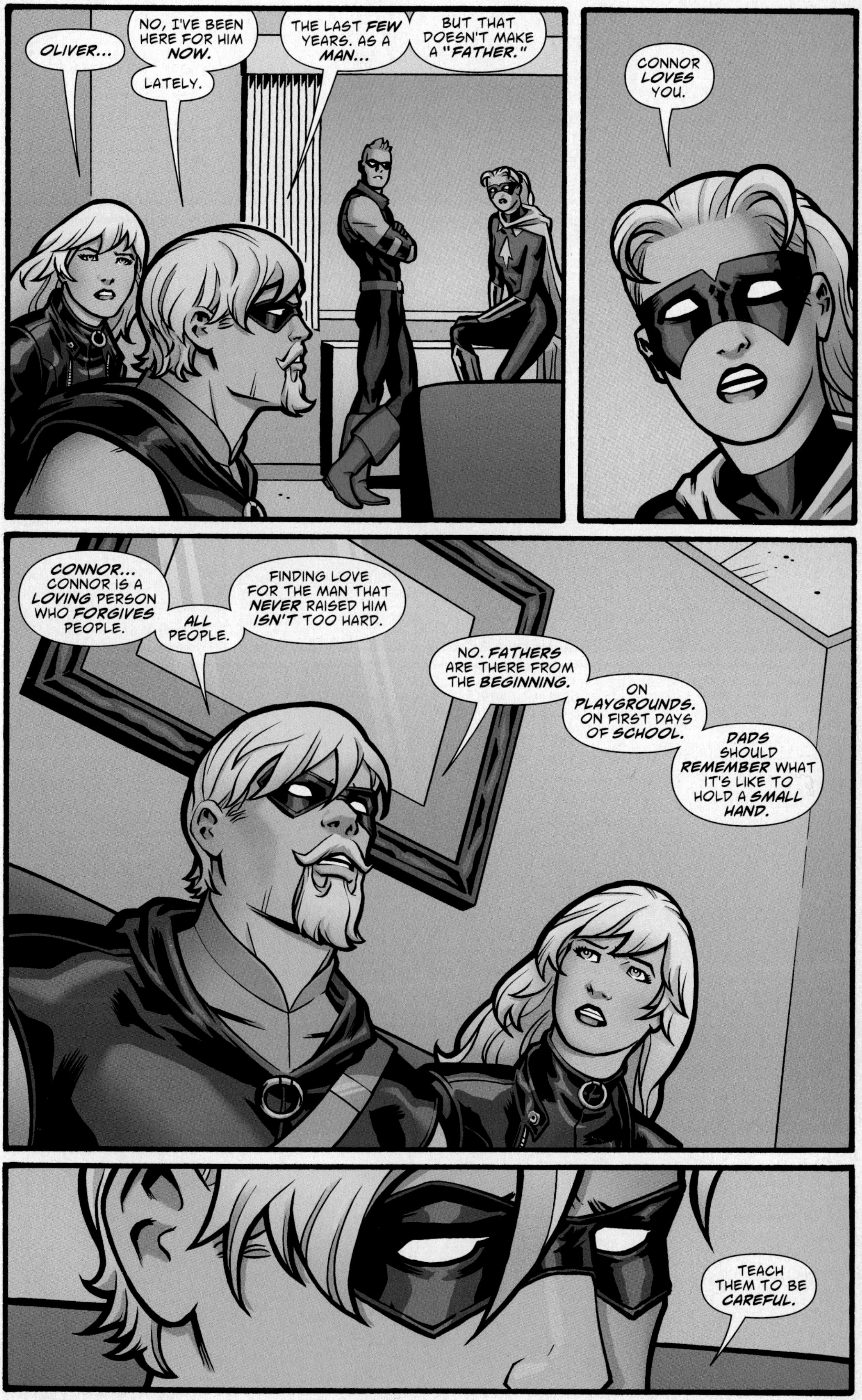

OLIVER...
NO, I'VE BEEN HERE FOR HIM NOW.
LATELY.
THE LAST FEW YEARS. AS A MAN...
BUT THAT DOESN'T MAKE A "FATHER."
CONNOR LOVES YOU.
CONNOR... CONNOR IS A LOVING PERSON WHO FORGIVES PEOPLE.
ALL PEOPLE.
FINDING LOVE FOR THE MAN THAT NEVER RAISED HIM ISN'T TOO HARD.
NO. FATHERS ARE THERE FROM THE BEGINNING.
ON PLAYGROUNDS. ON FIRST DAYS OF SCHOOL.
DADS SHOULD REMEMBER WHAT IT'S LIKE TO HOLD A SMALL HAND.
TEACH THEM TO BE CAREFUL.

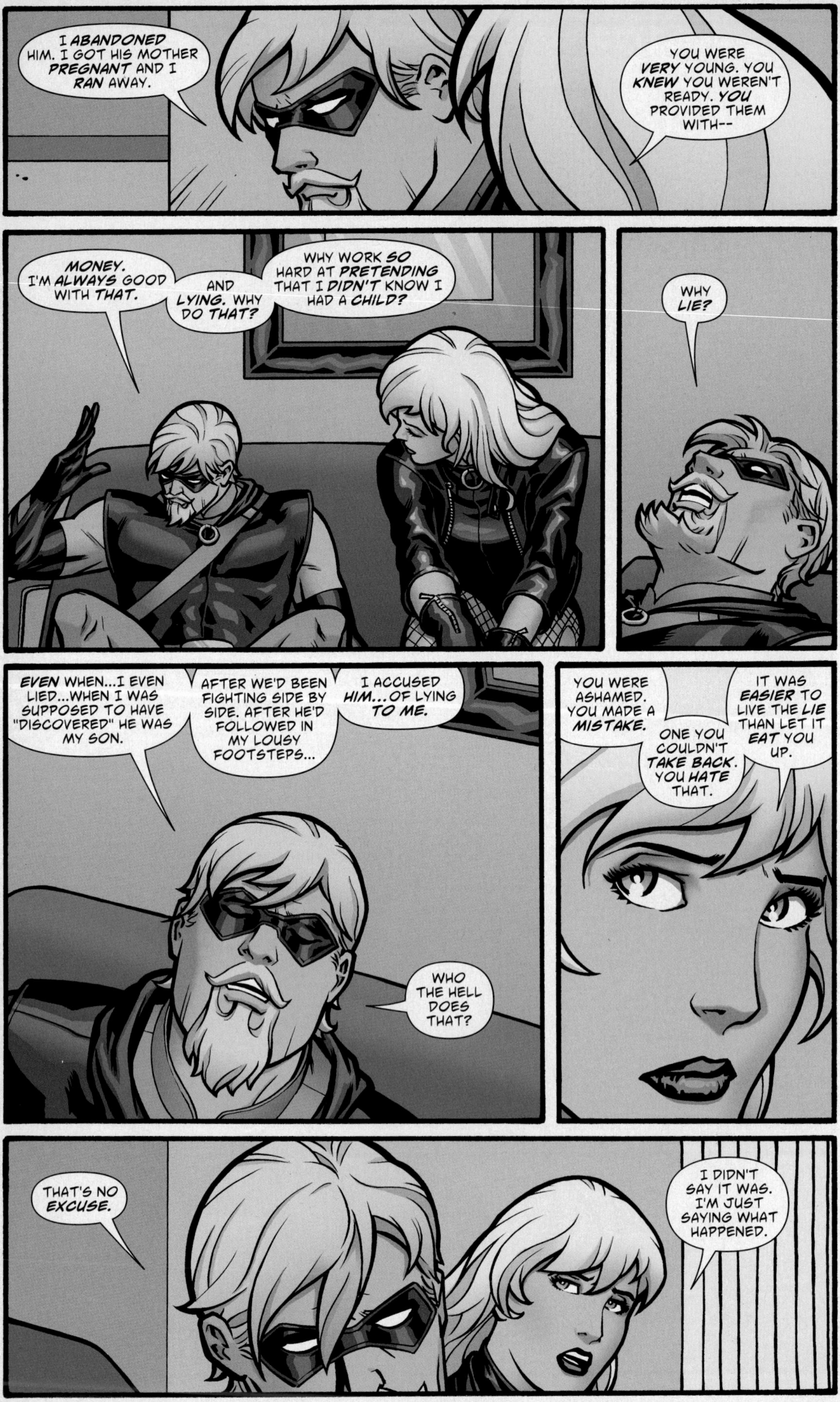

I ABANDONED HIM. I GOT HIS MOTHER PREGNANT AND I RAN AWAY.
YOU WERE VERY YOUNG. YOU KNEW YOU WEREN'T READY. YOU PROVIDED THEM WITH--
MONEY. I'M ALWAYS GOOD WITH THAT.
AND LYING. WHY DO THAT?
WHY WORK SO HARD AT PRETENDING THAT I DIDN'T KNOW I HAD A CHILD?
WHY LIE?
EVEN WHEN...I EVEN LIED...WHEN I WAS SUPPOSED TO HAVE "DISCOVERED" HE WAS MY SON.
AFTER WE'D BEEN FIGHTING SIDE BY SIDE. AFTER HE'D FOLLOWED IN MY LOUSY FOOTSTEPS...
I ACCUSED HIM...OF LYING TO ME.
WHO THE HELL DOES THAT?
YOU WERE ASHAMED. YOU MADE A MISTAKE.
ONE YOU COULDN'T TAKE BACK. YOU HATE THAT.
IT WAS EASIER TO LIVE THE LIE THAN LET IT EAT YOU UP.
THAT'S NO EXCUSE.
I DIDN'T SAY IT WAS. I'M JUST SAYING WHAT HAPPENED.

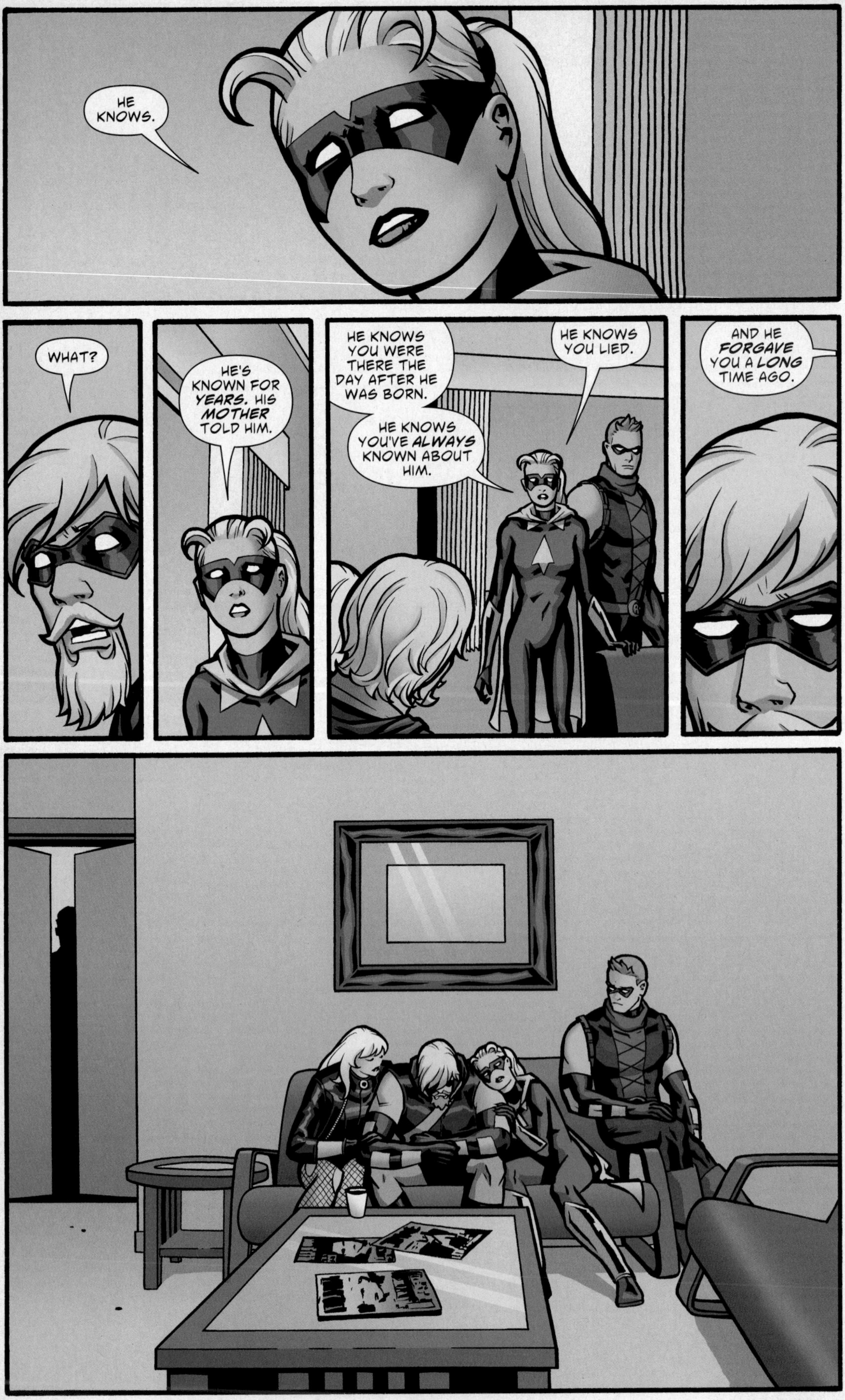

HE KNOWS.
WHAT?
HE'S KNOWN FOR YEARS. HIS MOTHER TOLD HIM.
HE KNOWS YOU WERE THERE THE DAY AFTER HE WAS BORN.
HE KNOWS YOU'VE ALWAYS KNOWN ABOUT HIM.
HE KNOWS YOU LIED.
AND HE FORGAVE YOU A LONG TIME AGO.

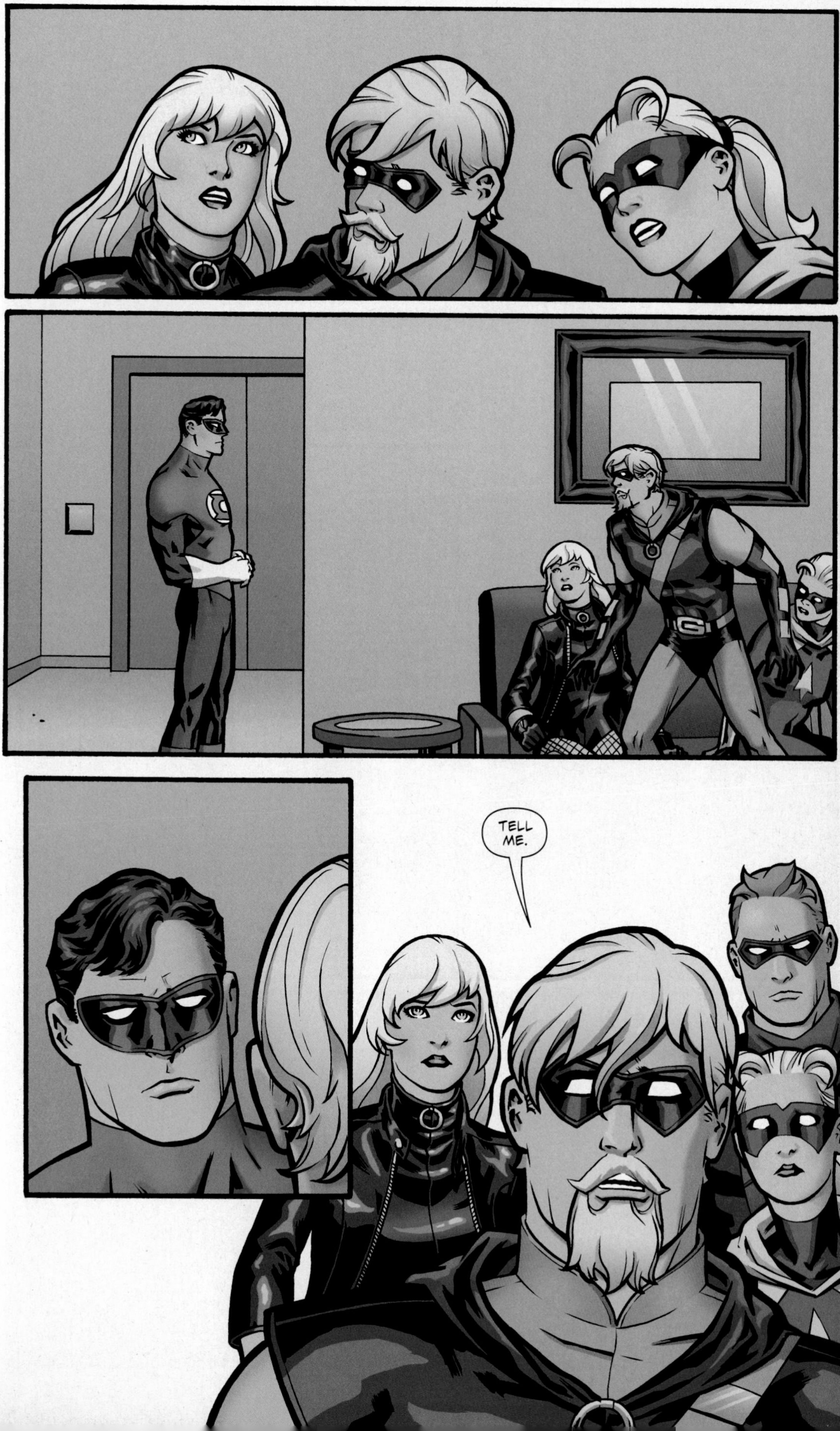
TELL ME.

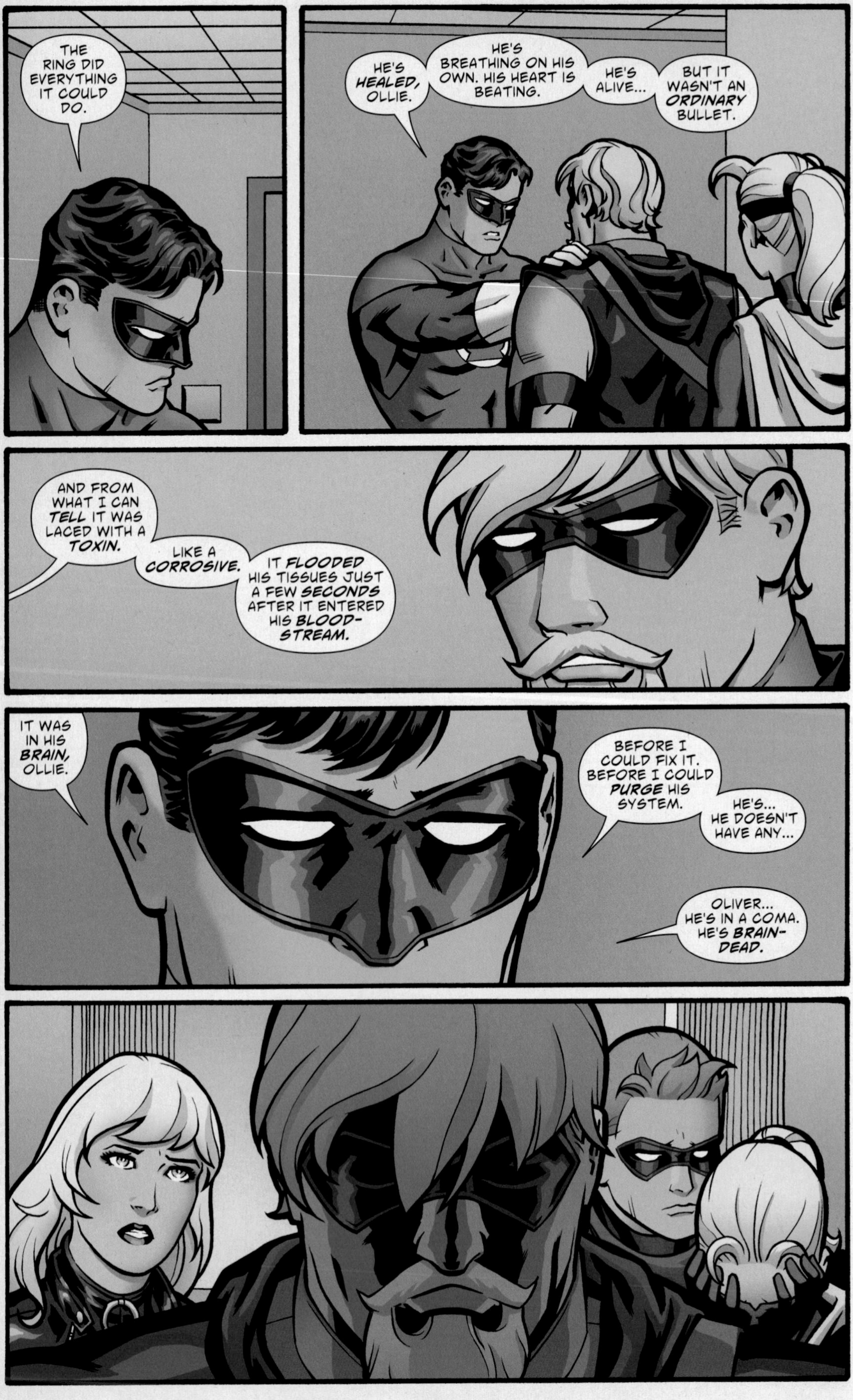
THE RING DID EVERYTHING IT COULD DO.
HE'S HEALED, OLLIE.
HE'S BREATHING ON HIS OWN. HIS HEART IS BEATING.
HE'S ALIVE...
BUT IT WASN'T AN ORDINARY BULLET.
AND FROM WHAT I CAN TELL IT WAS LACED WITH A TOXIN.
LIKE A CORROSIVE.
IT FLOODED HIS TISSUES JUST A FEW SECONDS AFTER IT ENTERED HIS BLOOD-STREAM.
IT WAS IN HIS BRAIN, OLLIE.
BEFORE I COULD FIX IT. BEFORE I COULD PURGE HIS SYSTEM.
HE'S... HE DOESN'T HAVE ANY...
OLIVER... HE'S IN A COMA. HE'S BRAIN-DEAD.

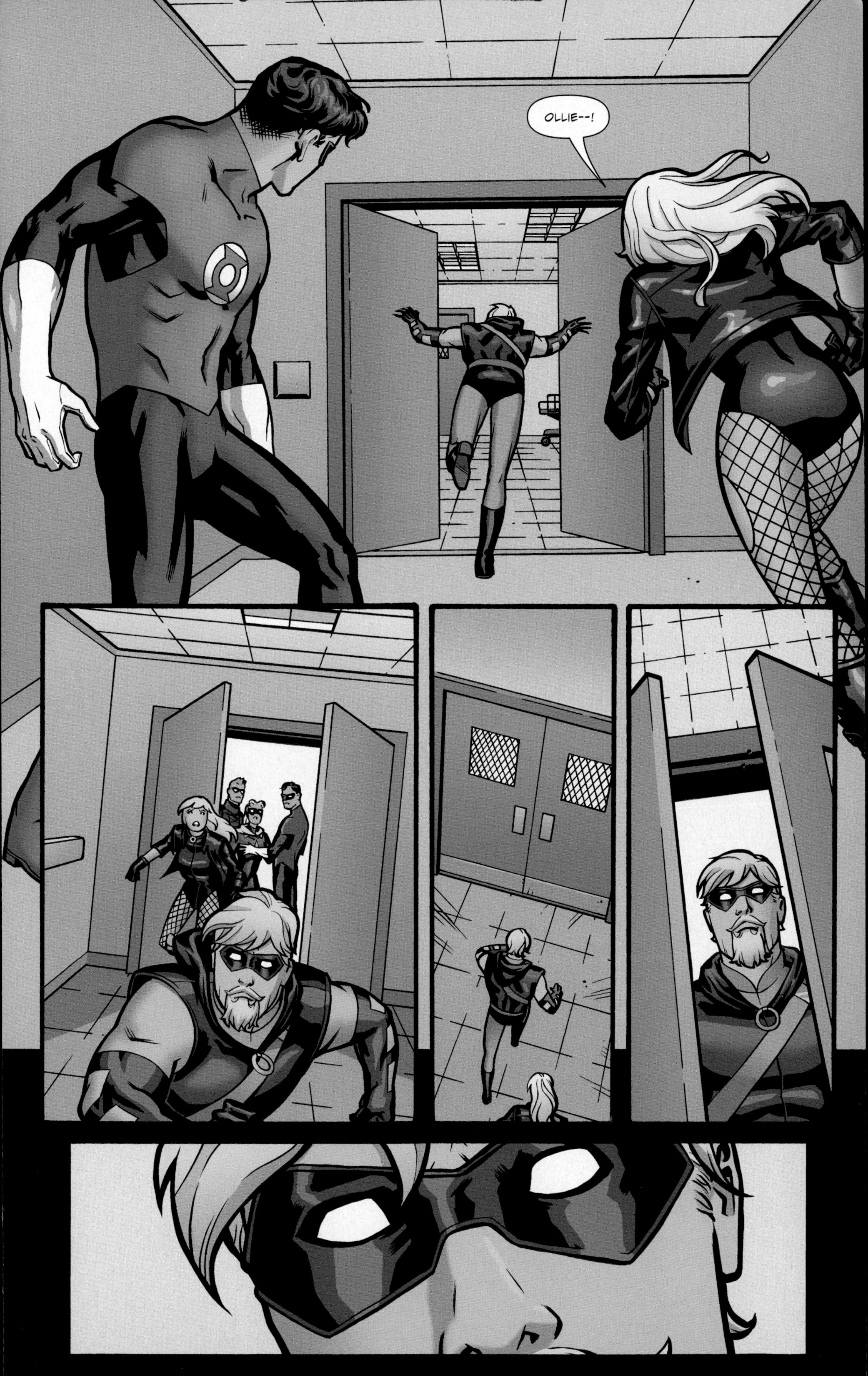
OLLIE--!

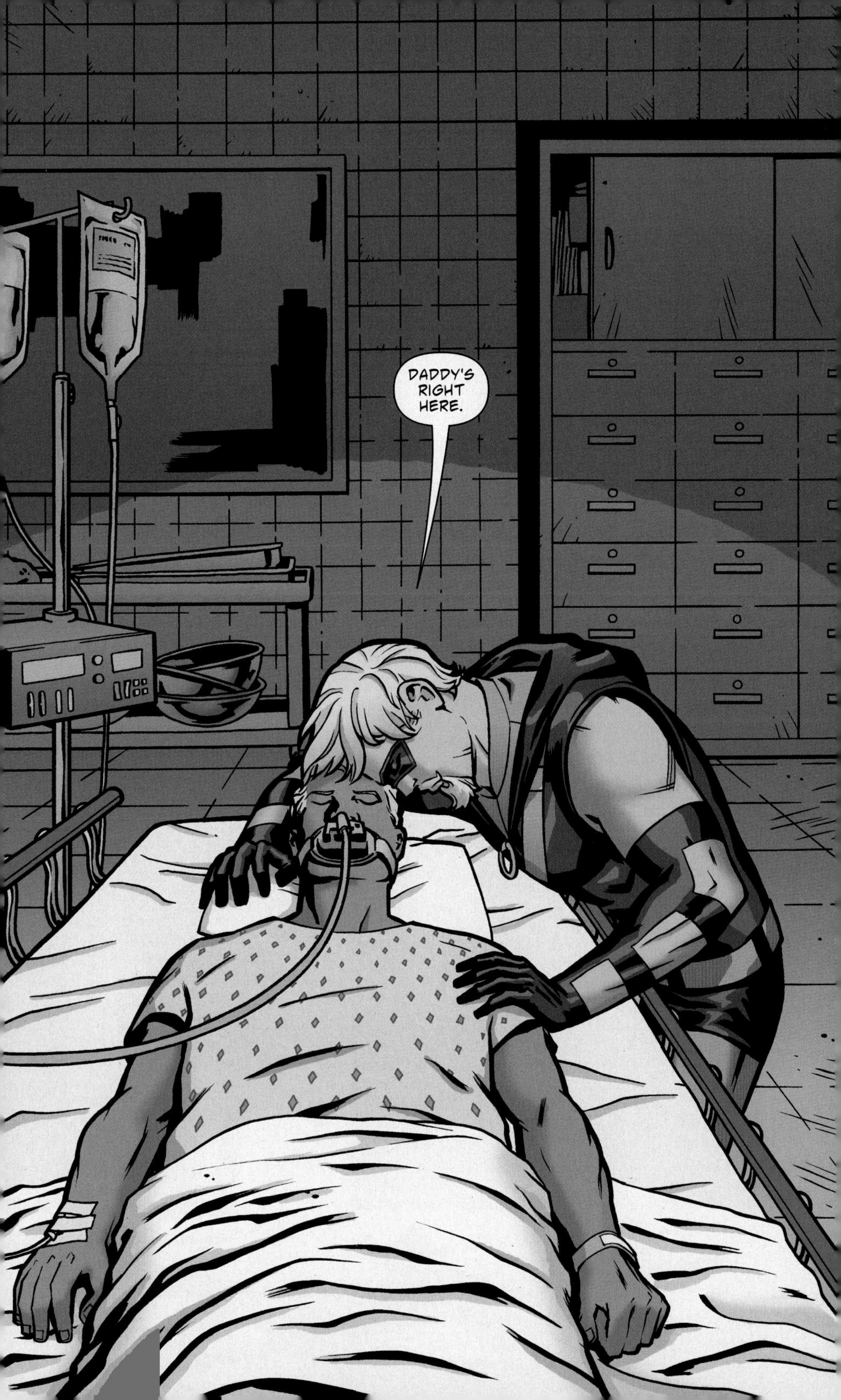
DADDY'S RIGHT HERE.

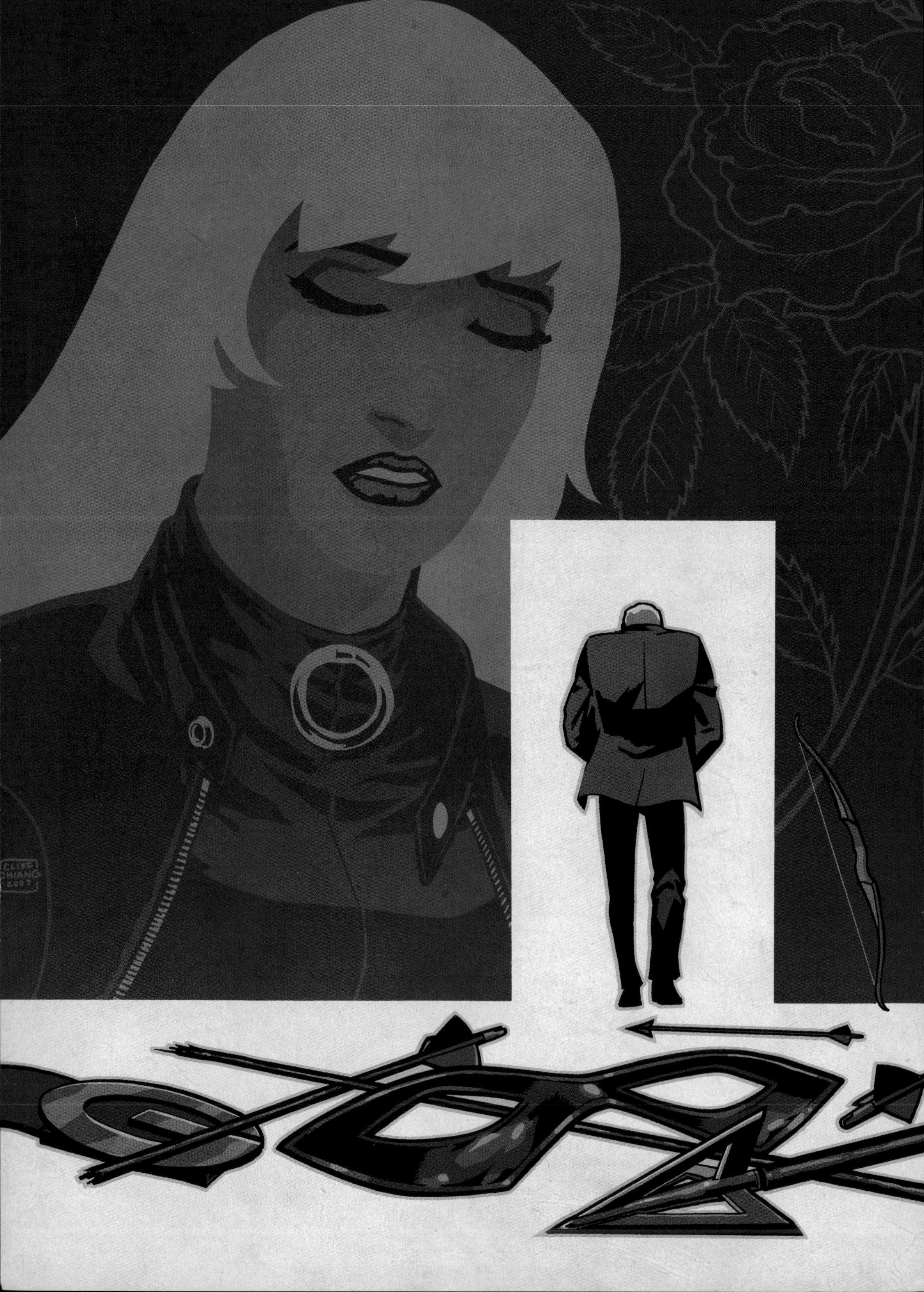
CLIFF CHIANG 2007

CHILD SUPPORT

Story: **Judd Winick** *Art:* **André Coelho** *Color:* **David Baron**

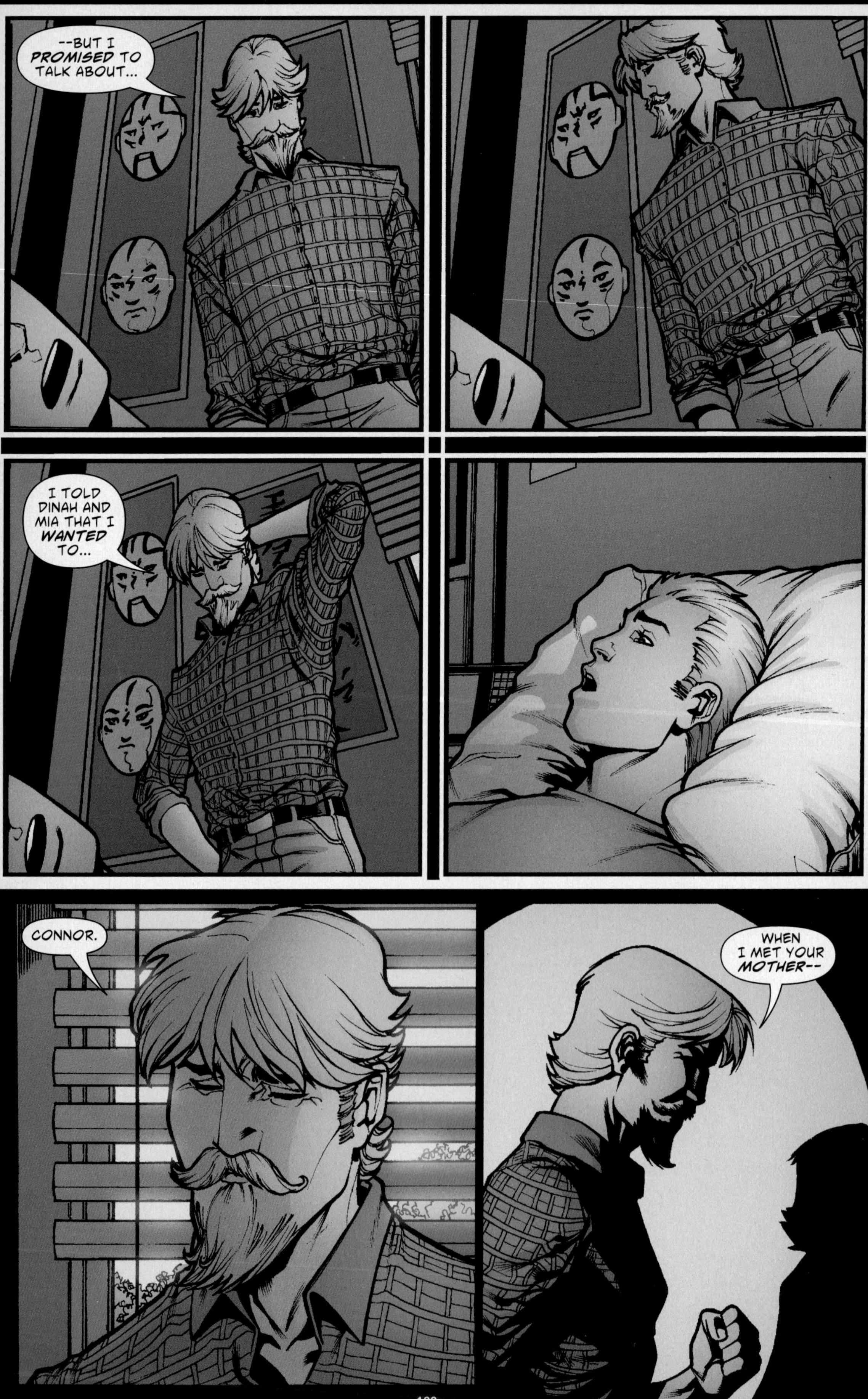
--BUT I PROMISED TO TALK ABOUT...
I TOLD DINAH AND MIA THAT I WANTED TO...
CONNOR.
WHEN I MET YOUR MOTHER--

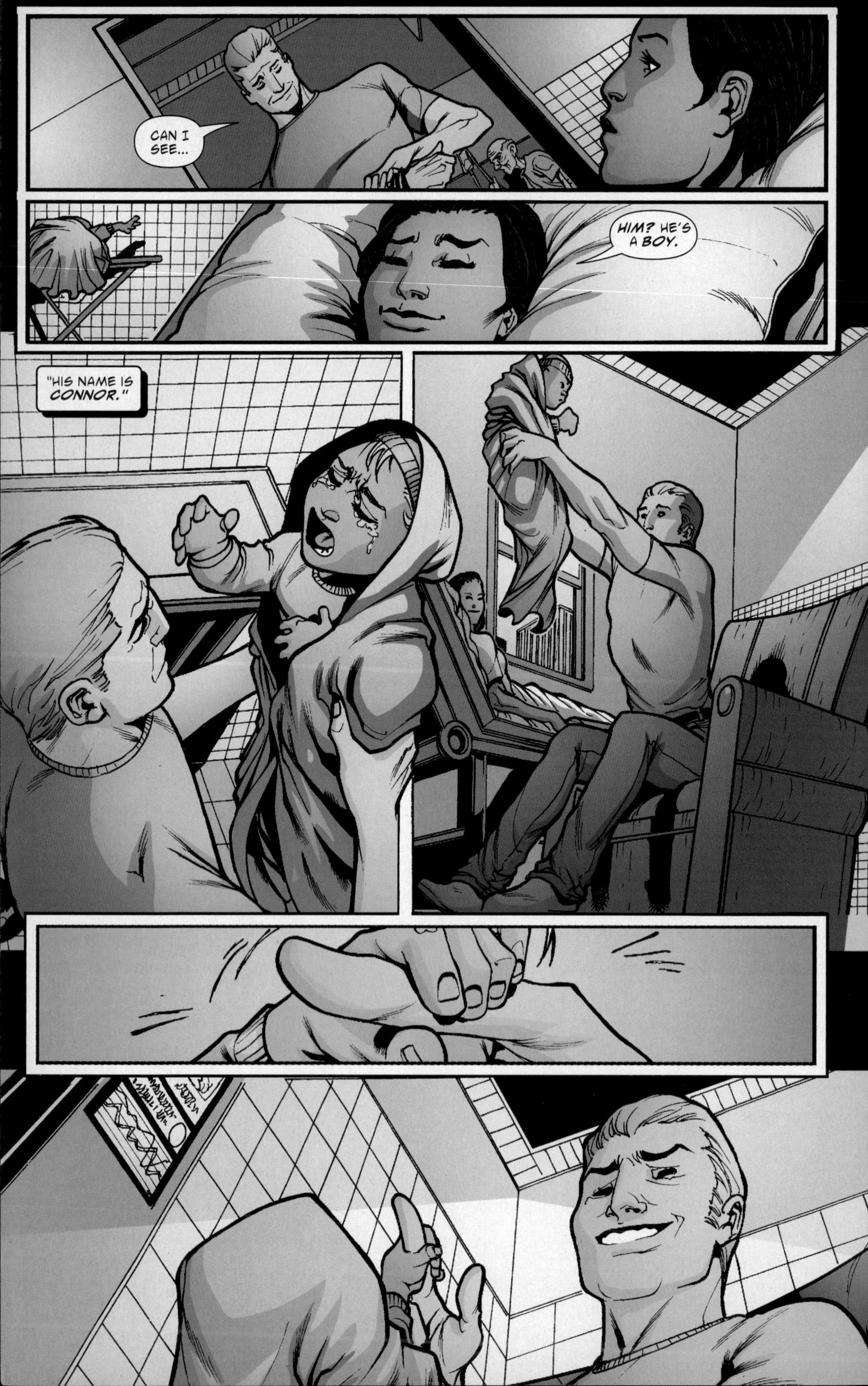
CAN I SEE...
HIM? HE'S A BOY.
"HIS NAME IS CONNOR."

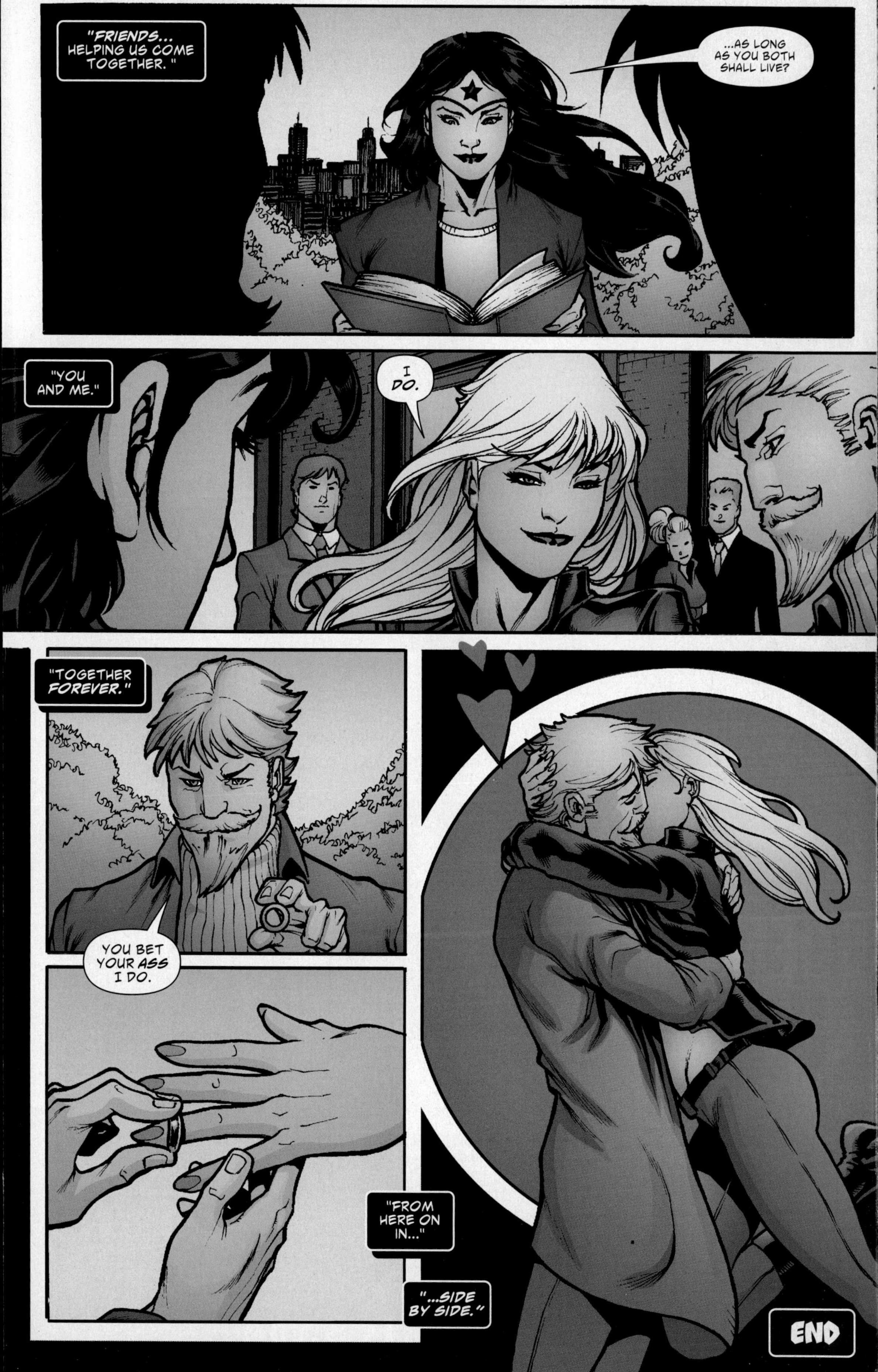
"FRIENDS... HELPING US COME TOGETHER."
...AS LONG AS YOU BOTH SHALL LIVE?
"YOU AND ME."
I DO.
"TOGETHER FOREVER."
YOU BET YOUR ASS I DO.
"FROM HERE ON IN..."
"...SIDE BY SIDE."
END

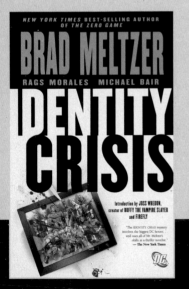